CONTAINING Draughts of Elevations of above 200 Buildings erected in thefe Colonies, & defigned by the most fkilful Architects be- ore Mr. *Thos. Jefferfon,* including 43 Churches & other Houfes of Worfhip, 14 Schools, Col- eges & Hofpitals, 18 Capitols, State-houfes & Courthoufes, 8 Markets & other Public Buildings, nd countlefs Dwelling-houfes & Manfions. THE Defigns for thefe Buildings were pre- pared by: SIR *Chr. Wren* & his Affociates; *John Prince; Jas. Porteus; Rich.ᵈ Taliaferro; Henry Cary* II; *Edmund Woolley; Rich.ᵈ Munday; John Smibert; Sam.ˡ Cardy; Wm. Naylor; Ezra Waite, John Arifs; Jas. Wren; John Hawks; Wm. Buck- land; Horatio Anderfon; Rob.ᵗ Twelves; Sam.ˡ Rhoads; Rob.ᵗ Smith; Thos. McBean; Godfrey Malbone; Rich.ᵈ Boulton; Gov.ʳ Bernard; Peter Harrifon; Chas. Carroll; Simon Duff; Pat. Creagh; Rob.ᵗ Key; Rob.ᵗ May; Jos. Brown,* nd divers others who are yet Anonymous.

12/05

o wilson web

o RRB,... 2000

o Rf. sources...

o EM

o FR

L = 5

BY JOHN FITZHUGH MILLAR

*With Drawings rendered by Suzanne Carlson*

BARRE PUBLISHERS MCMLXVIII

THE

# Architects

## OF THE

# American

# Colonies

## OR

# *Vitruvius Americanus*

*Copyright © Barre Publishers, Barre, Massachusetts 1968*
*Library of Congress catalogue card number 68-17068*
*Printing: The Lane Press, Inc.*
*Composition: Anthoenson Press*
*Design: Shirley Errickson*

## ERRATA

Page 105 — Line 1 should be last line on page,
not first.

Page 111 — Caption should read *Miles Brewton*,
not *Miles Brenton*.

Page 182 — Caption should read *Town House*,
not *Colony House*.

I owe a great debt of gratitude to the many kind people who have given so freely of their time and knowledge towards the compilation of this book; I owe far more, I'm afraid, than can be expressed in a simple list such as this. I wish to thank the Reverend Canon Lockett F. Ballard, John Betjemann, Carl Bridenbaugh, Reuben Brower, Paul Buchanan, H. M. Colvin, Francis Comstock, John Coolidge, Mrs. George (Antoinette) Downing, Wendell Garrett, Ivor Noel Hume, Harold Kirker, A. Lawrence Kocher, Mrs. Moira B. Mathieson, Mrs. George Maurice Morris, Hugh Morrison, Elliott Perkins, Samuel Gaillard Stoney, John Sweeney, George Tatum, James Waite, Walter Muir Whitehill, and many others. I hope at least that they will not be disappointed.

John Fitzhugh Millar

To Betsy Fryatt

Such a nice guest!

with best wishes,

John F. Miller

Also to Betsy, who's one of the very finest women I've ever known, and to our unique and beautiful friendship. May it exist forever.
with tremendous affection,
Bill Cassell

# CONTENTS

BOOK III

## Architects of the American Colonies: North

## Illustrated Glossary

## Bibliography

## Index

# FOREWORD

*Over the years there have been many books about 'American Colonial architecture,' some for entertainment, some for instruction, some dealing in great detail with a small number of buildings, and others attempting to spread a loose blanket over the whole subject. The purpose of this book lies somewhere in between: it is both to entertain, and to educate; it attempts to cover a large number of buildings systematically, and yet also to include as much detail as is needed.*

*There were originally two reasons for writing this book. The first was the result of some haphazard research which I had undertaken on Peter Harrison. Almost by accident, I came across a number of buildings that I felt were designed by Harrison, but which were not included in* Peter Harrison, First American Architect, *a work by that eminent American historian Carl Bridenbaugh. I had no wish to compete with Mr. Bridenbaugh in trying to sell books about Harrison, but nevertheless wished to publish my discoveries. I therefore contrived to write a book on all the architects of the Colonies, and put Harrison in his place in the middle.*

*The second reason, perhaps considerably more important than the first, is that when I wanted to learn about American Colonial architecture, I found to my great amazement and dismay that Harvard offered no course that so much as mentioned the subject. A course called* History of American Architecture, *offered for one term and never repeated, seemed to pass over the whole Colonial period in less than a lecture. Some careful inquiries around the University produced the disturbing information that none of the appropriate professors or instructors was in the least bit interested in the architecture of the eighteenth century; furthermore, it was soon clear that even if such a subject were to be included in a course, none of them knew enough about it to teach it. A further check revealed that anyone who tried to teach it would be subject to yet another handicap: there was no adequate text. Therefore I decided to write a text that would cover the most important parts of the subject.*

*Bearing in mind my two reasons for writing this book, I have had to walk a literary tightrope. I have had to make the material palatable to the casual reader, to the research-scholar, and to the students who might have the misfortune to be assigned this as a text. Naturally, I can not hope to have walked the whole length of the tightrope without treading on the toes of my different kinds of readers. However, I beg them to bear with me through the parts that may be difficult for them to read, and hope that they will be lucky enough to find as much enjoyment in reading it as I have had in preparing it and writing it.*

*One fact easily apparent from a quick glance at this book is that it deals with only the works of architects. Most books on the subject do not see any distinction between one kind of Colonial building and another, but this book is an attempt to study only one kind. No more than one would expect to find mass-produced ranch houses in a book that deals with the skyscrapers of Ludwig Mies van der Rohe, one should not find New England saltboxes alongside the academic work of Peter Harrison in any scholarly work. This is not to play down the importance or beauty of a New England saltbox, but it has its own place, which is not here.*

*Now there are those who say that there were no architects in the Colonies, and that all architecture, so-called, was the dabbling of amateurs. Jefferson, they say, was the first architect in America. This, of course, all depends on one's definition of architect. Many will no doubt disagree with my interpretation of the word, but to my mind there is usually a sharply discernible line between the works of my architects and the works of carpenters or master-builders.*

*The difference is more than one of quality; it is also a matter of being up-to-date. My architects were usually about 25 years behind their English counterparts; buildings like the American buildings were found in England about 25 years before they were built in the Colonies. The work of local master-builders (even if it is of the same quality, which it is usually not), is another 25 or so years later than the work of the Colonial architects. The difference is often a difference in price, too: if one is going to spend over a certain amount of money on a structure, it pays to hire an architect, not only for extra beauty but also as insurance that the building will stand surely. Consequently, most of the buildings designed by architects were for wealthy gentlemen, for the Anglican Church or for the government. In a way, then, the history of American Colonial architects is also a view of the history of upper-class life in the Colonies, and of ecclesiastical and governmental activity. Closely connected with these is the history of hospitals, schools and colleges, for they, being a cooperative venture also could afford, and found it advisable, to hire an architect.*

*'Si monumentum requiris, circumspice,'[1] reads the epitaph of Sir Christopher Wren in St. Paul's Cathedral. For one version of the history of the American Colonies, look around you at the works of the Colonial architects; about two-thirds of their buildings remain, and among them they tell an interesting story.*

*Many readers may claim that my attributions represent an oversimplified view of Colonial architecture, but I believe that the extraordinary lack of mobility in the eighteenth century justifies my view. Whatever one thinks of the attributions, one can hardly dispute the value of including such a large collection of period academic designs inside one cover.*

*The name Vitruvius Americanus is based on two eighteenth-century British architects' pattern books. The first was Vitruvius Britannicus by Colin Campbell (    -1729), and it contained drawings of buildings designed by Campbell and of a few designed by others that illustrated his point of view about architecture. The second was Vitruvius Scoticus by William Adam (1689-1748), with drawings of major eighteenth-century buildings in Scotland, especially those done by Adam himself. Vitruvius Scoticus, since it included a fair number of smaller buildings, was used as a handbook in the Colonies; John Ariss of Virginia used it extensively. Vitruvius Britannicus, on the other hand, contained almost exclusively colossal palaces that were far too large for use in the Colonies, aside from minor details. Vitruvius, of course, was the Roman architect and engineer of the first century B.C. who set down at great length all the information he considered important for architects and engineers to know.*

*The aim of Vitruvius Americanus, however, is slightly different. It is to present drawings and verbal descriptions of all the buildings built in the Colonies by people who deserve the title of architect. Obviously, in spite of all the efforts made to find all the buildings in this category, some must have escaped detection. Perhaps they will never be found, but whether they are or not, there are probably few not mentioned in this book that ought to be.*

*March 1968, Newport*                                                      *J. F. M.*

---

[1] Translation: 'If you are looking for his monument, look around you,' i.e., at the cathedral he built, and at the city churches and other buildings around the cathedral.

# SCALE

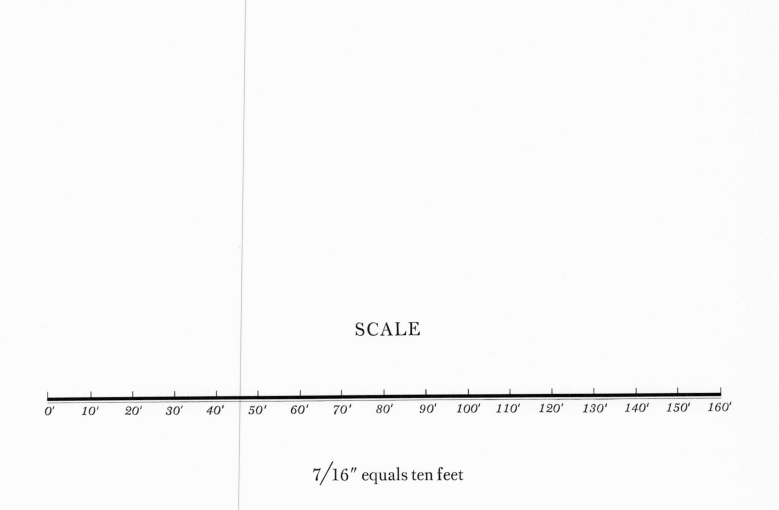

0'  10'  20'  30'  40'  50'  60'  70'  80'  90'  100'  110'  120'  130'  140'  150'  160'

7/16″ equals ten feet

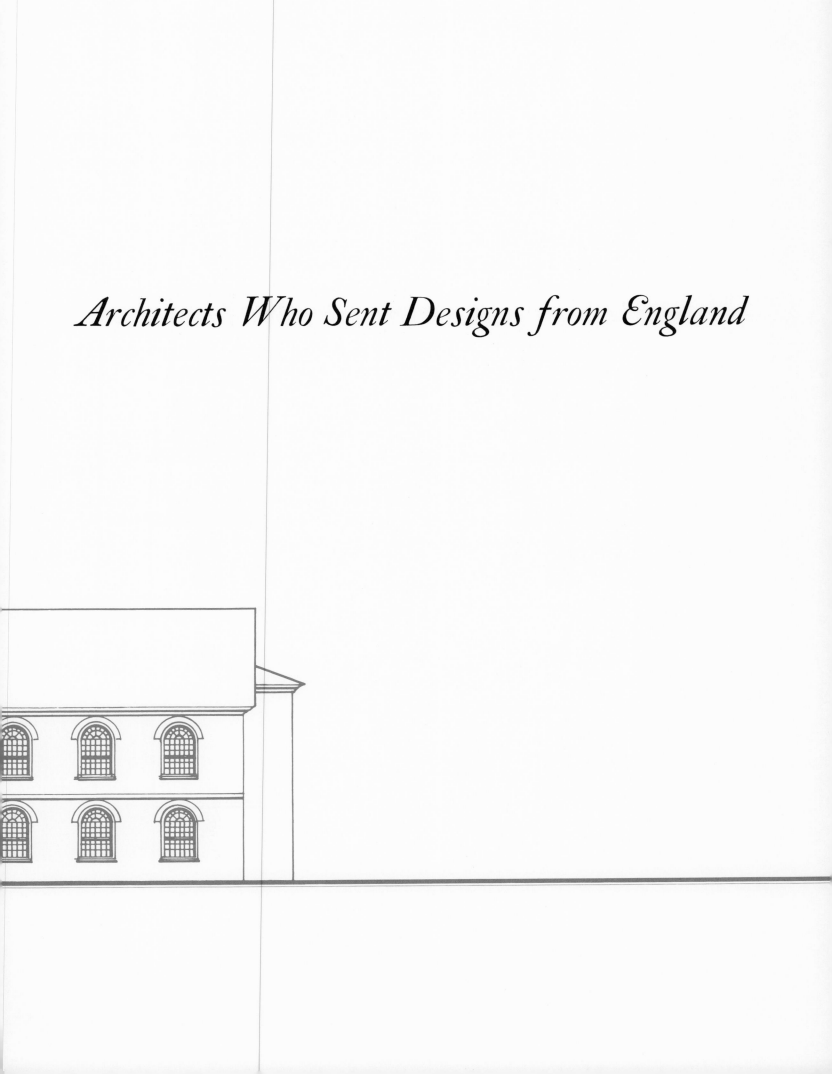

# Architects Who Sent Designs from England

*Throughout the whole history of American Colonial architecture, the style employed is most simply characterized as 'Wren,' named after the English architect Sir Christopher Wren. Although this simple characterization, like most general statements, is not absolutely correct, it does go a long way towards showing where the history of Colonial architecture differs from English architectural history. In fact, with very few exceptions, Colonial architecture was dominated by the schools of Wren and of his pupil James Gibbs. England, on the one hand, was subjected to the futuristic, ponderous experiments in mass of Nicholas Hawksmoor and Sir John Vanbrugh, who were also pupils of Wren, and who influenced Wren for a time at the end of his life, and to the English school of Palladianism, which was both a search for purity in architecture and an experiment in frivolity at the same time; the Colonies, on the other hand, had little use for the massive buildings of Hawksmoor, and had not the time, inclination or money to adopt the Palladian style to any extent, especially since it too was generally confined to enormous buildings in England. Instead, the Colonists, conservative as they were, delighted in the simpler, more natural styles of Wren and Gibbs.*

*Neither Wren nor Gibbs, nor any of their entourage save John James, ever came to the Colonies. This, however, did nothing to prevent their influence from being felt in the Colonies. In the case of Wren, one suspects that the influence was not a result of his work, but merely that the Colonial architects arrived at the same conclusions and solutions to their problems as Wren did. In the case of Gibbs, on the other hand, his influence is easy to trace, for he wrote a number of pattern books and builders' handbooks which were full of plates of his designs; Gibbs' books were not used in the Colonies until about 1750, although they were written a long time before that.*

THE history of the first building in the Colonies to have a claim on the name of Wren, the so-called Wren Building at William & Mary College in Williamsburg, begins around 1695. This original college building burned down soon afterwards in 1705, and was promptly rebuilt using most of the original walls. Its connection with Wren stems from two sources. The first was a statement by Rev. Hugh Jones, former Professor of Mathematics at William & Mary, published in 1724; he wrote: "The Building is beautiful and commodious, being first modelled by Sir Christopher Wren, adapted to the Nature of the Country by the Gentlemen there; and since it was burnt down, it has been rebuilt and nicely contrived, altered and adorned by the ingenious Direction of Governor Spotswood; and is not altogether unlike Chelsea Hospital." This statement can be interpreted in many different ways. Marcus Whiffen, who has probably done as much research on the buildings of Williamsburg as anyone in order to write his two excellent books on the subject, thinks that Jones was telling a white lie to try and 'sell' Virginia to the English reading public, and that the architect probably was not Wren—who could not refute Jones' remarks because Wren died the year before Jones' book was published. I personally am less skeptical than Whiffen, as we shall see.

A problem involved in interpreting Jones' quote is the question of whether Wren designed the first, the second or both of the buildings, for the second one was quite different from the first, even though they did use mostly the same walls. The most ardent supporter of the Wren theory might read Jones' remarks as follows: Wren designed the first building, but it was too hard for the locals to construct it, so they freely altered it to suit their needs, tastes and ability. After the fire, Governor Spotswood wrote Wren, telling him all that had happened, and Wren replied with plans for the second building, which of the two far more closely resembles Chelsea Hospital. This theory is attractive to me, except for the fact that there is absolutely no trace of correspondence or other records to support it.

Quite apart from Jones' remarks, one would be tempted to attribute the building to Wren in some way or other for different reasons. Most important is the fact that the College was a Royal foundation, meaning that the Crown would be likely to call upon the Surveyor of the King's Works to design such a building; the Surveyor was Wren. It is also significant that the Wren building was the first structure in Virginia of academic design; such a building would have quite a chance of being the work of the leading architect in England if the design was sent from England, as it almost certainly was. Other authors have argued far more fully than this about the Wren building, and since it is certainly not my purpose to compete with them we shall proceed to a description of the building.

The plan of both buildings was a small quadrangle that was to have been completely enclosed. However, it was never finished that way in either the first or second building. According to a copy of a sketch by a Swiss traveller named Ludwig Michel, the façade of the first building was quite plain and very different from the second one. It was the same length, and the windows and chimneys were in the same places, but it was of a different height. The walls of the old building had four storeys of windows in them, while the present building has but two on top of a high basement. The difference was made both at the top and at the bottom, for after the fire the top storey of masonry, being unsafe, was removed, and at the same time earth was piled up around the basement, eliminating that as a principle storey; the arched front doorway was moved up a storey to compensate. Perhaps the most striking change was the addition of a one-bay pedimented pavilion in the center of front; this gives a much-needed focus

A curious parallel between two government buildings in two different Colonies but designed the same year provokes our next attribution to Wren. Of the City Hall in New York we know very little except what we can see from one eighteenth-century sketch of it. The Capitol at Williamsburg, by contrast, has been thoroughly researched. In neither case is there the shred of documentary evidence as to the name of the architect, but from the appearance of the two buildings it is quite obvious that the same man was responsible for each. Marcus Whiffen in his account of the Capitol says that there is no attribution to Wren at stake, and backs this up by claiming that Wren's office was concerned at that time only with the maintenance of royal buildings; even so, he admits that the design probably came from England. Now, if Wren was the official architect for the Crown, and one man was appointed to design public buildings in Crown Colonies, would that man not be Wren? That is my opinion, but since there is no evidence to support it, it would be useless to labor the point. Significantly, Whiffen neglects to mention the connection of the New York and Williamsburg buildings, which in turn is probably their most plausible connection with Wren.

In plan, the Capitol is like an H; 2 two-storey blocks are joined by a cross member resting on three arches; a tall, hexagonal cupola surmounts this cross member. Semicircular apses with round windows at the ground floor form the ends of the two blocks on one side of the building. The New York City Hall was also H-shaped, or possibly U-shaped, but it is not clear

*Capitol   Williamsburg   1701-1705*                    *burnt 1749   reconstructed 1931*

*Attribution:   probable*

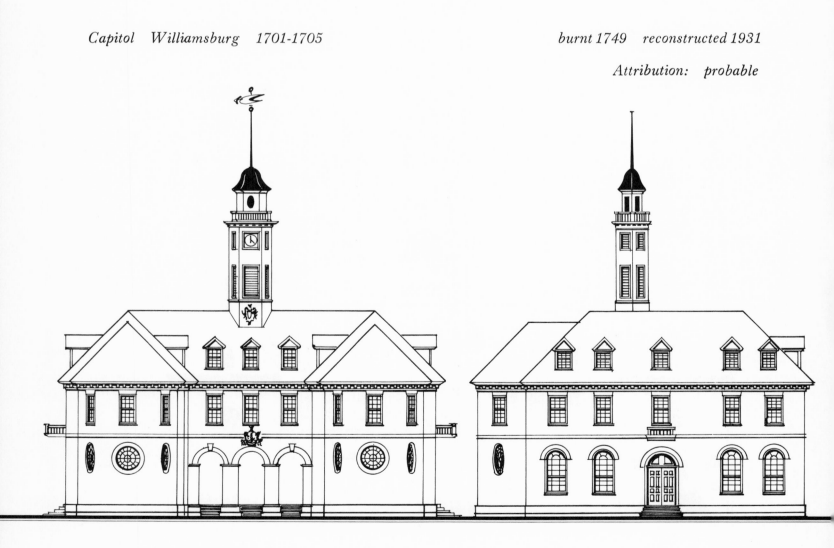

from the only existing view of it. The cross member here too was supported on three arches and was crowned by a cupola that may have been hexagonal, but it was a much lower cupola, just as the New York roof is lower than the Williamsburg one. An interesting contrast between the two buildings is the window glazing; these buildings were built at a time when sash windows were replacing casements, and as far as can be determined from available evidence the Capitol was originally provided with sash while the City Hall was given the old-fashioned casements.

The Capitol was burnt in 1749; a new building was immediately constructed on most of the old foundations, but it apparently looked quite different from the old one. It was later fitted with a two-storey entrance portico, similar to the one at Shirley, and possibly an early work of Thomas Jefferson. This building also burned down, and there are fewer records of its appearance than of the first Capitol, a fact which helped Colonial Williamsburg to decide to reconstruct the first rather than the more historic second Capitol when they began the restoration of the town in 1931; the first was also the more interesting architecturally speaking. The New York City Hall was completely rebuilt in the Federal style some time during the latter part of the eighteenth century; George Washington was sworn in as President on the upstairs porch of the altered building. This structure in turn was demolished around 1810 to make way for the enormous City Hall built in the French style by Mangin & McComb.

*City Hall    New York    1699*                                    *demolished about 1810; reconstruction*

*Attribution:    probable*

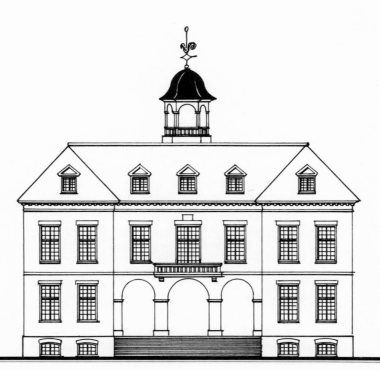

The third building in Williamsburg that can be attributed to Wren is the Governor's Palace. Again, there is not a shred of evidence for such an attribution, but it nevertheless remains an attractive hypothesis. The closest English equivalent was Edial Hall in Staffordshire, now gone, but the resemblance was probably coincidence. The design almost certainly came from England, especially since no other building of its style or sophistication appeared in Virginia at that time. Again, Wren being the Royal architect would be the logical choice for the Royal Governor's architect. It was begun in 1706 and finished in 1720, and Henry Cary (*q.v.*) was appointed to oversee the construction, for he had apparently done such a good

*Governor's Palace   Williamsburg   1706-1720*                    *burnt 1788*

*Attribution:   possible*                                        *reconstructed 1931*

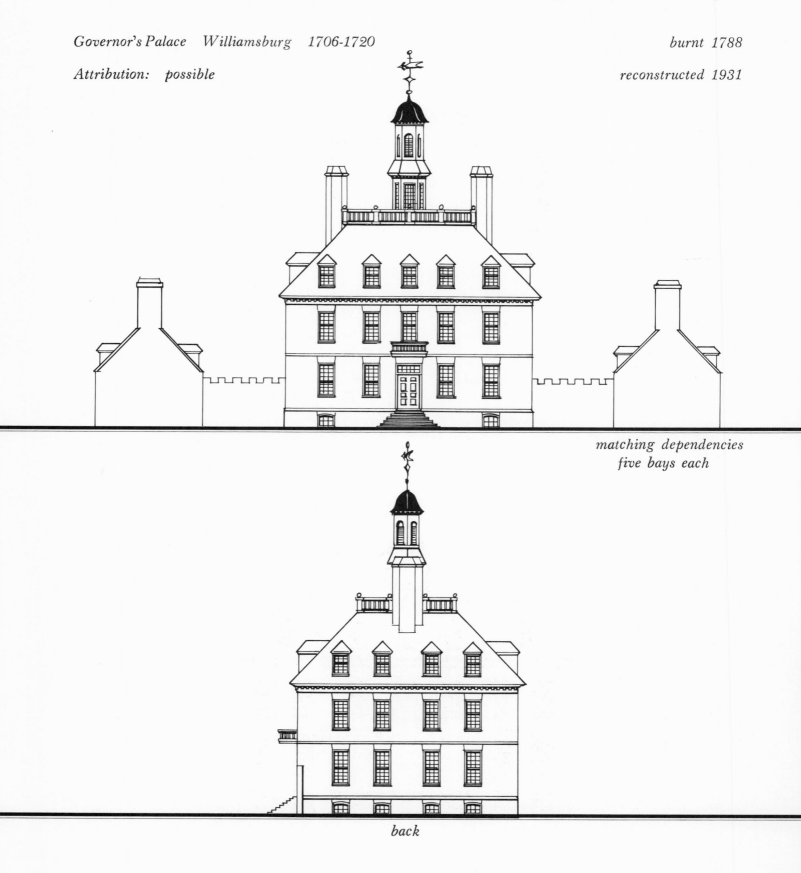

*matching dependencies*
*five bays each*

*back*

job with the Capitol a few years earlier. The Palace is a tall rectangular building, 2½ storeys high, with a pair of forecourt dependencies arranged formally. The steep deck-on-hip roof is studded with hipped dormers, and massive chimneys at the break stand at either end of the roof deck balustrade; in the center of the deck a two-storey hexagonal cupola of unusual design reaches high above the Palace. The Palace was altered around 1750 by the addition of Taliaferro's ballroom wing on the back, and by various internal changes which were recorded by Jefferson when he was Governor and when he drew plans for further alterations, which happily were never executed. In 1788, the Palace burned to the ground, to lie undisturbed until it was reconstructed in 1931.

The remaining two buildings in the Colonies by Wren are quite obviously a pair. They are both churches; Christ Church, built in Boston in 1723, and Trinity Church, built in Newport in 1725. If Wren designed these buildings at all, he would have to have designed them long before they were built, for he died in 1723, and his last buildings were in the heavy style of Hawksmoor, which these two delightful churches most certainly are not. Fortunately, some evidence has been found to support this proposition. It is alleged that a scholar not long ago came across a letter from the Bishop of London to Wren asking him to design some churches for the Society for the Propagation of the Gospel to build in the Colonies. The letter dated from the first decade of the eighteenth century. Unhappily, the letter has again been lost, and so is not admissible as concrete evidence, but if Wren ever did design any churches for the S. P. G., these certainly must be they.

From an architectural standpoint, the evidence for Wren's authorship is very strong. Wren designed some fifty parish churches in London following the Great Fire, and these two fit in with them better than any other churches anywhere. The interior arrangement of the two Colonial churches is basilical, with galleries surrounding three sides of the building, and an apse at the east end. The galleries are supported on piers, and they in turn support the ceiling with another tier of pillars, using architraves and cross barrel vaults. This arrangement is seen in a number of Wren's churches, including St. James' Piccadilly, St. Andrew's by the Wardrobe, St. Andrew's Holborn and St. Clement's Danes. Above the cross barrel vaults the two Colonial churches differ from each other; Trinity has a flat ceiling into which the vault ribs flow as at Wren's St. Dionis Backchurch, and Christ Church has a longitudinal architrave supporting a high barrel vault, as at St. Bride's Fleet Street. Even though Christ Church's acoustics are better than Trinity's, yet one suspects that if there was only one set of plans the builder of Trinity followed these plans more closely than the builder of Christ Church, but this is sheer speculation, for there could easily have been alternative plans provided by Wren.

Outside, Christ Church is of brick, five bays long, with an external tower supporting a tall wooden steeple. The design of the steeple is reminiscent of those on St. Lawrence Jewry, St. Augustine Watling Street and St. James' Piccadilly, but it is also not far different from the tower on the Boston Town House, now known as the Old State House. Trinity was built to the same arrangement, only it is completely of wood. The proportions and details of Trinity's steeple are better than those of Christ Church, but not really very different. Many words have been written about which of the steeples is the earlier and about their having been added some twenty years after the building of the churches. Most recent evidence indicates that at least Trinity's steeple was built contemporary with the rest of the building, although it was replaced later on by an identical copy. Certainly the design of the steeples accompanied the design of the churches, regardless of the date of execution.

A Boston print seller named Price has been variously credited with procuring or actually drawing the designs for these churches; his real involvement seems to have been no more than as an agent of the parish with the S. P. G. Similarly, the carpenter-architect Richard Munday (*q.v.*) has been credited with 'improving' upon Wren's design for Trinity; actually, he being a skilled craftsman was able to build the church more accurately to Wren's designs than the craftsmen of Boston who had had little practice with such intricate work. In 1762, Trinity was cut in two, and the east wall was moved out two more bays. Although this completely alters the visual and acoustical effect—probably for the worse—the extra bays match the old ones, and most visitors do not notice the change. Trinity has never needed any large-scale restoration. In the rear gallery stands the Bridge organ presented by the philosopher George Berkeley in 1733; all the old pipework has been replaced, but it is hoped that a new organ can soon be built on the old principles inside the old case. Christ Church has one of the first organs made

*Trinity Church    Newport    1725-1726*                    *enlarged 1762 from    five to seven bays*

*Attribution:    certain*

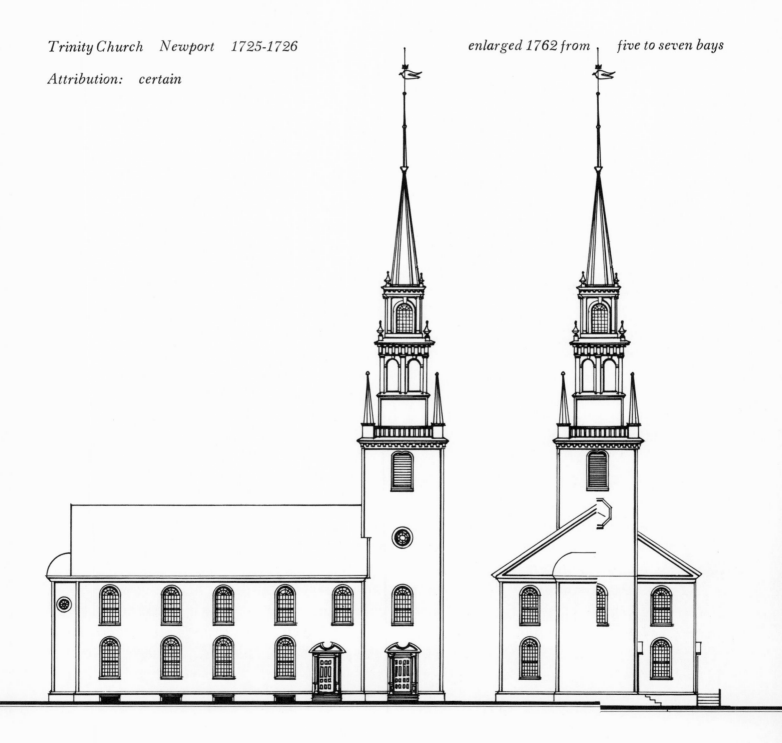

in the Colonies; although all the old pipework has long since been removed, a new organ in the old case is a fitting companion for the excellent acoustics of the church. Christ Church is known as the Old North Church, and the celebrated lanterns of Paul Revere's ride were shown from its steeple; this steeple was replaced by a slightly different one by Bulfinch in the early nineteenth century, and it was this one that blew down in the hurricane of 1954. Fortunately, a new steeple was soon erected along the lines of the original one.

Of all the buildings in the Colonies, these two churches are the most likely to have been designed by Wren, and now they are being joined by a third, for Westminster College in Fulton, Missouri, has imported stone by stone Wren's St. Mary the Virgin, Aldermanbury, from London to commemorate the 'Iron Curtain' speech of Sir Winston Churchill made at Fulton. St. Mary's was bombed during the war, and until Westminster College bought it the church was not going to be rebuilt.

*Christ Church    Boston    1723*

*Attribution:    certain*

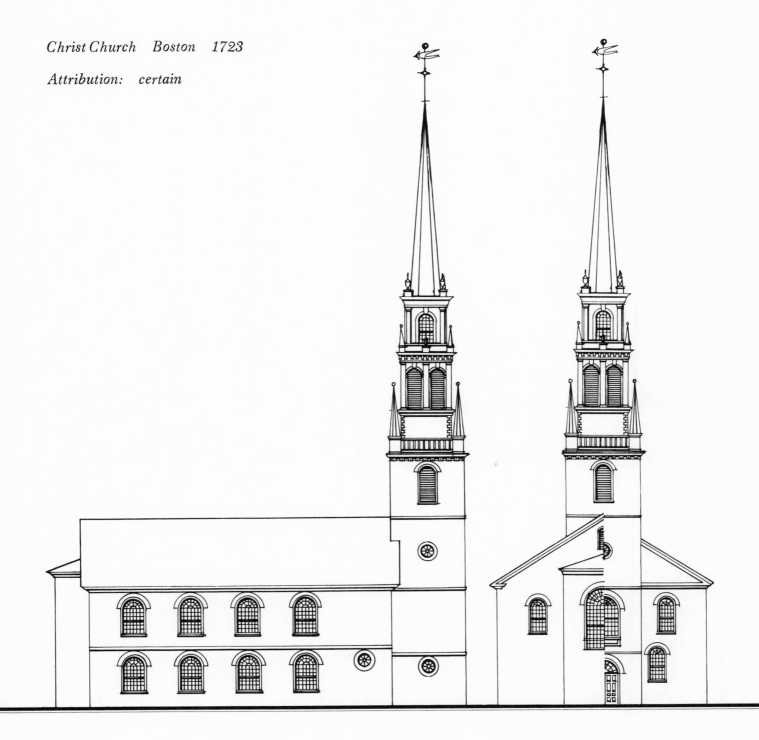

## James Gibbs    1682-1754

JAMES GIBBS was a pupil of Wren's who spent some time in Italy. Of all the buildings designed by Wren's assistants and pupils, those of Gibbs reflect most closely the style we have come to know as the 'Wren' style, although it should be pointed out that Wren himself, especially in his later years, did not always stick to the 'Wren' style.

Wren, who was above all a scientist and therefore a busy man, and who had many assistants in his architectural work, never set down for posterity his ideas concerning architecture. Gibbs, however, published many of his ideas and designs in two books called *Book of Architecture* (1728) and *Rules for Drawing* (1732). These books were widely used in the Colonies after 1750, whether for details as in the case of Peter Harrison and John Ariss or for complete buildings, such as St. Paul's Chapel in New York and the First Baptist Meeting House in Providence. In spite of his great success in the Colonies with his books, Gibbs only designed one building directly for construction in the Colonies, and even this is conjecture for it does not rest on documentary evidence.

*St. Philip's Church    Charleston    1723*    *demolished 1835, reconstruction*

*Attribution:    probable*

*west*                                    *east*

St. Philip's Church in Charleston was built in 1723 to replace an earlier church that had become too small. It was of brick with stucco trim. The inside was five bays long, but considerable length was added to this on the outside by three entrance porticos and a thick tower. These Tuscan entrance porticos mark the first use of giant-order porticos in the Colonies, although it is widely supposed that the portico on Peter Harrison's Redwood Library in Newport, built 25 years after St. Philip's, was the first.

The side of the nave had four giant round-headed windows and a matching door in the center; each window was separated from its neighbor by a giant pilaster of the Tuscan order. Above the roof line, the tower was in three stages, all octagonal. The lowest was the bell stage; above that was the clock stage, capped with a dome, and above that a heavy lantern. The tower is slightly reminiscent of that on St. Nicholas' Worcester, in England, built between 1726 and 1730 by Thomas White from an idea by Gibbs.

So far, there has been nothing to give Gibbs the nod over the local designer of such houses as Archdale Hall. However, it is the interior that has the telling mark of Gibbs. The only trouble about it is that the Kirk in Aberdeen, Scotland, whose interior was identical with that of St. Philip's, was not built until about twenty years after St. Philip's. This, however, does not preclude the possibility that Gibbs actually did the design of the Kirk long before it was built. Massive piers supported longitudinal arches, on top of which was an architrave supporting a barrel vault; pilasters on the inside face of the piers stretched from a plinth to the architrave. Gibbs seems to have copied this arrangement almost exactly from Wren's St. Peter's Cornhill in London, but there is no possibility of Wren's having designed St. Philip's: quite apart from the late date (Wren died the year St. Philip's was started), Wren never put giant-order porticos in front of his churches, while such porticos were commonly used by Gibbs. Both St. Philip's and the Aberdeen Kirk had galleries abutting on the piers.

St. Philip's caught fire during the eighteenth century, but was saved by the courage of a Negro, who was set free for his trouble. His efforts were partly in vain, however, for the church caught fire again in 1835, and this time there was no one to save it. A new church has been erected on the old foundations, but both externally and internally it is slightly different from the old one; outside, the new one has a tall spire, and an apse at the east end, and inside, the massive piers have been replaced by light columns in a scheme copied ironically enough from a contemporary of St. Philip's, Christ Church in Philadelphia (q.v.).

It is sad to note that of all the great early churches in the Colonies the only two we have lost were both dedicated to St. Philip, and both were in the Carolinas; perhaps it is best to rejoice that we have not lost more.

THERE remain a few more buildings that are tagged 'plans sent from England.' One of these is the Holden Chapel at Harvard University. A small rectangular building, it was built of brick in 1742 as a result of a bequest. It is shaped like a temple, and is three bays long. Ridges of brick between each pair of tall round-headed windows recall pilasters, but they are not dressed with the capitals or bases of pilasters; above them is a Doric entablature around the eaves. The door in the end is round-headed, and it is surrounded by a pair of Doric pilasters supporting an entablature. The building has been used for practically everything but its original purpose, and has most recently served as headquarters for the Glee Club.

*Holden Chapel   Cambridge, Massachusetts   1742*

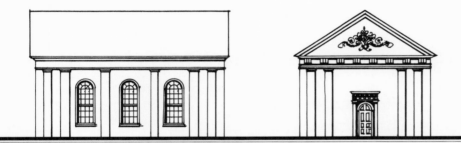

*Robert May and Company, London*

**D**ELAWARE situated next to two richly endowed neighbors Pennsylvania and Maryland, is poor in academic architecture of the Colonial period. There is some work, however, designed by the firm of Robert May & Company, variously described as from London and from Philadelphia. May is not mentioned in H. M. Colvin's *Biographical Dictionary of English Architects 1660-1840*, which may indicate that his work was not highly enough regarded to qualify him as an architect by English standards. This can be confirmed by a look at some of his buildings, which although quite attractive yet are not up to the best work done in the other Colonies at this date. Among May's buildings are the Old Drawyers Presbyterian Church and the Corbit House, both built around 1773 in Odessa. The church is a simple, brick, rectangular building, two storeys high, with a low gable roof. At the back, it has a pair of round-headed windows that shed light on the pulpit, but all the rest of the windows are rectangular, although those on the lower floor are arched on the soffit.

*Old Drawers Presbyterian Church    Odessa, Delaware    1773*          *Attribution:    certain*

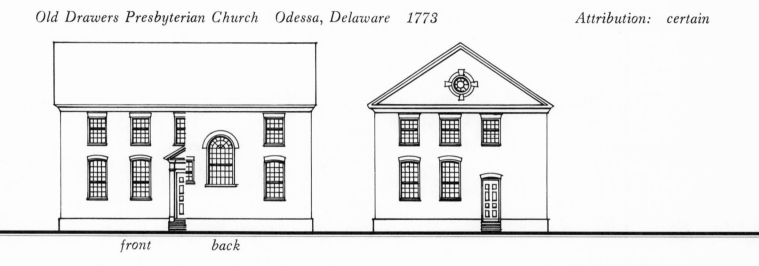

    *front*       *back*

The Corbit House is five bays long and 2½ storeys high. It is rather tall for its size, although this is offset by its attractive composition and appearance. Certain features of its decoration classify it as being in the Chippendale style, named after the Georgian English cabinetmaker; these features include the elegant dormer windows and the Chinese Chippendale roof-deck balustrade. There are probably other Delaware houses by May, but little research has been done in this direction; anyway it is likely that these two are his best.

*Corbit House    Odessa, Delaware    about 1773*          *Attribution:    certain*

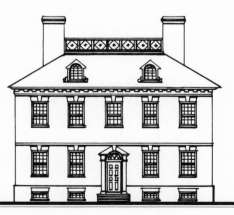

# Architects of the American Colonies: South

*John Prince    fl. 1705-1730*

THOMAS T. WATERMAN is probably the first architectural historian to have seen that there were certain architectural connections between some of the early buildings of Virginia, and that these buildings most likely had a single architect. Waterman calls this architect 'John Prince,' because of the similarity of the Virginia buildings with some contemporary houses built in Shropshire in England by a man named John Prince. This theory is but a speculation, although not necessarily a poor speculation; we are no more than honoring Waterman's theory by calling the Virginia man 'John Prince.'

Whether or not his name was Prince, one thing is almost certain: that all or most of the buildings in question were designed by one man. Many of their similar features that lead us to this conclusion are internal, and so unfortunately we shall not be able to devote much space to discussing them in this book.

By far the most important of this group of buildings is Rosewell Hall. Situated across the York River from Williamsburg in Gloucester County, Virginia, Rosewell was the seat of the Mann Page family. It was begun shortly after 1715, but construction delays forced the mansion to remain uncompleted for half a century. The main part of the mansion was a large rectangle with a bold pavilion on each face. The main block was the focus of an impressive complex, which included two 1½-storey forecourt dependencies, one of which was the kitchen and the other the servants' quarters. Each dependency was five bays long, with gable roof, hipped dormers and end-chimneys. The mansion itself was 3½ storeys high with a tall deck-on-hip roof. At either end of the roof deck, which was surrounded by a balustrade, were cupolas. This arrangement of two cupolas has no parallels in the American Colonies, and there are very few examples of it in Britain.

All the buildings at Rosewell are of brick laid in Flemish bond. The brickwork is exquisitely done; the two main doors are decorated with elaborately rubbed and moulded brick, the one at the front having a triangular pediment, and the one at the back a segmental pediment. Over the windows are carved stone keystones set in segmental brick arches. There is a tall round-headed window in the center of each side pavilion; it and the window above it are wider than most of the rest of the windows. Similarly, the windows in the center of the front and back pavilions, over the doors, are wider. The round-headed windows at the sides were to light the stairways, which were placed in the side pavilions.

This is the feature that most relates Rosewell to a house in England by Prince; except for the number of windows, the ground plan of Rosewell is identical with that of Cound Hall near Shrewsbury in Shropshire. There is the same arrangement of pavilions, and the same arrangement of rooms and staircases inside, as far as the difference in size between the two houses permits, for although Rosewell was one of the largest houses built in Colonial America yet it was very much smaller than Cound, which in turn was not enormous by English standards.

If the architecture of Rosewell is outstanding, the mansion also has claim to an interesting history. One of its owners, Mann Page, Governor of Virginia, was a best friend of Thomas Jefferson, and the latter spent many long hours at his friend's home. The two were interested in science, and among other things constructed a tank for measuring rainfall on the roof. It is said that Jefferson, in a playful mood, stocked the tank with fish so that the two could fish up on the roof. It is also said that Jefferson composed the Declaration of Independence while sitting up on the roof, staring out over the York River.

In 1838, the house was altered; the cupolas, high roof and parapet around the roof were removed and replaced with a low hipped roof, with gable pediments over the side pavilions. Most of the beautiful walnut and mahogany panelling was also removed at this time, and installed in a small house nearby. Finally, in 1916 the mansion burned down; the whole interior was destroyed, including the huge carved main staircase, which had three twisted balusters per step.

Today, the house remains a picturesque ruin, and although all four walls stand for most of their extent, the building can not expect to survive much longer. The dependencies have long since been swallowed up by the surrounding jungle, but some fine family tombstones remain nearby.

*Rosewell Hall    Gloucester County    1715-1740*          *burnt  1916, reconstruction*

*Attribution:    probable*

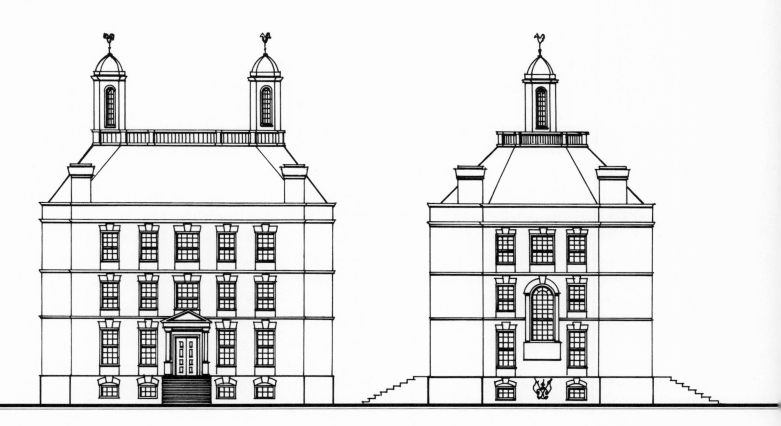

*two matching forecourt dependencies, five bays each*

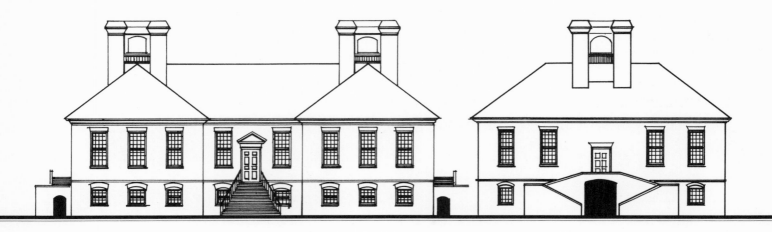

Stratford Hall, near Montross in Westmoreland County, was built at about the same time as Rosewell. Although the two are equally attractive and equally unique in Colonial American architecture, there could hardly be more of a contrast between them in many ways. Stratford is a monumental house built on an H-plan, surrounded by four small dependencies. The house is one main storey set on top of a high basement.* The hipped roof has no dormers, but is crowned at each end by a cluster of four chimneys; a balustraded platform stands inside each cluster. The whole has a massive quality about it reminiscent of the work of Vanbrugh and Hawksmoor in England.

In the middle of the front and back façades rise rather severe flights of steps in Portland stone; the steps are tapered in a straight line to the top, and have heavy balustrades. At the top of the steps is a large doorway surmounted by a crude brick pediment.

The door leads into a large hall that runs the length of the bar of the H. The hall has very fine panelling from floor to cornice, and is broken up with Corinthian pilasters. The ceiling is a high cove that sticks up into the roof. At each end of the central hall are the living quarters, with small stairways descending to the basement, in which is the kitchen.

The house is built of brick, laid in Flemish bond. The bricks of the basement storey are of a larger size, and have glazed headers. The basement windows have a segmentally arched soffit, but the taller windows of the main floor have flat lintels. The trim is all of brick, including the floor belt course and the soffit lintels. Much of the detail on the house resembles detail on houses in and around Shrewsbury, and so again the finger points to John Prince as architect.

The mansion was built for Thomas Lee in about 1725; Thomas' sons Richard Henry and Francis Lightfoot were born and raised here, as was his grandson Robert E. Lee. The house is restored and is open to the public.

Tucked away on a side road near Kilmarnock in Lancaster County is Christ Church, obviously a strong contender for a title of 'most perfect building of the American Colonies.' It was built in 1732 to replace an outgrown older church a few miles away. Robert 'King' Carter, the local grandee, had found the old site inconvenient, and so he agreed to pay for the new church if it were built near his mansion of Corotoman. He died before the church was even started, but his heirs confirmed the gift. Because it is so out of the way this church has survived almost untouched since the eighteenth century.

The building is in the shape of a Greek cross; that is, the distance from the altar windows

* This arrangement is often called *Piano Nobile*.

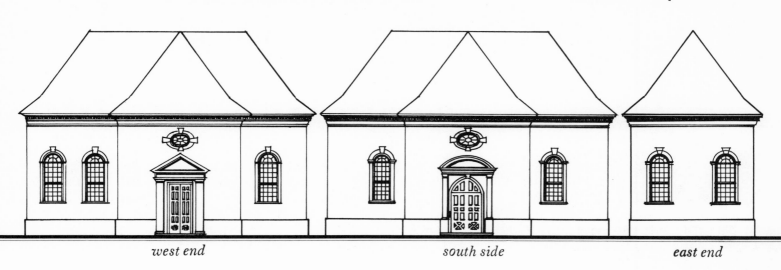

*west end*                              *south side*                              *east end*

to the west door is the same as the distance from transept door to transept door. However, the transepts are nearer the east end than the west.

The brickwork is of the highest quality. It is laid in Flemish bond with occasional glazed headers. The trim is very similar to that on Rosewell, especially on the transept doorways and the round-headed windows. The west door is more elaborate: it has a segmental pediment resting on a detailed architrave over well-proportioned Doric pilasters; the door itself has a round-headed arch with stone keystones. Over the three doorways are oval bull's-eye windows with the same stone and brick trim. The cornice with triple-plane architrave, cushion frieze and block dentil course is boldly conceived and delicately executed. It supports a steep hipped roof with splayed eaves that gives an effect reminiscent of a Chinese pagoda, although the passion for things Chinese had not yet materialized.

Inside, the ceiling is a cross barrel-vault, beautiful in its airy simplicity. The walls are three feet thick, which gives an atmosphere of coolness and solidity. With the exception of the addition of galleries in Victorian times, the interior woodwork is original. Especially noteworthy are the high panelled box pews, the pulpit with sounding board and the chancel trim, all done in walnut and pine. The floor is of Purbeck stone. Under the chancel wall is Carter's superb marble tomb.

Of all the buildings in Virginia that we have ascribed to the man we call John Prince, none owes more than Christ Church does to the drawings in William Salmon's builders' guide, *Palladio Londinensis*. Among the helpful drawings in Salmon's book are doorways, entablatures, windows, and even the splayed-eave roof with barrel-vault ceiling underneath found at Christ Church. Various designs from this book also appear in the trim of all the other buildings attributed to this architect. The use of pattern books from England was popular among Colonial architects, and there were a great many different publications. This particular architect may have used some of the others too, but he seems to have relied chiefly on Salmon.

While speaking of English precedent and patterns for American buildings, one might mention a little church in Farley, Wiltshire, which bears at least a superficial resemblance to Christ Church. This was built in 1688, and has been attributed to Sir Christopher Wren, although without any certainty. It is simpler in treatment than Christ Church, and has a tower on the west end, but the similarities are enough to make one wonder whether Prince hadn't perhaps seen Farley Church; after all, Wiltshire is not far from Shropshire.

*two matching forecourt dependencies, river side*

In an old frame house called Morattico in Lancaster County, Virginia, now destroyed by the erosion of the river, was a painting done on a wooden overmantel panel. It is of a large mansion with dependencies near a river. It has been said by those who know that this mansion is not in Britain. If therefore the painter was not inventing such a house—admittedly a possibility—then it must have been a Virginia mansion. There are, however, many gaps in the archaeology of Virginia still to be filled, and it is quite likely that the foundations of something like this house will some day be discovered and excavated. The most logical Virginia mansion to have had this form was Robert Carter's Corotoman, already mentioned as being close to Christ Church in Lancaster County. Other possibilities were Rippon Hall, Warner Hall and Turkey Island.

Allowing quite a bit for the crudity of the overmantel painting, a not unreasonable mansion can be reconstructed. It resembles Rosewell in plan, but is larger and more elaborate. It is 3½ storeys on top of a high basement. The front and side pavilions of the lower two floors are decorated with pilasters between each bay, with heavy entablatures on top of each row of pilasters. The massive front door is surmounted by a heavy balcony. The roof, surrounded by a parapet and studded with dormer windows, is a deck-on-hip of steep pitch. On the center of the deck is a complicated two-storey cupola, set off by four heavy but tall decorated chimneys. The dependencies echo this arrangement, being 2½ storeys with pilastered trim on the ground floor; the deck-on-hip roof is topped by a simple cupola between two massive chimneys at the break of the hip.

The whole, as far as we can tell, was of brick with stone trim. The windows probably became smaller as they went up the façade, as at Rosewell and at many other Virginia mansions. However, because of the dubious nature of this interesting building, probably the less said the better.

The Carter family has appeared a number of times so far, and is to appear many more times, for the Carters were well-to-do, and used their wealth to build houses. One such house is Sabine Hall near Warsaw in Richmond County. It is situated high on a hill overlooking the Rappahannock River, a rectangular building of 2½ storeys and four end-chimneys. It has been altered, but it originally had a high hip roof. It is of brick laid in Flemish bond with glazed headers, and with a profusion of stone trim. Central pavilions one window wide are outlined in the front and back in stone, but they actually do not project from the façades. The windows are all covered by stone lintels in a manner quite like some Shrewsbury houses, but unlike anything else found in America. Like Rosewell, the main stairway is in the center of a side, and this stairway is lit by a tall, wide window, but unlike Rosewell this window has a flat top. Many of the interior details seem to come from Shrewsbury houses, notably the Judge's Lodging.

Since it was built in 1729 Sabine Hall has undergone a number of minor alterations. The dependencies have been replaced; the hip roof has been made lower in pitch, and wide pediments have been added over the central pavilions. The pediment in the front has been projected forward to rest on four large columns, while at the back a one-storey porch has been built the length of the house.

*Sabine Hall   Warsaw, Richmond County   1729*                    *now slightly altered*

*Attribution:   probable*

Very like Sabine Hall in shape, but considerably larger, was Nomini Hall near Montross in Westmoreland County. This was another Carter home. Since it was destroyed by fire many years before photography, we have little evidence about its appearance. It seems to have had four end-chimneys and a deck-on-hip roof with splayed eaves. Verbal descriptions and a crude drawing show us that it had two storeys with seven bays in the front, but only four bays in the rear. The front door seems to have resembled the one at Rosewell, while the two doors at the back were glazed. Carter may have installed the two Venetian windows alongside the glazed doors at the back at a later date, but if they are original they are certainly the first instance of such windows in an American private house, although Christ Church in Philadelphia, designed before 1727, has such a window.

The house was of brick, covered in lime soon after it was built. As far as we can tell, there were stone keystones over the windows. However, very little is really known about this house, and it would be wiser to move on to the next one.

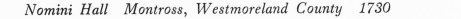

*Nomini Hall   Montross, Westmoreland County   1730*     *burnt 1850, reconstruction*

*Attribution:   probable*

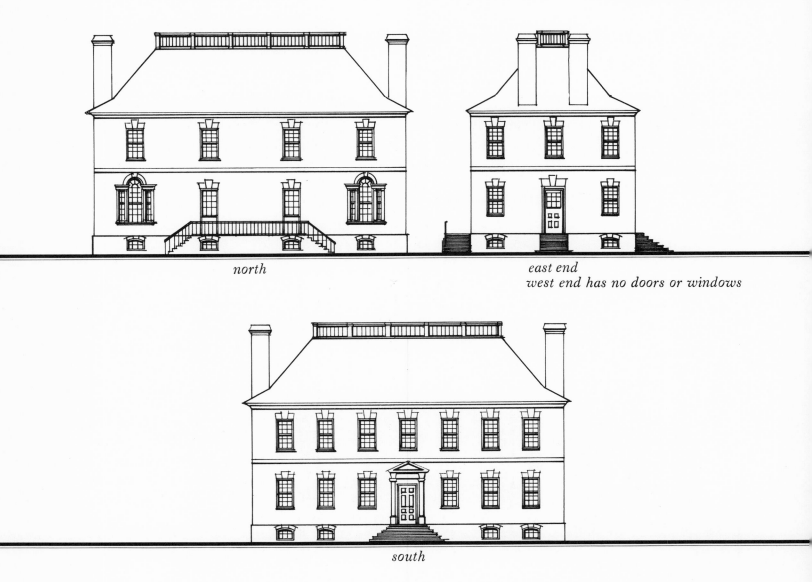

*north*

*east end*
*west end has no doors or windows*

*south*

Most formal houses in the Queen Anne and Georgian styles in this country have hipped roofs in some form or other. However, in later Georgian architecture, such as that ushered in by Jefferson after the Revolution, many houses were given gable roofs with a formal pediment in the gable end. Nevertheless, there were at least three Virginia houses built in the first quarter of the eighteenth century that had gable roofs that were meant to be formal. The first of these was Berkeley, in Charles City County, built in 1726.

Berkeley is the largest of the three buildings of its type. It has two chimneys along the ridgepole, set in a bit from the ends of the house, and is five bays long. The bricks are laid in Flemish bond with random glazing. The present doorways are modern, being gauged brick pediments supported by pilasters; there is evidence that they were once done in stone. The horizontal cornices of the pediments on the gable ends are covered by little roofs of their own that run into the gable ends as if the gables were hiding a hipped roof underneath; this is an interesting and attractive feature that is also found in the other two buildings of this type.

*Berkeley   Charles City County   1726*          *now much altered internally*

*Attribution:   probable*

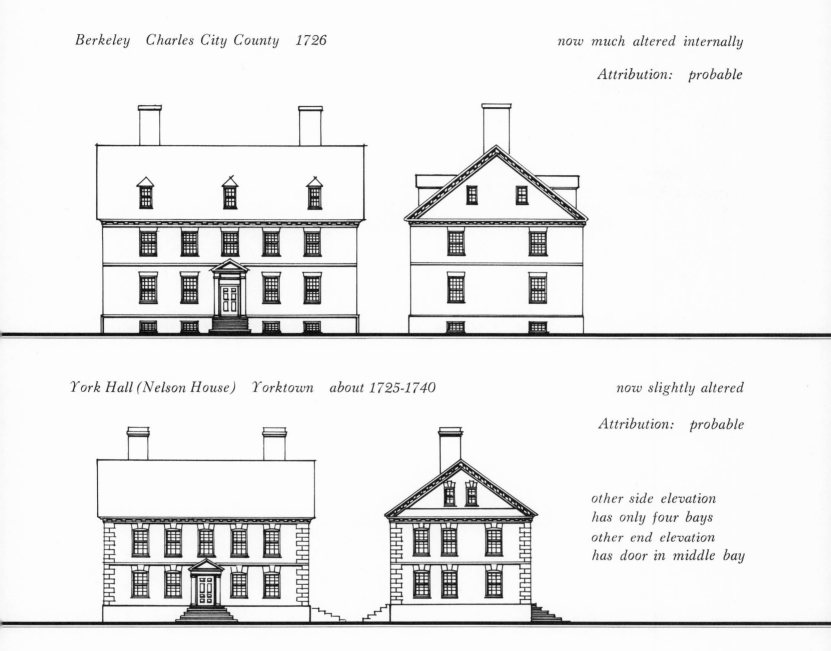

*York Hall (Nelson House)   Yorktown   about 1725-1740*          *now slightly altered*

*Attribution:   probable*

*other side elevation
has only four bays
other end elevation
has door in middle bay*

In plan, the house is four rooms and a central hall on each floor; the main staircase is in the hall, which runs from front to back. While the basic elements of the house have not changed much, the house was rebuilt after a fire around 1800, and so all the decorative features are of that date. Little can therefore be said about its original trim, but it seems that the sashes in the windows were like the big ones at Nomini Hall (not the Venetian windows at Nomini, of course). Berkeley was the home of both Presidents Harrison.

Similar in type, but totally different in feeling, is the Nelson House in Yorktown, now known as York Hall. It was built at about the same time as Berkeley, and was definitely finished by 1735. It has much richer detail than Berkeley, but is a little smaller. The front elevation is five bays of two storeys, but the back is only four bays. Trim, such as corner quoins, window sills and keystones, is of stone. The brick is laid in Flemish bond, and the effect is slightly reminiscent of Rosewell. The windows are arched on the soffit, and the cornice is bold with its row of precise modillions.

Inside, the plan is like that of Berkeley, but it is asymmetrical, both from front to back and from side to side. Although the chimneys are symmetrically balanced in the front or back elevation, they are not balanced on the side elevation, and both rise on the rear side of the ridgepole. Almost all the interior woodwork, which is quite fine, survives. British and American troops made an effort to spare the house during the siege of Yorktown, and it was but slightly damaged during the Civil War. Dormer windows have been installed in recent years to provide more room, as was also done at Berkeley.

The other building in this category is not a major one; it is a dependency for an older house that was soon destroyed, although a second mansion was built close by at a later date. This is Shirley. Actually, there are two dependencies, but they are identical. Here the roof pitch is a little steeper, and the eaves are splayed. The chimneys are part of the gable ends. The buildings are each five bays long and two storeys high. The windows have shallow segmentally arched soffits, like Rosewell and the Nelson House. In addition are a pair of L-shaped carriage houses or stables, one storey high, that seem to belong to this group, but they are quite plain, although charming. All four are of brick laid in Flemish bond.

Another mansion once stood close by; this was Jacobean in style, rather like Bacon's Castle, but it was probably modified by Prince when he erected the dependencies. The mansion, however, was soon destroyed, and the present Shirley was built about 1770. Shirley was another home of the Carter family, so it is likely that they would have used the same architect. Certain parts of the alterations to the old mansion, such as a section of a chimney that is lying nearby, show similarity in detail to Rosewell and to patterns in Salmon's book.

*One of two matching forecourt dependencies at Shirley (south)   Charles City County        before 1740*

*Attribution:   probable*

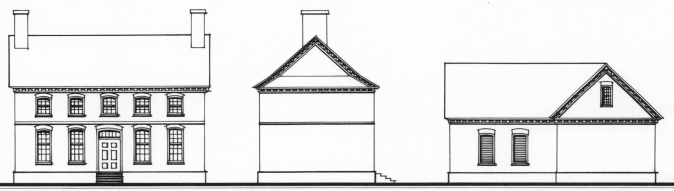

*two matching L-shaped stables*

The last two buildings which may have been designed by Prince are perhaps not of so great importance as those already discussed, but they are both charming buildings. The first is the Custom House in Yorktown, built in 1715. For its early date it is quite academic, having a hip roof and a well-defined modillion cornice. It is two storeys high, and two bays wide, the front being on the narrow axis. The bricks are laid in Flemish bond with glazed headers. The windows and low doors of the ground floor are arched on the soffit, but the bricks forming the lintel of the windows appear squashed by the low belt course. There is one chimney at the back. This building is in excellent repair, and is extremely reminiscent of some buildings by Prince in Shrewsbury.

*Custom House    Yorktown    1715*                                        *Attribution:    probable*

St. Mary's Church Whitechapel, Lancaster County, was once cruciform like its neighbor, Christ Church, but unfortunately in 1830, after the church had remained abandoned for many years, the nave and chancel arms of the cross were pulled down. The transept was then restored as a rectangular church. When St. Mary's was first built, it must have resembled Christ Church quite considerably, except that the latter had richer detail and was slightly larger. St. Mary's is built of brick laid in Flemish bond with much glazing. Inside, the woodwork has been altered. It is a pity that this church has been so changed that the original appearance beyond an outline is obscured to us.

*St. Mary Church    Whitechapel, Lancaster County    about 1732*          *conjectural restoration*

*Attribution:    possible*

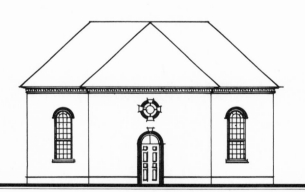

As we noted earlier, the story of John Prince and the first architect of Virginia is an enigma, and probably will remain so, but no one can deny the beauty and charm of the foregoing buildings. They are connected to each other by many similar details; is this a coincidence of a number of people using the same pattern book, or is it all the work of one man? Here is a problem that we will run into often in our discussion of early buildings. Just because there is no documentary evidence does not mean to say that a certain architect did not design certain buildings, and yet it is sometimes not enough to be guided by mere similarities in detail.

*Henry Cary & Son*

**T**HE distinction between a builder and an architect is often difficult to draw; many people think it is only in the eye of the beholder. Nevertheless, in this book we have tried to make such a distinction. Henry Cary truly has feet in both camps, for he designed a few buildings on his own, and also built some to the designs of others. Cary was roughly contemporary with the man we have called Prince, and may even have been the builder or overseer of building for the buildings designed by Prince. This, however, is not too likely, since Cary plainly learned from building according to designs of some buildings, while there seems to be no trace of his having learned from anything designed by Prince. Cary's history is a little hazy, in spite of the great effort made by the authorities at Williamsburg to obtain complete documentation for all their buildings. However, we can make educated guesses to fill in the gaps.

Cary was probably involved in the building of the College of William & Mary, the first and second times (*q.v.*), especially since his brother Miles was on the board of directors. He supervised the construction of the Palace (*q.v.*), the Gaol and the Capitol (*q.v.*), and possibly did other minor buildings around Williamsburg. No doubt his son, Henry Cary, Jr., helped his father and learned from him by working with him on these projects. Henry Jr. was almost certainly involved in work done to Bruton Parish Church and to the Powder Magazine at Williamsburg, although he was not the leading figure in either (the Magazine was designed by Governor Alexander Spotswood, as far as can be known). Henry Jr. also did two other churches, based on the design for the transept of Bruton Parish Church. They are St. John's in Hampton (1728) and St. Paul's Norfolk (1739). Both are cruciform buildings, and are so closely modelled on parts of Bruton that Cary's services can not really be described as those of an architect; therefore these churches have been arbitrarily omitted from the illustrations in this book; Henry Jr.'s chapel wing of the College is also omitted, as it may have been part of an original design.

Henry Jr. built Ampthill in Chesterfield County before 1732 with the help of his father; it was their family residence. Ampthill is discussed later in this book because it was altered by Richard Taliaferro, who made it into a more substantial house. The other three buildings

*Brafferton Hall   The College of William and Mary   1723*            *Attribution:   certain*

we are ascribing to the Carys are illustrated under their names. The first is Brafferton Hall, or the Brafferton, as it has sometimes been called, at William & Mary College. This was built in 1723 as a dormitory for Indian students at the College. It is a two-storey hip-roofed building five bays long, with well-shaped chimneys in the ridgepole. The proportions are rigid but simple. The roof is of very steep pitch, and has three gabled dormers on the front, and one at each side. Over the door is a large transom light below a deep brick lintel, covered by a strange brick modillioned pediment. The brick of the walls is laid in Flemish bond with glazed headers. The whole exterior appearance is obviously inspired by the Governor's Palace, from the proportions of the sash to the pitch of the roof to the shape and position of the chimneys. The interior floor plan is quite unrelated to the Palace, it being three rooms with a central stair-hall that stretches from front to back of the house.

*President's House   The College of William and Mary   1732*          *Attribution:   certain*

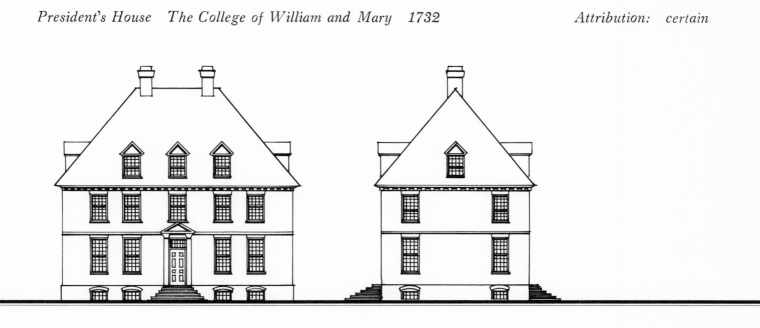

In 1732, Cary built another house in front of the College building and placed symmetrically to the Brafferton. This was the President's House. It is identical in appearance with Brafferton Hall, but upon close examination turns out to be a few feet bigger in all its dimensions. Inside it is similar to the other house, except that the large room on the right of the front door in the Brafferton has been turned into two rooms, because of the bigger dimensions of the newer house; the result is a typical four-room plan with central hall.

*Kingsmill   James City County   about 1730*                              *burnt 1900*

*Attribution:   probable*

*two matching four-bay forecourt dependencies 166' apart*

The last building connected with Henry Cary, Jr., is the plantation of Kingsmill outside Williamsburg. This is only a conjecture, but circumstantial evidence points strongly to Cary. The mansion was a house about the size of the Palace, with two advance dependencies, as at the Palace. Kingsmill's dependencies, however, are 1½ times as far apart as those of the Palace, indicating that the builder had learned a lesson from the slightly cramped effect of the Palace forecourt.

Kingsmill was built for the Kingsmill family around 1730. It was later owned by the Burwell family. In 1900 the main building was destroyed by fire, and since there is no written or pictorial description of it we can only conjecture that it looked like Brafferton Hall or the President's House, from the shape of the foundations. The dependencies are in poor shape, and one of them was burned, although it has now been rebuilt. The site is owned by Colonial Williamsburg, and it is hoped that detailed excavations may give some clue to the original appearance of the mansion.

*Richard Taliaferro   1705-1779*

RICHARD TALIAFERRO (pronounced 'Toliver') was a Virginia gentleman, like the men for whom he designed houses, and a burgess. Actually, the evidence for his being an architect is very scanty, but since a large number of buildings from 1730 to 1762 seem to have been designed by the same man, and we have no documentary evidence giving us a name for this man, we are calling him Taliaferro on the strength of the slight evidence that we have.

This evidence is in documents relating to the mid-century additions and alterations to the Palace, and in three houses owned by Taliaferro and his family that belong in the group under discussion. Taliaferro, who lived in a house on the Palace Green, apparently designed the ballroom wing of the Palace in about 1750, for he is described as Virginia's 'most skillful Architect' in connection with the building of this wing. He also is recorded as having been in charge of renovations to the President's House at the College.

Practically nothing is known about the appearance of the ballroom wing of the Palace. The floor plan, of course, was found by excavation and from plans drawn by Jefferson, but apart from that the reconstruction built in the 1930's is a complete guess. In fact, although the reconstructed rooms are indeed beautiful, it is quite obvious now that the man who designed this large group of Virginia houses could not have designed the wing to the Palace the way it has now been built; for one thing, the Chinese Chippendale motif is quite foreign to the methods of Taliaferro, and for another he did not use cove ceilings anywhere else, although they do seem to be most applicable in this situation.

The only other clue that indicates that Taliaferro may be the undocumented architect of this group of buildings is that he designed two houses for himself that fit perfectly into the group, as does a third house designed for a cousin of his. These are, respectively, Powhatan in James City County (1735), the Wythe House in Williamsburg (1750), and Brooke's Bank in Essex County (date uncertain). We shall come to these later.

Taliaferro almost certainly learned his architecture from John Prince, just as Thomas Jefferson later learned from Taliaferro. The learning in each case must have been from a mixture of actual experience on the job with the teacher and from pattern books and builders' handbooks sent from England. The early work of Taliaferro seems to have many of the qualities of Prince's Virginia buildings, but does not seem to be up to Prince's standard. Later, Taliaferro's architecture matured, but he never got far away from the style he developed in the beginning. In his later buildings Taliaferro shows himself to be a master of the medium of brick; most of his later buildings have their architectural details in brick, with little or no stone or wood ornamentation beyond the roof cornices.

Westover in Charles City County is assumed to be Taliaferro's first work. It was built for the Byrd family in 1732, and although scholars dispute whether the house was burned twenty years later or not, it is almost certain that if it was burned it was also rebuilt exactly as originally.

Westover is a beautiful mansion, especially in its setting surrounded by tulip poplars above the river. The main house is of brick, laid in Flemish bond, and is two storeys high set on a high basement. The front and back are seven bays wide. The hip roof is of extremely steep pitch, and has a row of hip-roofed dormers. Chimneys in the end walls are part of all of Taliaferro's early houses; Westover has four. The windows, which are diminished in size quite subtly on the upper floors, are arched on the soffit, and have brick lintels. Other exterior trim includes a fine modillioned cornice, a narrow stone belt course, and stone doorways from Salmon's book. The south doorway is a split ogee pediment of the type so often poorly imi-

tated, set on pilasters of the composite order; the doorway on the north side has a more graceful segmental pediment set on fluted Corinthian pilasters. Obviously the inspiration for Westover came from Sabine Hall, but the effect is totally different.

*Westover   Charles City County   1730*                                    *slightly altered*

*Attribution:   probable*

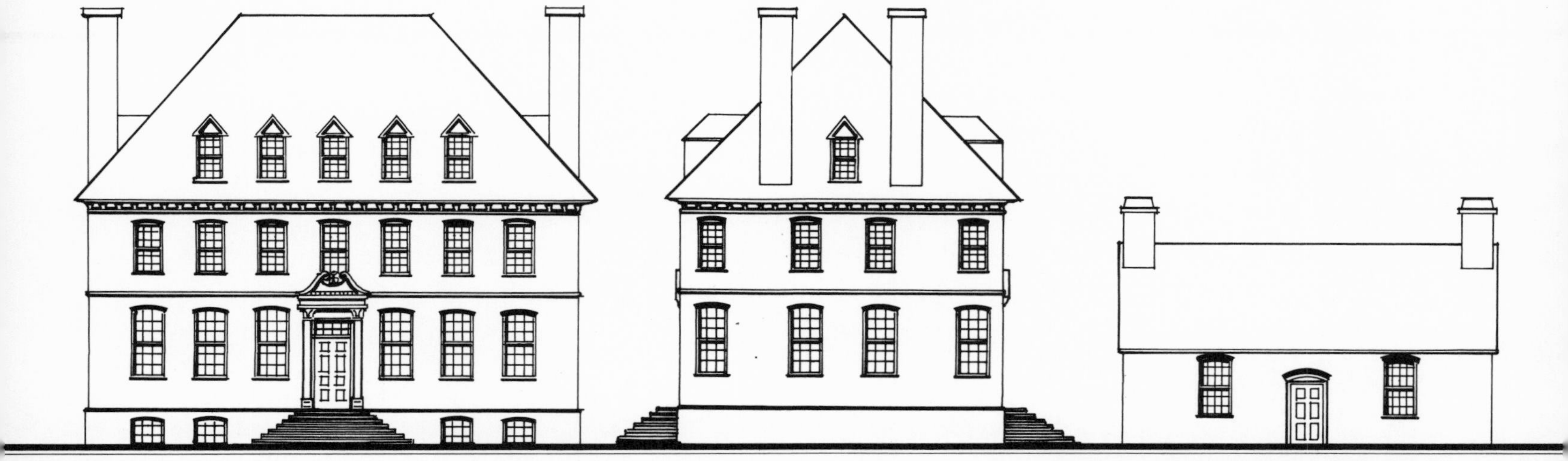

two matching side dependencies

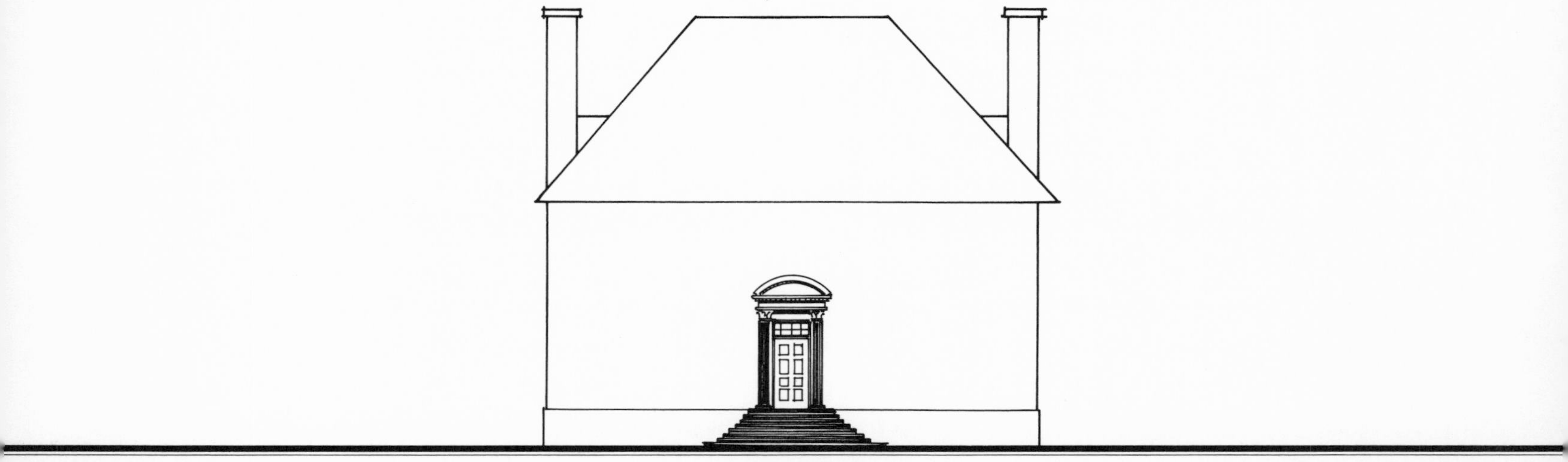

north door

The main house is flanked by two simple three-bay dependencies of one storey each; they
have gable roofs, and a chimney at each end. These have been joined to the house by enclosed
corridors in recent years, but originally they were detached. One flanker now has a gambrel
roof.

Inside, the main house has a wealth of detail. There are exquisitely carved wood and stone
mantels, plaster ceiling decoration (of a later date) and a fine staircase with twisted balusters.
There are some archaic features about the design of the panelling and the arrangement of the
pilasters, but generally the effect is more than satisfactory. In plan, the house has four rooms
to the floor with an off-center stair-hall, a plan that Taliaferro was to modify in his later
buildings.

*Eppington    Chesterfield County    about 1732*                    *slightly altered*

*Attribution:   possible*

Eppington in Chesterfield County was built for the Jefferson family around 1732. It is a simple wooden building, but obviously connected to Westover in concept. There is a central pavilion of two storeys with high hip roof and end-chimneys; this pavilion is only three bays wide, but it has a one-storey wing on each side of it, two bays wide. Beyond a modillioned cornice, there is no other exterior detail. The appearance of the house has now been altered by the addition of a porch.

*Wilton    Henrico County    1753*                    *moved to Richmond 1934*

*Attribution:   probable*

Wilton, built in Henrico County in 1753 and moved to Richmond in 1934, is transitional between Taliaferro's two styles. It has the four end-chimneys and white doorways of Westover, and the lower pitched hip roof of later buildings. It is built of brick laid in Flemish bond, and in almost all dimensions is exactly the same size as Westover; Wilton, however, has a façade of only five bays to Westover's seven. The window lintels at Wilton are also different from those at Westover: they are flat while Westover's are arched. The doorway at Wilton, repeated at the back of the house, is of wood, and is in the same family of design as Westover's.

In plan, the houses are almost identical, with four rooms around an off-center hall. The staircase and panelling, too, are related to their counterparts in Westover, but show slight changes in the direction of the more academic Georgian period from the rather warmer Queen Anne period. There is really the same sort of difference between the outsides of the two houses.

Wilton was built for the Randolph family, and is now the headquarters for the National Society of Colonial Dames of America in the State of Virginia. It is open to the public.

Carter's Grove, in James City County, perhaps represents the acme of Taliaferro's designs. It was built around 1750 by the Carter family, who naturally wanted the latest in design. It is of brick laid in Flemish bond two storeys high, seven bays wide at the front and only five bays at the back; this feature was repeated in a number of Taliaferro's later houses, as it produced a rather attractive arrangement for the central stair-hall, and allowed the hall to have some light.

The main house had a hip roof about the same height as the one at Wilton, and therefore was much lower than that at Westover. The two chimneys come out of the side faces of the hip, just outside the ridgepole. However, the whole arrangement has now been altered: a high roof like Westover's has been added, together with a row of hipped dormers, and the dependencies at the side have been enlarged and linked to the main house. It is hoped that some day the mansion will be returned to its original appearance. The fine doorways are of brick.

Inside, Carter's Grove has four rooms around the central hall; the hall is wider at the front of the house than at the back, so as to let some light in; the staircase is in the narrower section of the hall. There is a graceful arch across the hall at the foot of the stairs where the hall changes its width; the arch rests on panelled Doric pilasters and is surmounted with an attractive modillioned cornice that goes around the whole hall. As at Wilton, the panelling has taken on a Georgian formality lacking at Westover, and the staircase here has replaced the twisted balusters of the earlier houses with plain shafts and vases in the Georgian taste. Carter's Grove is open to the public.

There were two other houses very similar in design to Carter's Grove. These were Cleve in King George County, and Peckatone in Westmoreland County, both built between 1750

*Carter's Grove   James City County   1750-1753*                    *altered 1928*

*Attribution:   probable*

*back has only five bays*                    *two matching side dependencies*

*back has only five bays*

and 1755. In spite of the similarity of their designs, these houses were very different in feeling from Carter's Grove, and to a lesser extent from each other. Cleve had elaborate stone trim as quoins at the corners of the house and around all the windows and doors; this must have produced an overpowering contrast between the white stone and the soft salmon-colored brick of the house. The basic idea of this decoration comes from Sabine Hall, but at Cleve it is not so successful. One reason may be that the house is quite small; it is smaller than Carter's Grove, but retains the same proportions and the same shape of floor plan—also the same variation in fenestration of seven bays on the front and five on the back.

Cleve was built for the Carter family, and was burned twice. The first time, in 1800, it was rebuilt with a gable roof, and the second time, in 1917, a new house was built on the site from pieces of the old house.

*Peckatone   Westmoreland County   about 1750*

*burnt 1886, reconstruction*

*Attribution:   probable*

*back probably has only five bays*                    *two matching forecourt dependencies*

Peckatone, as far as we know, was a little bigger than Cleve but smaller than Carter's Grove. It had the same floor plan and fenestration as the other two, but its stone trim was different. Instead of the lavish use of stone trim that was found at Cleve, Peckatone had only stone lintels and keystones above the windows and doors. Peckatone also had another feature that was unusual among houses designed by Taliaferro: this was forecourt dependencies, two storeys high. Most other houses in this group, if they had dependencies at all, had them flanking laterally the main house, and had only one-storey structures; the second storey, however, was possibly a later addition.

Peckatone, built for the Corbin family, burned down in 1886, and was claimed by the ravages of time and the eroding river.

*Powhatan    James City County    1735*

*Attribution:    certain*

*burnt 1865, rebuilt*

*conjectural restoration*

Powhatan, built in James City County in 1735 for Taliaferro himself, is of the early style of Westover. It is smaller than Westover, and has only five bays and simpler detail than the Byrd mansion. It had a very steep hip roof like Westover, and single L-shaped end-chimneys. It was built on the site of the famous Indian Chief Powhatan's village. Although it was burned in 1865 it was rebuilt, but with a gable roof. It has now been restored to its original shape.

In sharp contrast to the early style of the first house Taliaferro built for himself is the Wythe House in Williamsburg, which he built for himself in 1750. The Wythe House is quite small and simple, but it has the elegant sophistication of Georgian design found at Carter's Grove. It is five bays wide at both front and back, and has a hip roof with a chimney part way up the slope of each side face of the hip. The brickwork, laid in Flemish bond, is well executed, but simple in detail. Inside, it has four rooms around a central hall that remains the same width from front to back. The stairs have the same plain shafts for balusters that are found at Carter's Grove.

Taliaferro gave a life interest in the house to his son-in-law, George Wythe, who was Jefferson's law tutor, and it has since been called after that more famous man rather than after its owner. It is now restored, and is one of the exhibition buildings of Colonial Williamsburg.

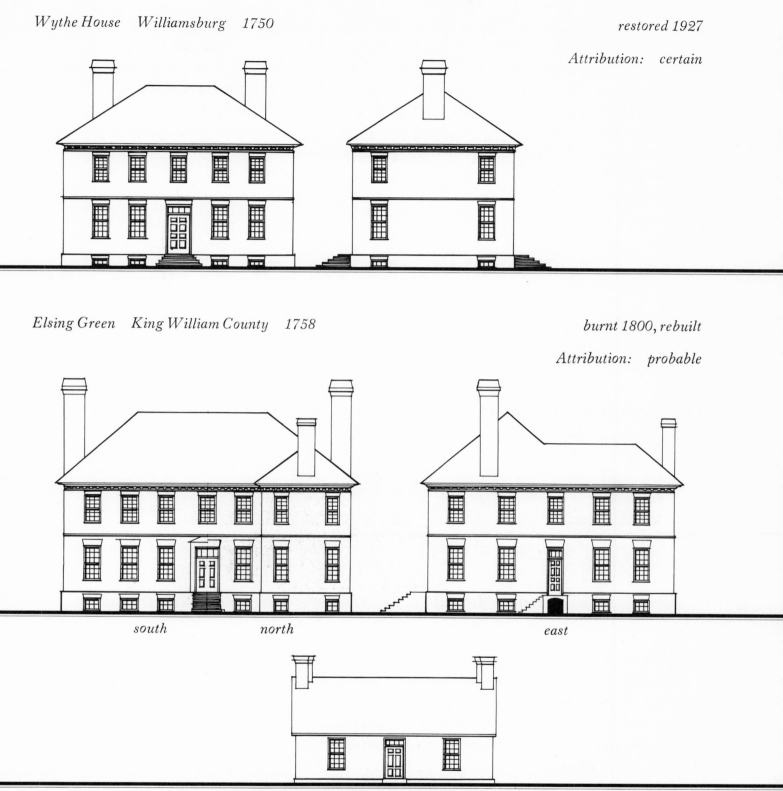

*Wythe House    Williamsburg    1750*

*restored 1927*

*Attribution:   certain*

*Elsing Green    King William County    1758*

*burnt 1800, rebuilt*

*Attribution:   probable*

*south          north                            east*

*two matching side dependencies*

Elsing Green, built in 1758 in King William County by the Braxton family, who were related to the Carters, is the largest of the houses designed by Taliaferro. It is also unusual in that it is U-shaped. The façade of the main house is seven bays long, and the side elevations are five bays long, of which two bays represent the wings of the U. The house has hipped roofs over the main part and the wings, and one main chimney at each end of the front elevation, and a minor chimney in the center of the back wall of each wing. There is a pair of flanking dependencies, each three bays long with a gable roof and end-chimneys. The brickwork, which is well done, is laid in Flemish bond.

Inside, there is a large T-shaped hall, with the upright member of the T slightly offset to the left; this part of the hall connects the front door with the cross-hall at the back of the main part of the house. In front of this cross-hall are two rooms of unequal size, and behind it there is one room in each of the two wings. The cross-hall contains a flight of stairs at each end.

No detail remains from the original house inside, as the building is said to have burned twice, once before it was finished, and once around 1800. However, the exterior of the house has hardly changed at all from its original appearance.

*Ampthill    Chesterfield County    rebuilt about 1750*                    *now altered and moved to Richmond*

*Attribution:    probable*

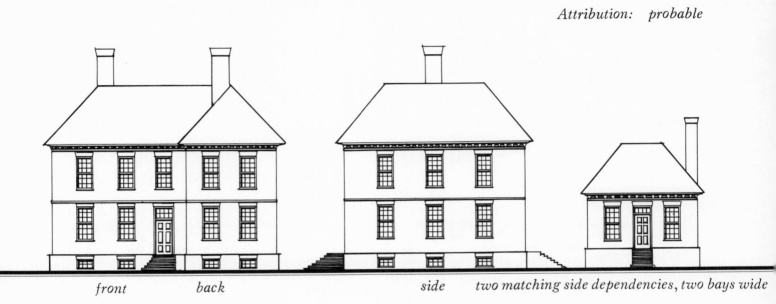

*front          back                                    side      two matching side dependencies, two bays wide*

Ampthill, originally built in Chesterfield County, was only rebuilt by Taliaferro. It was originally built by the Cary family (*q.v.*) for themselves before 1732, and is unique among the formal houses of Virginia in that it has the more archaic English bond for its brickwork. When originally built, it was a simple house with one room on each side of a central hall; later a wing was added at each side of the back of the house to form a U-plan. Still later, but before 1760, the space between the arms of the U was walled in and roofed over, the resulting roof shape being a hip-on-hip. It is not certain which of these alterations was done by Taliaferro, but his hand can be seen in the design for the interior trim. In 1929 Ampthill was moved to Richmond and restored; strangely enough, its neighbor on the old site, Wilton, is now a neighbor in Richmond.

The third Virginia mansion that was torn down and rebuilt in Richmond is Rocky Mills, now called Fairfield. It was built around 1750 in Hanover County for the half brother of Patrick Henry, John Syme II. In detail, it is much like Cleve on the exterior, and like Carter's Grove on the interior, although the quality of execution is not so good as at the other houses. In plan, it is also similar to this group, with a central hall that is wider at one end than at the other.

On the outside, there is lavish use of stone trim, in quoins at the corners of the house, and around the edges of the doors and windows. However, since Rocky Mills had only five bays at the front and the back, this stone trim has not produced the cluttered effect found at Cleve. At the front of the house, the door was round-headed, and above it was a Venetian window. At the back, the door had a horizontal soffit, and a pediment built onto the roof, yet with no pavilion below to support it. The pediment was once removed and stored in the attic, but in 1928 when the house was moved to Richmond it was rebuilt with the pediment supported by a three-bay pavilion; the back façade was also altered at this time to have seven bays instead of five. A one-storey porch has been added to the pavilion at the back.

*Rocky Mills (Fairfield)   Hanover County   about 1750*   *moved to Richmond and altered, 1928*

*Attribution:   possible*

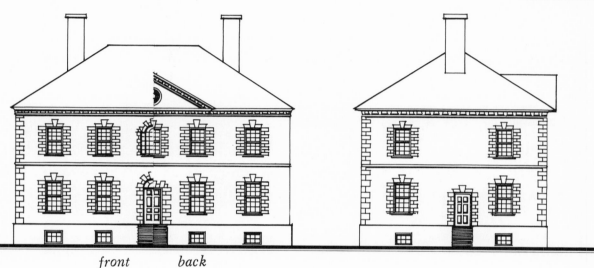

*front          back*

Brooke's Bank in Essex County belongs to the earlier group of Taliaferro's designs, although the date of the house is unknown. It was built for a member of the Taliaferro family, and originally resembled Powhatan. It may have had a high hip roof as at Powhatan, but the present roof is low in pitch.

*Brooke's Bank   Essex County   1735-1765?*   *slightly altered*

*conjectural restoration*

*Attribution:   certain*

Weyanoke, in Charles City County, could be said to be a wooden version of Wilton, except that it was Wilton that was built ten years after Weyanoke. It is simpler than Wilton, without any elaborate doorways, and lacking two of the four sets of narrow windows that Wilton has on the end elevations.

*two matching side dependencies*

Eltham, built for Burwell Bassett in New Kent County around 1745, resembled Peckatone, but had end-chimneys instead of the more graceful chimneys at the break of the hip that we saw at Peckatone. It had small flanking dependencies, but evidence as to the original appearance of the mansion is slim, because it burned down in 1876, and although one flanker survived until recently, it was torn down to provide bricks for the Williamsburg restoration, unfortunately without records as to its appearance.

Chelsea, built in New Kent County around 1735, looks like a slice of Wilton. It has Wilton's front elevation, albeit without the elegant doorway, and half the side elevation of Wilton. The bricks are laid in Flemish bond, with glazed headers on the sides. The house has been altered by the addition of a wing at the back.

*Abingdon Church Gloucester County 1754*                    *now slightly altered*

*Attribution: probable*

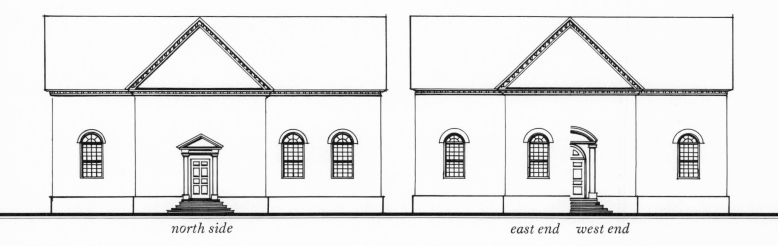

*north side*                                              *east end    west end*

Abingdon Church, built in Gloucester County in 1754, presents almost as perfect an appearance as Christ Church, Lancaster County, by which its design was no doubt influenced. It is cruciform like Christ Church, and has almost the same fenestration. The doorways, too, are reminiscent of those at Christ Church. One important difference, though, is that Abingdon Church has a gable roof all around, whereas Christ Church has an elegant hip roof. Like Berkeley, the Nelson House and the dependencies at Shirley, the horizontal cornice of the gable is covered by a little roof of its own, implying that the gable was built on top of an earlier hip, which of course it was not.

The side doorways are similar in design to the doorways at Carter's Grove, the Public Records Office at Williamsburg, and other buildings. This is supposed to be the mark of the bricklayer David Minitree. Minitree has often been credited with the design of all the buildings we have ascribed to Taliaferro, but all the evidence we have indicates that Minitree was no more than a builder, and that Taliaferro has the better claim to having been the architect of these buildings.

The inside of Abingdon Church has been much altered in Victorian times; the ceiling has been replaced by a really ugly one that looks as if it can be no more than temporary, but actually has been there for years. The altarpiece, box pews and other interior trim have all been removed, and the east wall has been pulled forward to form a small vestry and sacristy behind it; this is very unfortunate architecturally, though perhaps necessary liturgically, for it removes the two east windows over the altar, and leaves the windows on either side of the chancel stuck into recesses. It is fervently to be hoped that the church will some day be restored.

Now we have come to a large group of arcaded courthouses. Marcus Whiffen and A. Lawrence Kocher have done the most research on them, and very exhaustively, too, but there remains much that we would like to know about these buildings. They change little in appearance or plan from 1730 to 1762, which indicates the hand of one architect, especially since the design has certain academic features about it.

*Court House    Isle of Wight County, Smithfield,    1750*                    *Attribution:    probable*

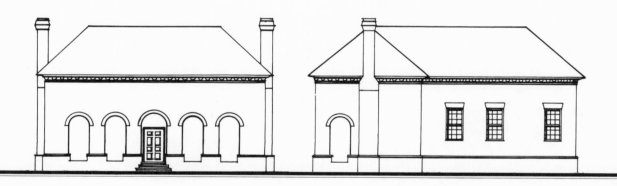

Basically, all these courthouses have a front elevation of a one-storey arcade, and a ground plan in the shape of a T. This concept is not traditionally English, and one wonders whence the idea came that was so suited to Virginia and the Common Law that it was not changed for at least thirty-two years, during the course of which more than six were put up in this style. These six include the ones at Charles City County, 1730, and now altered, York County, 1733, demolished 1814, King William County, 1746, Hanover County, about 1750, Smithfield in Isle of Wight County, 1750, and Martinsburg, around 1762, and now demolished. The last two showed some alteration from the earlier ones. The Smithfield Courthouse, now ably restored by Kocher, has an apse at the back of the wing that forms the upright part of the T-plan. This is an echo of the Capitol at Williamsburg, and itself was echoed in the courthouse in Edenton, Chowan County, North Carolina. The Martinsburg

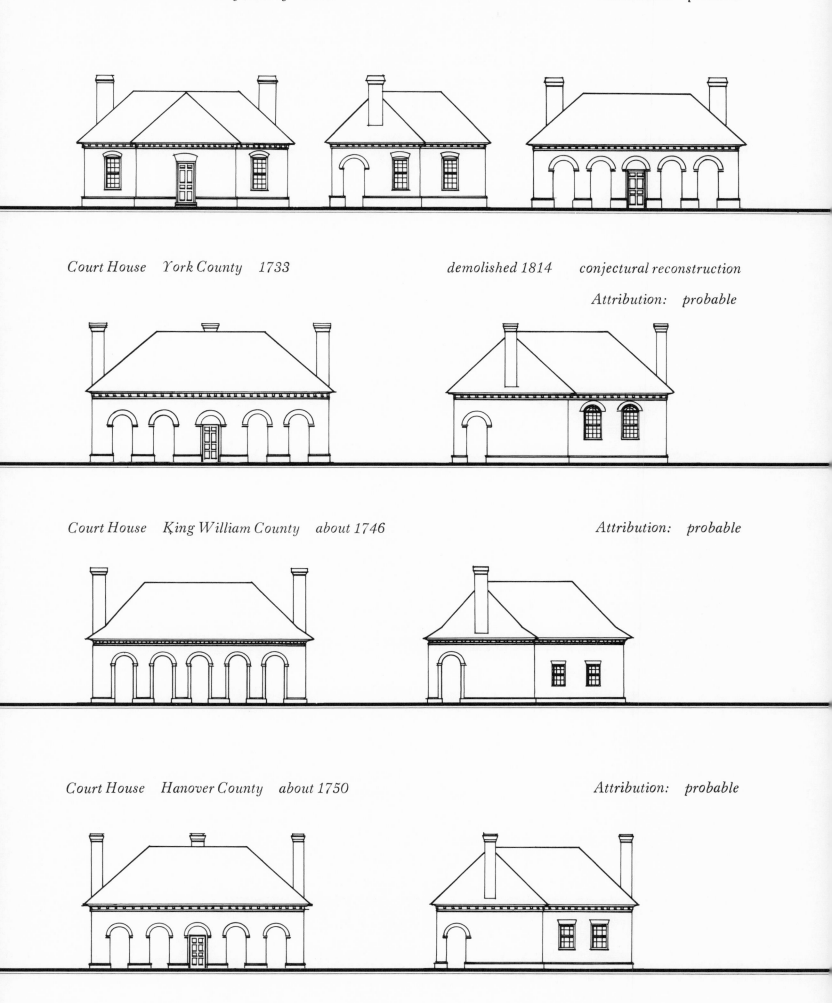

Court House    Charles City County    1730             *Attribution: probable*

Court House    York County    1733             *demolished 1814*    *conjectural reconstruction*

*Attribution: probable*

Court House    King William County    about 1746             *Attribution: probable*

Court House    Hanover County    about 1750             *Attribution: probable*

Courthouse differed from the others in that it had a small cupola in the center of the roof. All the courthouses had hip roofs, and end-chimneys, some of which are part of the end walls, and others of which are exterior to the walls. The brickwork is generally of very high quality, and some seems to have been laid by the man who did Westover. It is in Flemish bond, and the pattern of glazed headers running around the arches of the front arcade produces a very satisfactory effect.

According to Whiffen, the courthouses at Norfolk, 1726, and at Lancaster County, 1740, may have looked like these, and probably had apses like the one in Smithfield.

*Court House   Martinsburg   about 1762*          *demolished     conjectural reconstruction*

*Attribution:   probable*

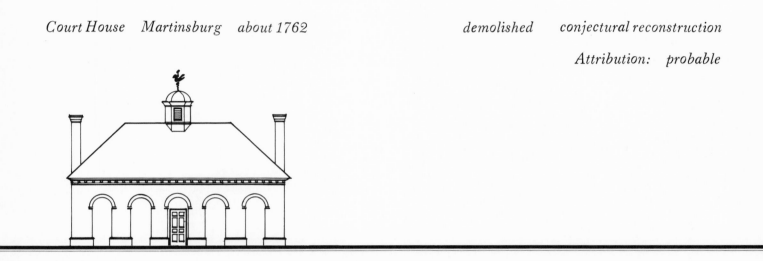

Among the other Virginia courthouses of note that we may perhaps also attribute to Taliaferro are those that once stood in Henrico and Chesterfield Counties. The Chesterfield Courthouse was ordered to be a copy of the Henrico Courthouse. The Chesterfield building was erected around 1750; the date of the other one is uncertain. These buildings resemble the arched courthouses in almost every way, but they replace the arcade with four windows and a low central door. The Chesterfield Courthouse was demolished in 1911.

*Court House   Henrico County (Chesterfield)   1752*          *demolished 1911*

*Attribution:   possible*

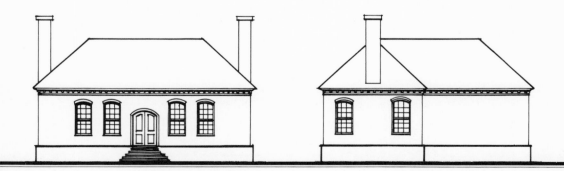

The last building we are attributing to Taliaferro is the Public Records Office in Williamsburg, built in 1748. It is a very dignified yet charming structure with hip roof and a T-shaped chimney at each end of the ridgepole. Set on a high foundation, it is one storey high; the front elevation contains four windows and a central door like those at Carter's Grove and Abingdon Church in design. The plan is rectangular, being divided into three rooms. There are no windows or doors on any wall but the front one. This building was constructed to preserve the records of the county and colony from fire, although it is by no means fireproof with its two chimneys and wood-framed roof; this is because it was realized that a fireproof building without fireplaces, and with a brick-vaulted roof, would have posed as great a danger to the documents, for such a building would have been extremely damp inside.

The last building we have attributed to Taliaferro was built around 1762, and yet the man lived until 1779. What did he do in that space of 17 years? We have no evidence at all; he certainly taught Jefferson the elements of architecture, and it is entirely possible that the houses that Waterman says are Jeffersonian[1] were actually done by Taliaferro in his late years. If so, why such a sweeping change in style? The answer would lie in the pattern books and builders' handbooks used. All of the buildings by Taliaferro that we have seen so far, like those by John Prince, were based on William Salmon's *Palladio Londinensis*. However, Jefferson did rely heavily on a book by Robert Morris, *Select Architecture*, published in London in 1757, and Taliaferro is known to have owned a copy of this book. It is conceivable that the late buildings were designed by the youthful Jefferson, with consultation and advice from his teacher, but it is equally conceivable that Taliaferro was the architect, and Jefferson the apprentice. We probably shall never know, but since these buildings really belong in the spirit of the years *after* the Revolution they are not illustrated in this book.

[1] *Shirley, the Capitol Portico at Williamsburg, Battersea, Nanzatico, Belle Isle, Brandon, Chatham, Monticello, Randolph-Semple House.*

*Public Records Building   Williamsburg   1748*                    *Attribution:   probable*

## John Ariss   c. 1725-1799

IN 1751, an advertisement appeared in a newspaper, claiming that the subscriber would design houses after the manner of the English architect James Gibbs (*q.v.*), who wrote books on how to follow his style. The subscriber, who claimed to have just returned from training in England, was John Ariss. His name has been spelled a number of other ways, including Ayres, Oriss, Orliss and Arris, and this fact has hindered research on him. Thomas Waterman pursued traces of this elusive man and arrived at a theory that Ariss was responsible for a group of buildings in Virginia in a mature Georgian style. Elevations and details of these buildings are mostly from William Adam's *Vitruvius Scoticus*, but substantial use was also made of books by James Gibbs and by Batty Langley.

Waterman sees these buildings falling into two groups, the formal ones and the smaller informal ones. The elevations of the formal ones are from the pattern books, while those of the informal ones are simply typical Virginia houses. The interiors of both groups are based on the pattern books. I agree with Waterman as far as that is concerned, but I disagree slightly on details. We shall come across these disagreements later.

It is certain that Ariss was a good friend of George Washington, of which more later. It is also certain that Ariss was no wealthy man drawing for fun and to please his friends, like Prince and Taliaferro, but rather that he was paid for his services, and that he had little money. Washington was a friend of his, and had him design for himself and his relatives, and paid him in part by giving him land to build on and houses to live in; no doubt Washington was a good friend to have, but he was also a good patron.

The only puzzle left about Ariss is that he advertised in a Maryland newspaper, and yet there is no building in Maryland that we are tempted to ascribe to him; all his buildings are in Virginia, as far as we know. The only possibility of his having designed Maryland buildings is that the joiner-architect William Buckland (*q.v.*), who worked with Ariss on a number of buildings in Virginia, may have asked his old comrade to help him out, but this is improbable.

One of the only two buildings actually built for which there is documentary proof that Ariss was the architect is Payne's Church Truro, Fairfax, Virginia, built in 1768. This is a small rectangular church, five bays long and three bays wide. It has one storey, marked by

*Payne's Church (Truro)   Fairfax   1768*                    *destroyed 1862-1864, rebuilt 1930*

*Attribution:   certain*

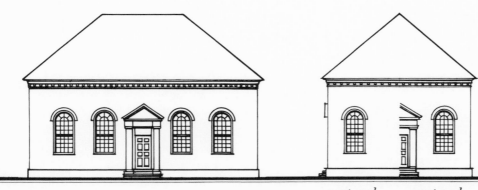

*east end      west end*

some high round-headed windows. The church is of brick, as is the trim. So are the doorways, whose pediments have a curiously high pitch to them. The roof is a hip sitting on a modillioned cornice. The church was destroyed in 1862 by troops fighting in the Civil War, but it was reconstructed about 1930.

Ariss is known to have designed two other churches, one of them called Cunningham's Chapel, but neither was built. However, there are two more churches about which we can be quite sure if we attribute them to Ariss. These are Lamb's Creek Church in King George County, 1769, and Little Fork Church in Culpeper County in 1776. These churches are very similar to Payne's Church, except that they are each seven bays long and Payne's Church is only five. They have the same end elevations and the same hip roofs, extended of course in the longer churches. Only the doors are different; in Lamb's Creek Church, the doorways are the same as those of Payne's Church, but their pediments are not so steep, while the doorways of Little Fork Church may have had a round-headed door enclosed by a pediment and two pilasters, although this is not certain. Lamb's Creek Church was used as a stable during the Civil War, but was later restored; Little Fork Church escaped that war unharmed, although both churches now have Victorian interiors.

*Lamb's Creek Church    King George County    1769*                                    *burnt 1865, rebuilt*

*Attribution:    certain*

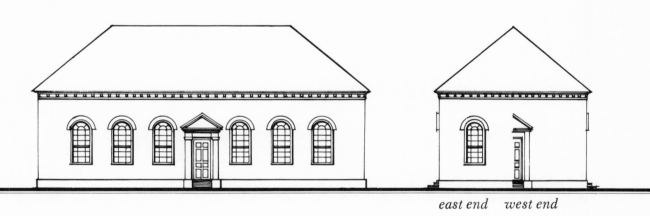

*east end    west end*

*Little Fork Church    Culpeper County    1776*

*Attribution:    certain*

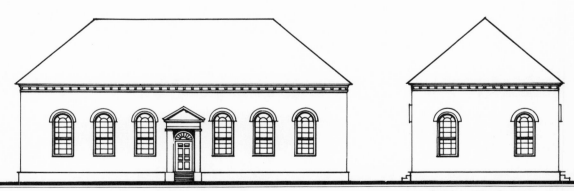

*both ends the same*

*Carlyle House    Alexandria    1751*                                    *now altered*

*Attribution:    probable*

*two matching forecourt dependencies*

Ariss' first building was probably the Carlyle House in Alexandria, which was built in 1751. This is a very formal mansion with forecourt dependencies. It has been much altered, so that its original appearance is not absolutely certain. It is of brick, now stuccoed, with stone quoins, which are placed at the corners of the three buildings, and at the corners of the pedimented pavilion in the center of the main house. The fenestration is unusual, in that the house is six bays wide, rather than five or seven; this is achieved by having two windows in the upper storey of the pavilion, above a Venetian door, itself unusual. The roof is a hip-on-hip, with a chimney on each side at the break of the roof. The dependencies no longer exist, but it is probable that they were joined to the house by covered passages.

While he was in Alexandria doing the Carlyle House, Ariss very likely also did the famous Gadsby's Tavern, but this is only conjecture based on architectural evidence that Waterman either did not notice or did not think important. It is five bays long and 2½ storeys high with end-chimneys; in fact, it is a large row-house. The trim is white stone on a brick building; there are stone lintels and keystones and a stone belt course. The doorway is particularly handsome, carved in wood. Part of the interior is like the remaining room at the Carlyle House.

*Gadsby's Tavern    Alexandria    1752*                            *Attribution:    probable*

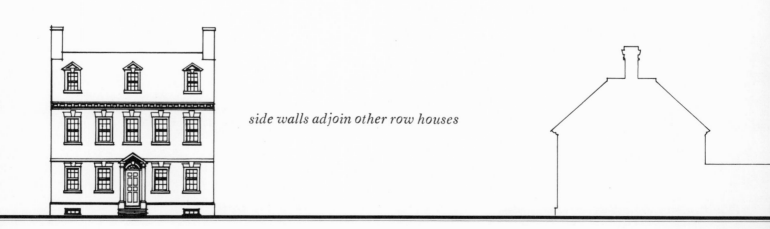

*side walls adjoin other row houses*

Waterman thinks that Ariss was in charge of the rebuilding of the 1741 house called Belvoir in Fairfax County; this was done around 1757. It is not certain what was done at that time, but excavations of the site have revealed many things about the appearance of the house, and the elaborate setting achieved through landscaping and correct placement of service buildings. The house was of brick, five bays wide and two storeys high with hip roof and end-chimneys. The doorway on the land side had a pedimented porch. Ariss undoubtedly was responsible for the landscaping as well as for the architectural refinements, for the plans for the garden are derived from plans in his books.

Perhaps the most impressive of the mansions designed by Ariss is Mount Airy near Warsaw on the Rappahannock, and across the road from Sabine Hall. It was built around 1758, and is of the same formal type as the Carlyle House, although it is much larger, perhaps because it is in the middle of the country, and perhaps because the Tayloe family were well enough to do that they could afford to construct such an enormous mansion. It is constructed of stone; the body of it is brown stone, but the trim, including corner quoins, window trim and the whole of the central pavilion on both façades of the house, are of a creamy colored

*Mount Airy Warsaw about 1758*        *roof and inside altered Attribution: probable*

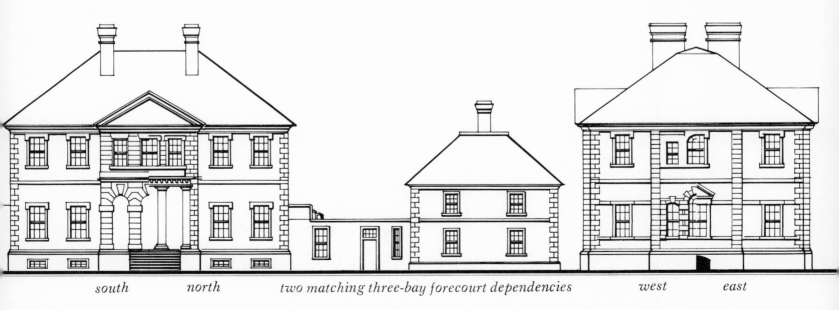

*south*        *north*        *two matching three-bay forecourt dependencies*        *west*        *east*

stone. The front and back elevations are each seven bays wide and two storeys high, but curiously enough the south face is from Gibbs, while the north face is from Adam. The difference between them is in the pavilion, for the south face has round-headed arches on the ground floor, whereas the north face has a horizontal architrave supported by pillars. The pavilions are rusticated. The dependencies are connected to the house by covered passages, and the effect of the forecourt thus enclosed is exciting; each dependency is two storeys high with a deck-on-hip roof and central chimney. The roof of the main house was once hip-on-hip, but is now a simple hip as a result of a rebuilding after a disastrous fire; luckily the house could be rebuilt after the fire, but all the beautiful carving and joinery by William Buckland was lost. The fire was deliberately set by a disgruntled maid in the nineteenth century.

Mannsfield, near Fredericksburg, was rather like Mount Airy in appearance, but it was destroyed during the Civil War. It was built sometime between 1760 and 1770. It was of stone, a dignified building material suitable for its owner, Mann Page, whom we met before at Rosewell. The house was seven bays wide, although the middle bays were a little squashed to fit into the pavilions, especially in the back where the pavilion was narrower than on the front. The back pavilion was rusticated, and there were quoins at the corners of all three buildings and both pavilions.

*Mannsfield    Fredericksburg    about 1760-1770*                    *destroyed 1863*

*Attribution:    probable*                                          *reconstructed drawing*

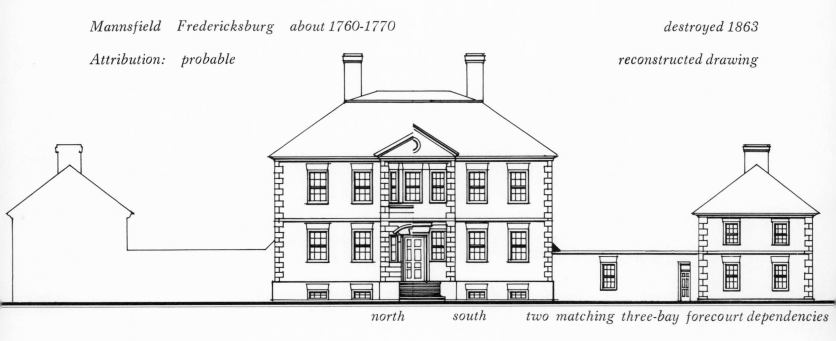

*north       south       two matching three-bay forecourt dependencies*

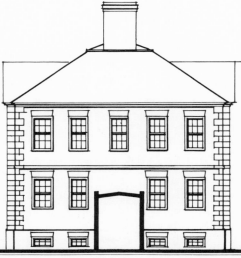

*east*

Another mansion in this group is Blandfield, built in Essex County in 1771 for William Beverley. Blandfield is in brick with brick trim, and is therefore simpler in detail than the last two mansions. It is seven bays wide and two storeys high with a hip-on-hip roof; there are four chimneys at the break of the roof. There is a central pavilion, three bays wide both at the front and the back. The connected dependencies form an attractive forecourt. The house has been altered on the outside by the addition in 1854 of one-storey porches in front of the pavilions, and by the substitution of large-light sash for the original ones. The interior was stripped at the same time, thus depriving us of more of Buckland's work, although it would have been destroyed a few years later anyway, when Civil War soldiers sacked the house.

More tempers have been aroused by the attribution of Mount Vernon in Fairfax County to John Ariss than any other attribution. Yet, it is not an attribution, but a documented fact, if only the document can be found. Waterman says that a descendant of Washington who did not then know of Waterman's interest in, or knowledge of Ariss claimed that she read in a family book that Ariss definitely was the architect of the house as it was built in 1774-1787. Even disregarding this, architectural evidence points to Ariss, and not Washington himself, as architect. I will not go into the details of the house, both interior and exterior, which support this, for they are cited at great length in Waterman: *The Mansions of Virginia.* Those

*Blandfield   Essex County   1771*                                 *slightly altered*

*Attribution:   probable*

*two matching two-bay (long) forecourt dependencies*

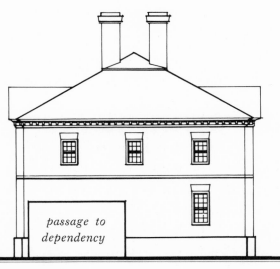

*passage to dependency*

who defend Washington as architect point to the mass of detailed correspondence Washington had with the workmen while he was away fighting in the Revolution, but this is inconclusive, because he could merely have been reeling it straight off the plans given him by Ariss. Furthermore, the only architectural drawing we do have by Washington, that of Pohick Church done for the other members of the vestry, shows a great lack of understanding of architectural principles and proportions; fortunately, the plans were properly drawn for Pohick Church by James Wren, its architect, whom we shall see in the next chapter. Therefore, all the conclusive evidence indicates that Washington, although extremely interested in the construction of his house, was not the architect of Mount Vernon, and that his friend John Ariss was.

However, when we refer to Mount Vernon, we must be careful which Mount Vernon we mean. A house existed on the site since the late seventeenth century; in 1758, that house was rebuilt and enlarged and made more formal, and again between 1774 and 1787 more enlargements, additions and refinements were made. It is my opinion that Ariss was responsible for both rebuildings of the house, not just the last one.

The first rebuilding produced a frame house five bays long and two storeys high, covered in wood that was chanelled and cut and painted to look like ashlar masonry. It had a hip-on-hip roof, and outside end-chimneys. The door, derived from Batty Langley's book, was off-center to the left.

*Mount Vernon   Fairfax County   1758   rebuilding of old house*          *reconstructed drawing*

*Attribution:   probable*

Inside, the 1758 house was much as the center part of the present house is now; the details were not changed in the second rebuilding, so we have a staircase and set of mantels that are characteristic of Ariss' early work; furthermore, they are in good scale and are well executed, which is more than can be said for the work done during the Revolution.

The second rebuilding was an attempt to convert a small manor into the seat of a leading Virginia gentleman. The alterations were drastic. The length of the house was extended by a different amount at each end, so that the door that was once off-center found itself lost in the absolute center of a huge façade; in order to help the door to be found again, a three-bay pediment was perched on the roof above the door—without, however, any pavilion to support it. The result was that the chimneys were off-center, so a cupola was placed on top of the roof above the pediment, so that the roof had a central focus. On the river façade, a two-storey portico was extended the whole length of the house, supported by giant Doric pilasters; dormers were placed symmetrically on the roof.

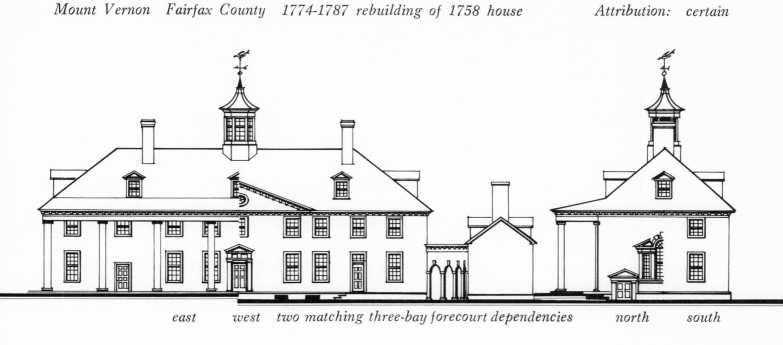

*Mount Vernon   Fairfax County   1774-1787 rebuilding of 1758 house*          *Attribution:   certain*

*east        west    two matching three-bay forecourt dependencies        north        south*

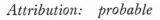

*Elmwood    Essex County    about 1774*                                    *altered 1852*

*Attribution:   probable*

*south              north*                                        *east*

Forecourt dependencies were constructed and connected to the house by covered, curved, arched trellis. The whole was finished in wood made to simulate ashlar. The landscaping around the house is considered to be very well contrived.

Inside, at the north end was built a large banquet room, with a Venetian window on the end. The mantels in the added rooms are quite fine, but perhaps a little out of scale, and not of as high quality workmanship as the earlier work.

A curious parallel to Mount Vernon in its last stage is Elmwood, built for Muscoe Garnett in Essex County around 1774. Ariss seems to have been the architect, because of similarities between Elmwood and some of his other buildings; the brickwork, for example, is the same as that of Blandfield. However, it is the plan of Mount Vernon that has the closest connections, not to mention certain interior trim that is repeated in both mansions. Both houses are long and thin; Elmwood seems to be a conscious attempt to improve on Mount Vernon, because the former was not tied down by having to include the plan of an earlier house in the middle like Mount Vernon. Consequently, in the middle, where Mount Vernon has four rooms and a central hall, Elmwood has a T-shaped hall and two rooms. This saves walking through the inner rooms to reach those at the ends of the house, which is one of the inconveniences of Mount Vernon; besides, one only needs a certain number of reception rooms.

On the outside, Elmwood is nine bays long and two storeys high, with a hip roof, and a chimney near each end of the ridgepole. Along the south side there is a porch on the east front as at Mount Vernon, but at Elmwood it is only one storey high. In the center of this façade the door, and corresponding window above, is surrounded by a narrow window on each side; this motif is repeated on the north front, but since the center bay here is on a gabled pavilion, there is room for the upper window set to be made into a Venetian window by the addition of a round head. This, while not altogether satisfactory, seems to be a better solution than Mount Vernon's to the problem of focus in a long façade. Elmwood may once have had dependencies, but no trace of any survives. The house itself has been altered and neglected, but is still a valuable example of late Colonial architecture.

Not all of Ariss' formal mansions were on the grand scale of the ones we have seen so far. Menokin, built for Francis Lightfoot Lee in 1769 on the occasion of his marriage to a Tayloe girl (the Tayloes built Mount Airy), is hidden in the woods near Warsaw in Richmond County. The front elevation is three bays wide and two storeys high. The house is of brown stone, but except for the corner quoins, belt courses and window trim, the brown stone is covered quite properly by a layer of white stucco. The interior was charming, and it has been suggested that William Buckland may have had something to do with that. However, it is extremely unfortunate that this lovely little house has been allowed to fall into ruins. The inside has been stripped, and the last time the author saw it the walls of the back left corner had fallen in; no doubt the roof will soon follow, and then it will not be long before the woods swallow up all traces of the house. There is already no sign of the dependencies. The roof, which is a hip-on-hip, has a chimney on each side just below the break. The author salvaged a fallen window sash, which is now the property of Colonial Williamsburg.

Camden, in Caroline County, was built around 1770 for John Pratt. The drawing here is a complete conjecture, for the house was almost entirely rebuilt in 1857 in an Italian Villa style. It is certain, however, that the house had end-chimneys, and roughly resembled the other mansions based on plates in *Vitruvius Scoticus*. It is not known how much the present frame building contains of the original building, but there are occasional details that come from the eighteenth century, such as the rounded corners of the halls. One two-storey pedimented dependency remains from the original house.

*Menokin    Richmond County    about 1769*                                    *now in ruins*

*Attribution:    probable*

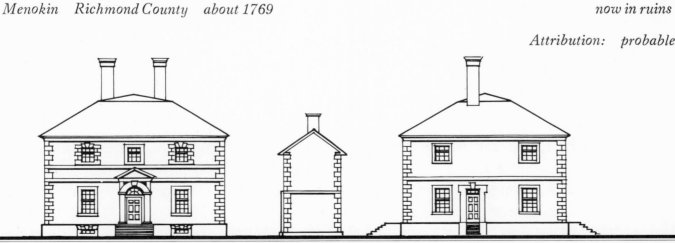

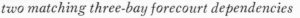

*two matching three-bay forecourt dependencies*

*Camden    Caroline County    about 1770*        *remodeled 1857    conjectural reconstruction*

*Attribution:    possible*

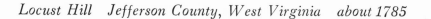

*two matching forecourt dependencies*

*Locust Hill    Jefferson County, West Virginia    about 1785*        *Attribution:    certain*

Another wooden house on fairly formal lines was Locust Hill. Ariss built this for himself around 1785 on land leased or loaned to him by George Washington. This was Ariss' last building, and he lived here in retirement until his death about fifteen years later. It is simple in elevation, and about as small as Menokin. It is five bays long and two storeys high. The hip roof seems to be held in by two massive end-chimneys that are contained within the house. The outside is covered in stucco. Inside, the staircase has been altered, but nearly everything else is as it was built, although the house is not well maintained.

*Sara's Creek House (Little England)    Gloucester County*        *about 1755 addition to older house*

*Attribution:    probable*                                        *now slightly altered*

There are three less formal houses that Waterman attributes to Ariss. The first of these is Sara's Creek House, or Little England, as it is now called, built in Gloucester County around 1755. It is a long, thin house, five bays long and two storeys high in brick laid in Flemish bond. Although it now has a gable roof, it originally had a hip roof. There is one chimney set in each end wall. It is said that this house is merely an older one rebuilt by Ariss, and although this is possible, it is highly unlikely, because of the close similarity it bears for Harewood, built at about the same time many miles away. What is most likely is that Ariss' building was added to the little wing at the back: that wing must be the older house.

*Harewood    Jefferson County, West Virginia    1756*                    *now altered    Attribution:    probable*

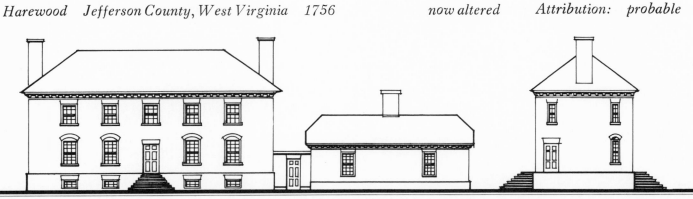

*two matching side dependencies*

Harewood, in what is now Jefferson County, West Virginia, formerly Berkeley County, Virginia, was built for George Washington's brother Samuel. It is constructed of a rough whitish stone, and the exterior resembles Sara's Creek House in every way except that Harewood has a pair of one-storey flanking dependencies with jerkin-head roof and central chimney, joined to the main house by a short passageway. Not only are the two houses alike on the outside, but also inside: they share the same staircase design, which itself is in the same family as other Ariss staircases, and they have similar overmantel designs, and panelling.

*Fairfield    Clarke County    about 1770*                    *now altered    Attribution:    certain*

The last of the informal Ariss houses is Fairfield, near Berryville in Clarke County. All information presently uncovered indicates that Ariss built this house for himself around 1770, and sold it to Warner Washington in 1783. Ariss is buried here in an unmarked grave, although he was living at Locust Hill at the time of his death. Fairfield is five bays wide and two storeys high, with a hip-on-hip roof and a chimney at each side just below the break. The central door has a semicircular arched light on top of it, but except for that and a modillioned cornice there is no architectural detail on the exterior. The exterior is of the same sort of stone as Harewood. The house is flanked by a gable-roofed wing on each side, with end-chimneys;

each wing is two bays long and one storey high, but it is not certain whether this was part of the original design or not, especially since the house has been considerably altered through the years. Some interior trim of the style of Ariss remains.

Waterman claims that Kenmore, built for George Washington's sister Betty in Fredericksburg in 1752, and originally named Millbrook, was designed by Ariss. The evidence to support his claim comes from the excellent interior trim, and the fact that Ariss was a good friend of the Washingtons. Furthermore, Waterman says that the floor plan is typical of Ariss. However, the exterior is most unarchitectonic; it is a typical Virginia builder's house of the period, and my guess is that Ariss was only responsible for the interior. It is highly unlikely that Ariss would have personally designed a house with a jerkin-head roof and such a plain exterior. On the other hand, Waterman has noticed two other houses that resemble Kenmore in plan and exterior appearance. These are Ratcliffe Manor and Pleasant Valley, both in Maryland, and they are not of such high quality interior workmanship. It would be wrong to disconnect Ariss' name completely from these three houses, but it would be equally wrong to give him the rather dubious credit for them. None of them has been illustrated in this book for the above-mentioned reasons.

*Chowan County Court House   Edenton, North Carolina   1767*          *Attribution:* **possible**

There remains only one more building that may have been designed by Ariss. This is the Chowan County Courthouse in Edenton, North Carolina, built in 1767. The history of the design of this building is obscure, but it is said that a certain Gilbert Leigh came down from Williamsburg to build this courthouse. Since, however, he is not known to have designed any buildings in Virginia, although he may have built some in the capacity of master-mason, we must conclude that Leigh was not the architect of this building. On purely architectural evidence, we might well ascribe this courthouse to Ariss. The general shape of the building is typical of Ariss, as are some of the details, such as the front door. The inside of the building does not match the outside; it is more than twenty years older in style than the outside, with its completely panelled room (the largest Colonial American completely panelled room) and bolection molding. This would be natural if Ariss drew the plans at long distance, and Leigh carried them out in the style he knew best, for the builders, as we mentioned above, were years behind the architects in style.

The Chowan County Courthouse is quite a large building. Basically, it is T-shaped, but with some modifications. The front is five bays wide, and two storeys high, with the center bays included in a pedimented pavilion. On the top of the hip roof is a short square tower with octagonal cupola. At the far back of the building is a semicircular apse, one storey high; this is reminiscent of some Virginia courthouses and of the Williamsburg Capitol. Inside the apse is where the judge sits on his throne, the design for which came from the throne in the Williamsburg Capitol, so the builder must have had extensive knowledge of that Capitol, because it had burned down years before, and was not rebuilt in its original shape.

So ends our glimpse of the architect who introduced the style of James Gibbs to Virginia. It is interesting that during the course of some forty-five years of designing Ariss' style changed little, and that he stuck to his original pattern books throughout his career. One must ask why he did this, for the new styles were readily accessible to him. Even if he did not or could not buy a copy of Robert Morris' book, he could always borrow one, for there were many around; furthermore, he only had to take a look at the buildings designed by Jefferson after 1760 or so to see Morris' principles applied to American materials in an American context. It is entirely possible that he was merely quite satisfied with the style he already used, and considered that it needed no improvement or alterations. Something that is hard for many to understand these days is that there is nothing wrong in holding to an older style if you like it; as Cicero said, 'De gustibus non est disputandum.'

*James Wren    fl. 1755-1770*

LITTLE is known about James Wren except that he lived in the area around Alexandria between 1755 and 1770. One legend says that he claimed descent from the great English architect Sir Christopher Wren, but whether he claimed it or not he was certainly no close relative, and may not have been related at all.

Documentary evidence ascribes three churches (Christ Church Alexandria, Falls Church, and Pohick Church) to his hand, and architectural evidence tends to add another church and two houses. Probably no more remain today than these six, though it is possible that he designed more buildings, especially in the town of Dumfries whose old buildings have almost all been destroyed.

*Aquia Church    Stafford County    1757*                    *Attribution:    probable*

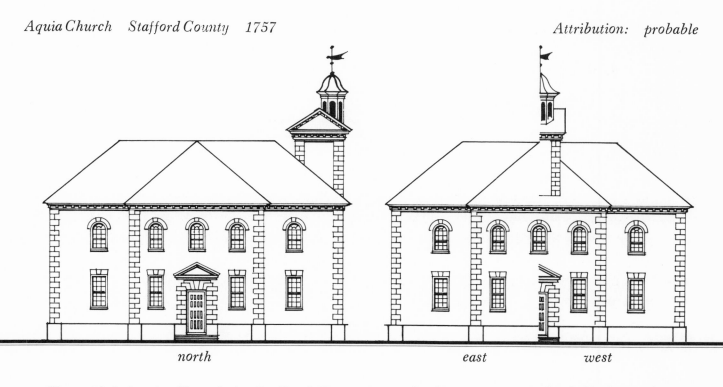

*north*                    *east*                    *west*

Beautiful Aquia Church in Stafford County was built in 1757 on the hill above Aquia Creek. The church is large and cruciform, and is built of brick with stone trim. The stones, brought from nearby Aquia quarry, are used for corner quoins, doorways and window keystones. The quality of the workmanship is excellent. The doors are particularly fine, and are the forerunners of the doors on Wren's later church, Christ Church in Alexandria; they are out of James Gibbs' book. There are two tiers of windows, the lower row being rectangular, and the upper row round-headed; this arrangement was repeated in all three of his later churches. The names of the contractor, Mourning Richards, and of the mason, William Copein, are recorded over the south door, but neither of these would have provided the designs. Since Aquia Church is not in the style of Ariss, the only other Gibbsian architect of the area, and since it is like the three churches that we know were done by James Wren, we must conclude that he was responsible for its designs.

Inside, the church is much as it originally was, with three-decker pulpit, elaborate altarpiece and box-pews, although the pews have been cut down a few inches from their original height. The ceiling is a graceful cove.

On the outside is a curious feature: sitting on the west hip of the roof is a little tower with pedimented roof, and out of the west slope of that roof sticks a small octagonal cupola, whence there is a good view of both the Potomac and the Rappahannock Rivers.

The town of Dumfries was established in the eighteenth century to help get the tobacco from the plantations to the ships. It soon grew in size, but in the nineteenth century it slumped. During its period of prosperity, James Wren probably designed at least two houses there, but we will never know, for only two survived until recently, one of those falling prey to a storm in 1933.

*Tebbs-Mundy House   Dumfries   about 1760*                    *destroyed 1933, reconstruction*

*Attribution:   probable*

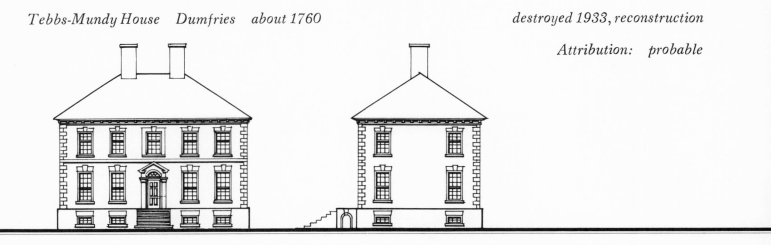

The first of these, the one that blew down in the storm, was called the Tebbs-Mundy House, and it was built on the side of a hill around 1760. It was of brick laid in an all-header bond with stone quoins and lintels, and was five bays long and two storeys high on a high basement at the front where the hill sloped away. The roof was a low hip with a pair of chimneys on the ridgepole. The plan was one large room and two small rooms with a central stair-hall. In one of the rooms was a typical Palladian mantel and overmantel, and a ceiling cornice with delicate dentils.

*Old Hotel   Dumfries   about 1765*                                           *now altered*

*Attribution:   probable*

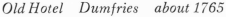

The other house in Dumfries, known as the Old Hotel, was built around 1765. It has the same kind of brickwork and stone trim as the Tebbs-Mundy House, and a low hip roof with four end-chimneys. The interior is not distinguished.

The three churches that we know were designed by James Wren are all very similar; this was to save money for the vestries of the three parishes, which are close to each other. The first and largest of the three is Christ Church in Alexandria, built in 1767. It was a rectangle five bays long and three wide, with the windows arranged in two tiers as at Aquia Church, the top row being round-headed and the bottom row rectangular. The east end has a large Palladian window over the altar, while the west end has a pair of doors like the doors at Aquia

Church. The roof is hipped, and rests on a modillion cornice. The brickwork, which is laid in Flemish bond, is set off by stone quoins and keystones.

*Christ Church   Alexandria   1767*                    *now slightly altered*

*Attribution:   certain*

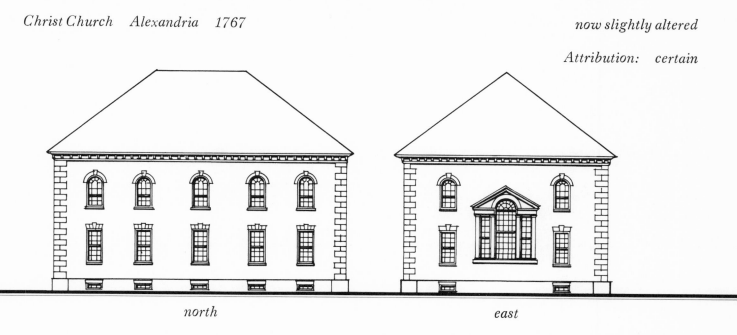

*north*                                        *east*

Inside, the pulpit and sounding board stand in front of the Palladian window, but behind the altar. There are galleries around three sides, and a tray ceiling above. It is said that William Buckland did some of the carving, and well he may have, for the dentilled cornice around the ceiling is very fine. The original appearance of the church has been altered by the addition of a tower with two-tiered cupola at the west end of the building.

*Falls Church   Fairfax County   1767*              *Attribution:   certain*

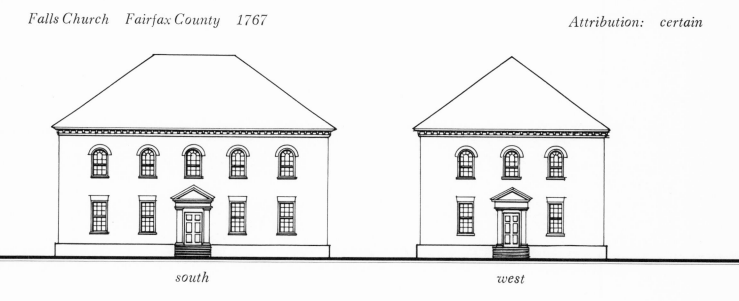

*south*                                        *west*

Falls Church is the plainest of the three; it has no stone trim, and the south door is of wood while the west door is of brick. It is a little smaller than Christ Church Alexandria, but is essentially the same design.

Pohick Church is also smaller than Christ Church, but retains its stone trim in places; the superb brickwork, laid in Flemish bond, is set off by stone quoins and stone doorways of a different design than those at Christ Church Alexandria. Pohick Church's doors, and those of Falls Church, are also in a different position on the building from the Alexandria Church.

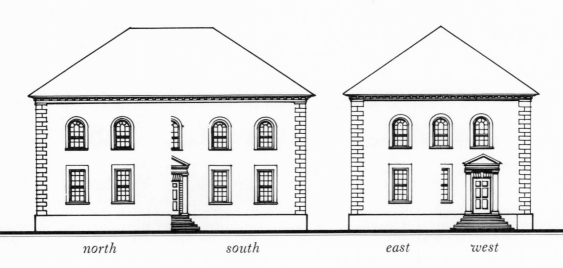

*north            south                 east        west*

Buckland is also said to have worked at Pohick Church; the man to whom he was indentured, George Mason, was an important figure in the politics of Pohick Church, and naturally volunteered the services of his indentured joiner and carver. The pulpit here is against the center of the north wall, and the altarpiece is in the shape of a Palladian window, although it only has glass at the top, for the rest of the frame is filled with the tablets inscribed with the Creed, the Lord's Prayer and the Ten Commandments. The church is well restored and a delight to the eye.

This is the building for which we have a drawing done by George Washington; as we noted earlier in our discussion of Mount Vernon, this drawing helps to prove that Washington was no architect and was therefore incapable of having designed Mount Vernon himself.

It is indeed a pity that we have no more buildings by James Wren than these six. He may never actually have designed others, however. It is curious to speculate on his relationship with Ariss, for both of them were friends of Washington, and both used Gibbs' handbooks for their designs.

*Simon Duff & Patrick Creagh    fl. 1730-1745*

OF all the Colonies, the most like Virginia in almost every way was Maryland. Maryland lived off the sale of tobacco, like Virginia, and like her neighbor Maryland had few towns, and the ones she had were small. The climate was also similar, if just a shade cooler, and so the architecture generally was governed by the same limitations in both places. In sharp contrast to this, however, is the documentation of Maryland buildings, compared with that of Virginia buildings. There is no book about Maryland, for example, like Thomas Waterman's *The Mansions of Virginia*. Whatever may be the shortcomings of that book, it is absolutely indispensable to the student of Virginia's Colonial architecture. The nearest are two books about William Buckland which are limited in scope.

Bearing in mind the limitations to our knowledge of the Maryland architects, it still seems surprising that there is absolutely no evidence of any work done by anyone worthy of the name of architect in the period that Prince was working in Virginia. The earliest building of architectural quality is 1731, about parallel with Taliaferro's earliest buildings, such as Westover. The earliest architects that we know of are the building team of Simon Duff and Patrick Creagh. The former was a Scot and the latter most likely was a Scots-Irishman. Together they did two houses in Annapolis, and may have done others.

*Dulaney House    Annapolis    about 1735*          *demolished about 1880, reconstruction*

*Attribution:    certain*

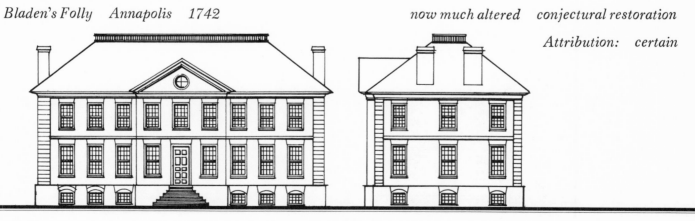

The first of these two buildings was the Dulaney House, built around 1735, and demolished about 1880. This house was of brick, seven bays long, and two storeys high, with a hip roof. There was a pavilion in the middle with only one window on the upper floor although it was as wide as any two other bays; the ground floor had a plain door with transom light, and a narrow window on either side. The pavilion was covered by a hip roof with a flat top. A chimney stood at each end of the ridgepole. The corners of the house and of the pavilion were outlined by verticle rows of brick ridges that gave the impression of quoins. Nothing is known of the interior of this house.

*Bladen's Folly    Annapolis    1742*          *now much altered    conjectural restoration*

*Attribution:    certain*

The other house by these men was a palace for Governor Thomas Bladen, but he never was able to complete it. It stood for years unfinished and rotting until it was bought by St. John's College. It now has three storeys and a cupola on the roof, but it was probably only intended to have two storeys when it was first built. The front of McDowell Hall, or Bladen's Folly as it was known, is nine bays wide, with the center three bays enclosed in a pedimented pavilion. There are two end-chimneys at each end. The corners of the building, but not of the pavilion, have the same brick ribbing found at the Dulaney House. Bladen's Folly was begun in 1742.

There are six other mansions roughly contemporary with these for whom we have no architect; of course, that is not to say that it could not have been Creagh and Duff, but there is no evidence either way.

The earliest is Readbourne, built in Queen Anne County in 1731. This brick house has a ground plan in the shape of a T. Each of the three wings of the T has an end-chimney. The house is five bays long and two storeys high. It used to have dependencies, but these are not the ones that are there now. The orientation of the house has also been changed: the front used to be the long river side, but now the 'front' door is in the side of the base of the T, at what used to be the back of the house. An interesting feature is the round-headed door with a round-headed window on the floor above in the center of the original front of the house. Some rooms from this house are now at the Winterthur Museum in Delaware.

*Readbourne   Queen Anne County   1731*                                    *Attribution:   possible*

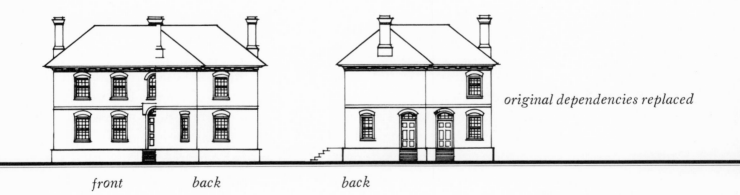

*front*          *back*          *back*          *original dependencies replaced*

*Belair   near Davidsonville   1746*                                    *Attribution:   possible*

A mansion in this group that has extremely academic proportions is Belair, built for Governor Ogle in 1746 near Davidsonville. It is of brick laid in Flemish bond with glazed headers, and is seven bays long and two storeys high. The center three bays are enclosed by a pedimented pavilion; the pediment, which has a bull's-eye window in it, stands out well as a foil to the hip-on-hip roof. The four chimneys are at the ends. The front door has a pediment supported on brackets, rather than the more customary pilasters; this fact may indicate that Governor Ogle himself did the designs, for he would have been *au courant* with the better English practices of the day. The mansion is now an office building.

A large mansion was built near Clinton around 1735; it has two names: Poplar Hill, and His Lordship's Kindness, the latter name because the Earl of Shrewsbury had it built for his niece and ward, Anne Talbot, on the occasion of her marriage. The front has two bays on either side of a pedimented pavilion, in which is enclosed a group of windows in the shape of a Venetian window, but without any formal architectural elements in the window's composition; on the ground floor underneath the Venetian window is a handsome door with a narrow window on either side. The back of the house repeats the window arrangement of the front exactly, except that there is no pavilion or pediment at the back. The roof is deck-on-hip, with massive chimneys, one on either side of the deck on the slope. The flanking dependencies are single-storey rectangles with hip roofs and a single end-chimney on the back façade. One of the dependencies used to be a chapel, probably Roman Catholic.

*His Lordship's Kindness (Poplar Hill)   near Clinton   1735*          *Attribution:   possible*

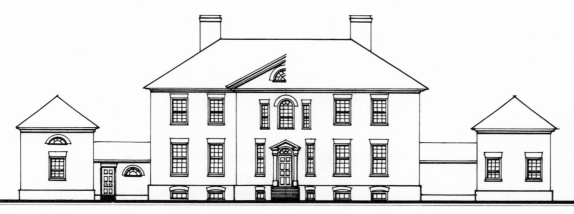

*front      back                two matching flanking dependencies*

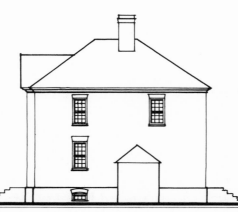

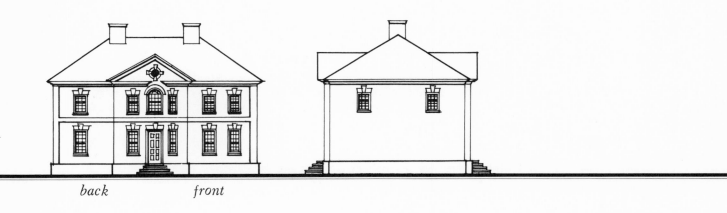

*back            front*

In Cecil County are two houses similar to each other. Greenfield is the simpler of the two. It is of brick, five bays wide and two storeys high. The central bay is enclosed in a pedimented pavilion. The hip roof has a chimney on each side just outside the ridgepole. The door and all the windows are surmounted by stone lintels and keystones. The modillions on the roof cornice are long and flat and are widely spaced. The house belonged to the Lusby family, but the date of construction is uncertain.

A neighbor of Greenfield in Cecil County is Bohemia. The two façades of Bohemia are totally different from each other; each has a central pedimented pavilion, but the pavilions are of different sizes. In the front there are two windows on either side of the narrower pavilion, and a door flanked by narrow windows in the pavilion. At the back, the pavilion is wider so there is only space for one window outside it; inside it is the door flanked by a normal window on each side. Above the door in both the front and the back of the house is a round-headed window; in the front this window forms part of an informal Venetian window. There is a bull's-eye window in both pediments. The hip roof has a chimney at each end of the ridge-pole. The corners of the house in the front and back are picked out by informal pilasters of brick that intersect with the heavy belt course. The brick is laid in English bond in the front but Flemish bond at the back, where there are glazed headers. The windows and doors have stone lintels and keystones; the plain roof cornice is broken to allow room for the tops of the round-headed windows in the center. To the right of the house is a 1½-storey gambrel-roofed wing.

Inside, most of the details were changed in the Federal period; there are Adamesque plaster designs on walls and ceilings, and the staircase has a lovely Chinese Chippendale railing.

*Governor's Mansion   Annapolis   before 1750   enlarged by Key 1768*                    *demolished 1902*

*Attribution:   possible*                                                           *reconstructed drawing*

Before 1750 a large building was constructed to serve as a Governor's mansion in Annapolis. In was enlarged by Robert Key (*q.v.*) in 1768 and demolished in 1902 because it was in the way of certain plans of the U. S. Naval Academy. This mansion was six bays wide and seven bays long. The central five bays of the front were enclosed by a wide pedimented pavilion. The two-storey house was topped by a hip roof. There were two chimneys in the front, one level with each edge of the pavilion, and a corresponding pair at the back of the roof. The pediment contained three windows, the middle one a round-headed window, so that the result was an informal sprawling Venetian window. The front door was covered by a porch straight out of James Gibbs' *Rules for Drawing*, which was not brought to America until after the house was originally built, so that the porch was an addition by Key. Another addition by Key was a rather awkward semioctagonal wing in the center of the back of the house.

## Charles Carroll

CHARLES CARROLL was a wealthy Roman Catholic. He had mansions in both Annapolis and Baltimore. A wing of the otherwise simple Annapolis house very closely resembled the whole of the Baltimore mansion, and since the two of them are like nothing else built in the Colonies it is reasonable to assume that Carroll designed them himself.

The wing of the Annapolis house was a five-bay gable-roofed structure of two storeys with end-chimneys. In the center of the front a pavilion stuck out from the second floor only; it rested either on a pair of columns or on pillars, thus forming a porch for the front door which was underneath. This pavilion, surmounted by a pediment, contained a large Palladian or Venetian window. Nothing much is known of this building, for it was torn down in 1850, but it was probably built around 1750.

The mansion Carroll built in Baltimore in 1754 is called Mount Clare. It is the back of Mount Clare that is so similar to the wing of the house in Annapolis. It is five bays wide, and the central bay has a pedimented pavilion jutting out from the upper floor, supported this time on an architrave over four Doric columns. The pavilion again has a Palladian window, and the garden door is covered by the porch formed by the pavilion above.

The house has a gable roof, but this time there are two chimneys in each end wall. The front of the house is also five bays wide, but the central three bays included in a large pedimented pavilion. The edge of the pavilion and of the house (on the front only) is set off by lines of darker brick made to look like pilasters. The pediments in both front and back each contain semicircular lights. Dependencies were added to the house at a later date. Mount Clare is now the property of the Society of Colonial Dames.

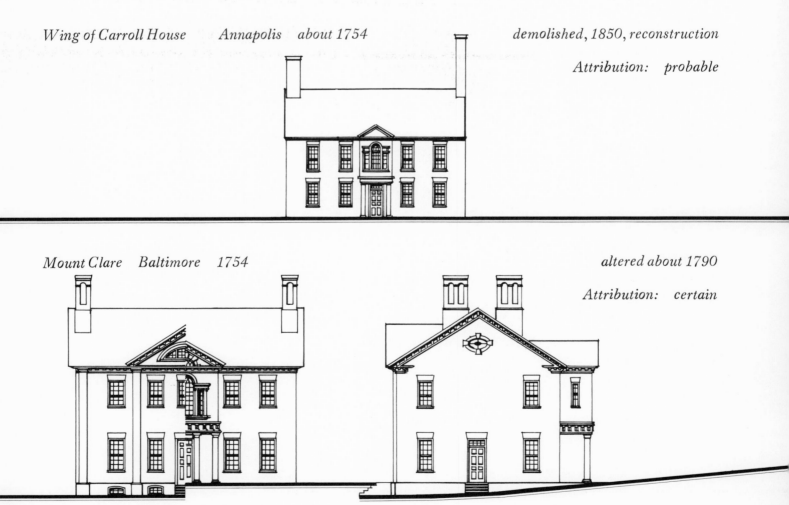

*Wing of Carroll House    Annapolis    about 1754*

*demolished, 1850, reconstruction*

*Attribution:    probable*

*Mount Clare    Baltimore    1754*

*altered about 1790*

*Attribution:    certain*

*front        back*

*Unknown*

TULIP HILL, built during the years 1756 to 1772 in Anne Arundel County for Samuel Galloway, is a most interesting sample of Maryland architecture, for the design changed during the course of construction. It is a five-bay two-storey mansion with high hip-on-hip roof. The chimneys, which stand above the break in the hip, are very tall with two flues apiece, joined together at the top by an arch. The only embellishment at the back is the Gothick canopy over the door, but because William Buckland was in charge of the construction of the house at the end, the front is considerably different. The plain cornice of the back and sides breaks out into a modillioned cornice in front, and it supports a large pediment in the middle; the pediment, however, looks a trifle awkward without a corresponding pavilion on which to sit. Over the door is a single-storey porch consisting of a wide pediment resting on four columns. The upper pediment has a bull's-eye window in the center.

Inside, the Buckland touch can readily be seen in such details as the double arch across the stair-hall (similar to the one he did at Gunston Hall, described in the next chapter), and perhaps in the dentilled cornice in the drawing room—certainly not in the full height panelling, which although attractive is archaic. Obviously when Buckland came on the scene the building was either almost finished or the owner was about to run out of money.

*Tulip Hill    Anne Arundel County    1756-1772*    *enlarged 1787*

*front        back — door off center*

*Peggy Stewart House    Annapolis    1763*    *now slightly altered*

There is an odd house in Annapolis with a few academic features. This is the Peggy Stewart House, built in 1763. The front is a simple one with five bays two storeys high, and a fairly high deck-on-hip roof; the chimneys are part of the end walls. However, it is the end walls that are unusual: in the middle of the three-bay elevation of each end there is a one-bay pedimented pavilion, with a little bull's-eye window in the pediment; the windows are offset in the pavilions to make room for the chimneys.

A few years later, two more buildings were erected in a more or less academic style, and although we have no hint of an architect for either one, they are still worth including. Furley Hall was built in Baltimore in 1775; it was partly demolished in 1870, and the site was ploughed under in 1953. It was a two-storey frame house with hip roof and end-chimneys. The main house was five bays wide, and the three center bays were covered by a large pediment which lacked a pavilion on which to sit. The pediment was pierced by a big round light. The windows of the upper floor were smaller than those of the ground floor, a trick pleasing to the eye that is often used in Colonial architecture. To the right side of the house was attached a two-bay brick wing crowned with a well-proportioned pediment. The cornice lines of the two parts of the house were not the same height in spite of the fact that they had the same number of storeys. The only pictures of the back of the house show it to have been most unacademic, and one can only assume that it must have been a later addition, and so it is omitted from our drawing of the house.

*Furley Hall   Baltimore   1775*                                       *demolished about 1870*

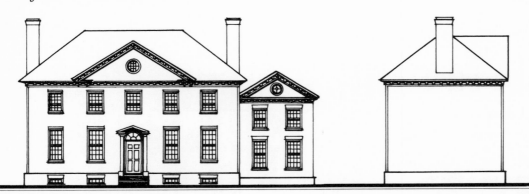

*St. James' Church   Herring Creek, Anne Arundel County   1762*

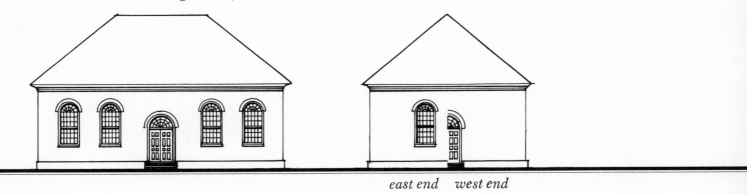

*east end   west end*

In Anne Arundel County there is a charming little church: St. James' Herring Creek Hundred was built in 1762. It is a low rectangular building, with a hip roof as high as the rest of the building. It is five bays long by two wide. There is a single row of round-headed windows. The brick is laid in an all-header bond on two sides, and in English bond on the other two sides. Inside is a barrel ceiling which is coved under the ends of the hip roof.

*Richard Boulton*

TWO more churches were built at about the same time to designs by Richard Boulton, about whom we know practically nothing. Of the two, St. Andrew's Church in St. Mary's County is the more elaborate. The other one, All Faith Church, also in St. Mary's County, is a simple brick barn with gable roof; it is five bays long and three wide with a single row of windows. The windows are arched on the soffit. The only piece of architectural decoration on the outside is a large Palladian window high in the gable of the west end over the entrance door. St. Andrew's is exactly the same, except for some embellishments. These consist of a chancel, at the east end, and two towers at the west end with stubby spires on top. Between the towers, under the Palladian window is a recessed entrance porch, the curtain wall of the gable being supported on an architrave over two Doric pillars, slightly reminiscent of the porches on the two houses by Carroll.

Inside each church is some fine detail, and a barrel vault supported on Ionic columns. These churches are perhaps the most fantastically odd designs to come from a Georgian Colonial architect. One feels like laughing at them, laughing with them, but they are serious. It would be interesting to see any other designs Boulton may have turned out, but we know of no others.

*St. Andrew's Church   St. Mary's County   1765-1767*                              *now altered*

*Attribution:   certain*

*All Faith Church   St. Mary's County   1765*                                        *now altered*

*Attribution:   certain*

## William Buckland   1734-1774

AT the age of fourteen William Buckland was apprenticed to his uncle in London to learn the joiner's trade. Six years later, he was indentured to Thomson and George Mason, two brothers who owned tobacco lands along the Potomac. They brought him to Virginia to finish what was to be the Mason country seat, Gunston Hall. Gunston Hall was a plain large 1½-storey brick house with gable roof and end-chimneys. Buckland added splendid porches to the front and back doors, and produced a perfect interior. He took the massive shapes of the current English Palladian style (for it was used in England mostly in large palaces, in which at times a single room could have swallowed up the whole of Gunston Hall) and fitted them to the small confines of Gunston Hall. There is something unpleasant about the large scale English Palladianism, but when Buckland reduced it in size to fit the small buildings in which he worked, it was transformed into a delicate thing of beauty as if by magic. Among the carvings by Buckland in Gunston Hall is an arch in the stair-hall that is two arches end to end; where they come together in the middle of the hall is a pendant pineapple. He used a similar device in Tulip Hill. Buckland probably also laid out the complicated but beautiful gardens at Gunston Hall.

While he was indentured to Mason, and afterwards when he was still living in the area, Buckland was persuaded to do work on other buildings, such as mansions designed by Ariss and churches designed by James Wren; unfortunately, not too much of this work has survived. After a while, Buckland decided to make his home and base of operations in Maryland, and so he settled in Annapolis. There he worked on a number of houses. While it is definite that he was responsible for the interiors of these buildings, it is not certain in every case whether he also designed the exteriors.

There is a group of three fine Annapolis Mansions with similar exterior characteristics on which we know Buckland worked. The grandest of the three is the Brice House. This is said to be a 1770 rebuilding of an earlier house that dates from 1740, but evidence is lacking. The Brice House is a large mansion in five parts. The center part is a five-bay two-storey brick

*Brice House   Annapolis   about 1770   rebuilding of 1740 house*            *Attribution:   probable*

*two matching five-bay flankers*

*Brice House, side view*

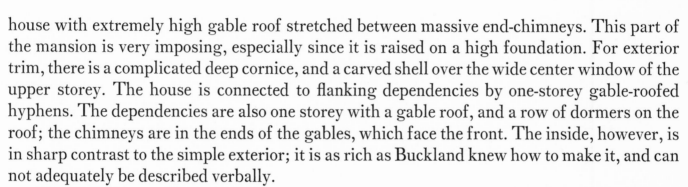

house with extremely high gable roof stretched between massive end-chimneys. This part of the mansion is very imposing, especially since it is raised on a high foundation. For exterior trim, there is a complicated deep cornice, and a carved shell over the wide center window of the upper storey. The house is connected to flanking dependencies by one-storey gable-roofed hyphens. The dependencies are also one storey with a gable roof, and a row of dormers on the roof; the chimneys are in the ends of the gables, which face the front. The inside, however, is in sharp contrast to the simple exterior; it is as rich as Buckland knew how to make it, and can not adequately be described verbally.

The Paca House, built in 1763, looks like a slightly simpler and smaller version of the Brice House; it replaces the Brice House cornice with a cove cornice, and omits the shell over the center window. It has also been stripped of nearly all Buckland's interior joinery, for until recently it was used as a hotel. Only one room still has its original trim.

*Paca House    Annapolis    1763*                                                    *now altered*

*Attribution:    probable*

*two matching five-bay flankers*

*front   back*            *two matching flankers*

The third in this group is the Ridout House, built in 1763. This house has more exterior trim than the other two. It has well designed doorways, with a small entrance porch on the garden side (the back). There is also a modillioned cornice at the back, but a plain cornice in front. The end-chimneys, which stick partially out of the end walls, have windows let into them between fireplaces. The flankers are not connected to the house as they are in the other two. The interior detail is restrained but lovely.

In spite of the impressiveness of the last three mansions, there are another three that are considered even better. The most famous of these is the Hammond-Harwood House. This is another five-part house, but the shape of each block is totally different than in the previous three mansions. The front of the house is Buckland's most educated façade; it is five bays wide and two storeys high. The center three bays are enclosed in a pedimented pavilion. The pediment is pierced by a bull's-eye window with elaborately carved trim around it; there is also much carving around the center window of the upper floor, and a superb doorway below, among the details of which is a large horizontal oak-leaf cluster forming part of the Ionic entablature. The fronts of the hip-roofed flanking dependencies are semioctagonal; the dependencies, which are a short two storeys high, are joined to the house by elaborately composed hyphens. At the back of the house, the whole arrangement is repeated with a few exceptions. The backs of the dependencies are roofed with a gable, and the pediment in the center of the back of the house does not rest on a proper pavilion like the one in the front, but on a pavilion only suggested by a row of four brick pilasters supporting a full entablature; a serious 'mistake' is made here, however, for the pilasters are covered by the belt course which runs over them rather than behind them. While this may be a mistake in academic style, it is nevertheless still attractive, and imparts a more relaxed air of the Queen Anne period to this otherwise stiffly correct Georgian house.

Inside, the carved wood details show Buckland at his best, and since they are described fully in other publications these details are omitted here.

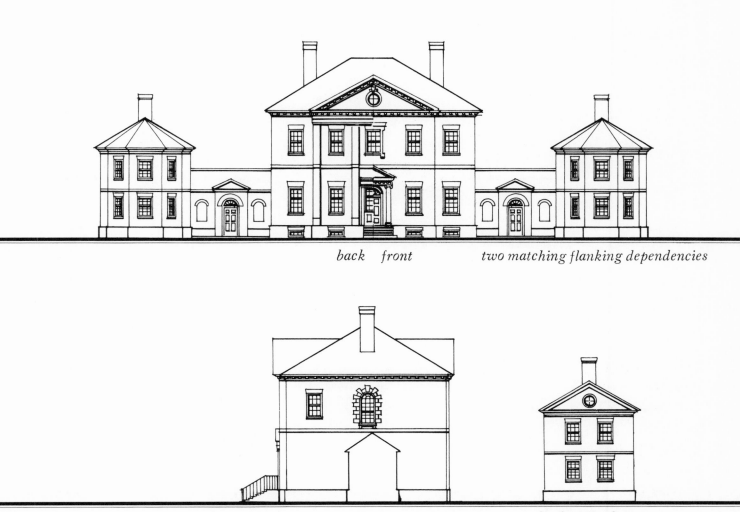

*back   front*               *two matching flanking dependencies*

*back of flanker*

The Hammond-Harwood House was built as a wedding present by the first owner for his bride, but before the house could be finished in 1774 the girl ran away with someone else, and so it was sold before ever being occupied. Two more architectural features of note are the jib door that leads out into the garden from the splendid dining room, and the rusticated round-headed window on the side of the house to light the stairs; this window is from James Gibbs, as are the bull's-eye windows in the pediments.

Directly across the street from the Hammond-Harwood House is the Chase-Lloyd House. This one was partially built when it changed owners, and the new owner employed Buckland to finish the house. It is three storeys high and five bays wide with a deck-on-hip roof. A massive flat chimney stands on each side of the deck. The front is broken by a one-bay pedimented pavilion, while at the back in the same place is a large Palladian window to light the stairs. The Palladian window motif is repeated elsewhere: the front door is a variation on that theme, and the central windows of the top floor both in front and in back are informal compositions along those lines.

Inside, apart from the usually brilliant Buckland carving, the most striking feature is the staircase, which ascends normally as far as the first landing, and then after a 180° turn breaks into a divided run as far as the next floor.

*Chase-Lloyd House   Annapolis   1769-1774*                    *Attribution:* **certain**

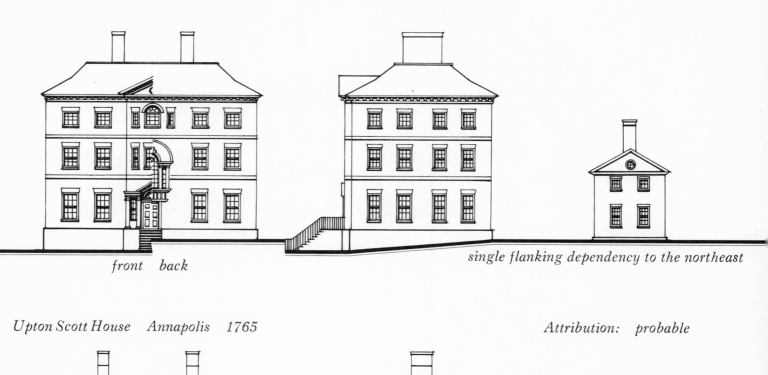

*front    back*                                      *single flanking dependency to the northeast*

*Upton Scott House   Annapolis   1765*                    *Attribution:* **probable**

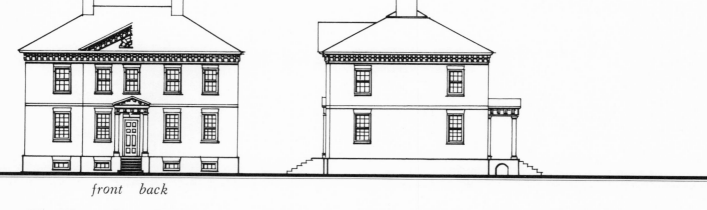

*front    back*

The Upton Scott House, also in Annapolis, was built in 1765, and has quite a formal front of five bays, the middle three of which are enclosed in a pedimented pavilion. The roof is a gable-on-hip, with a tall chimney on each side at the break. Inside, the entrance hall is perhaps the most beautiful part, but the rest of the house was probably as good before it was altered to serve as a convent. The brickwork is laid in an all-header bond.

*Adams-Kilty House   Annapolis   about 1770*          *now altered*   *Attribution:* **probable**

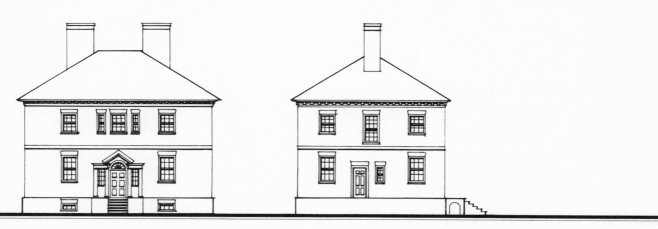

The Adams-Kilty House, often mistakenly called the William Pinkney House, is another of Buckland's Annapolis houses, but the date is uncertain. It is two storeys high with a low hip roof, and reminiscent of the Chase-Lloyd House, although it has not the latter's pavilion. The large flat chimneys, which are at the break of the hip, present their flat face to the front.

Another of Buckland's Annapolis buildings, Acton House, built in 1763, has almost the same roof and chimney arrangement, but the façade is otherwise quite different. The center bay is recessed between two pedimented pavilions each two bays wide. The pedimented porch over the front door, which is in the center bay, is supported by four Doric columns one storey high. At the middle of the back of the house is a semioctagonal pavilion. The interior trim has been altered or removed, as in the Adams-Kilty House.

Montpelier, in Prince George's County, is almost identical to the Hammond-Harwood House in its front elevation, except that the roof is steeper and the dependencies are lower at Montpelier. The carving is not so lavish, either. The original house was built in 1750, but Buckland completely rebuilt it in 1770, although strangely enough he left some of the earlier crude interior woodwork untouched and concentrated on the exterior.

*Montpelier   Prince George's County   1770   rebuilding of 1750 house*

*Attribution:  probable*

*back    front    two matching flanking dependencies*

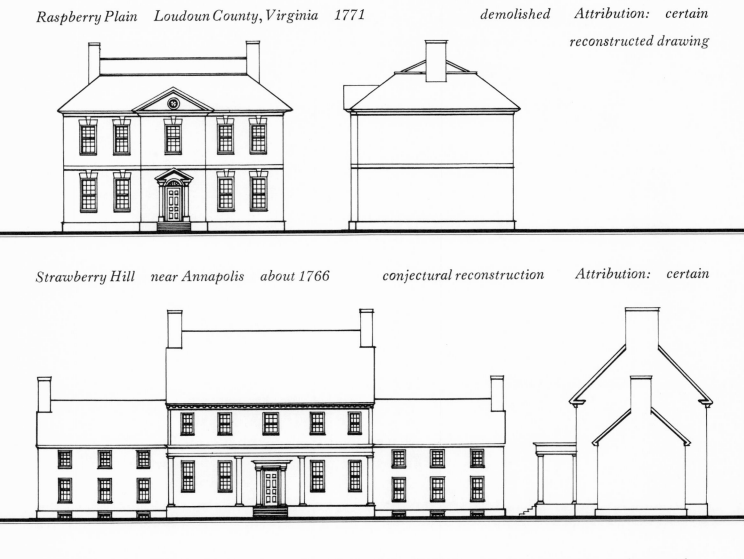

*Raspberry Plain    Loudoun County, Virginia    1771*          *demolished    Attribution: certain*

*reconstructed drawing*

*Strawberry Hill    near Annapolis    about 1766*    *conjectural reconstruction    Attribution: certain*

Two more houses were associated with Buckland in his capacity as architect, but neither of them is his best work. Raspberry Plain in Loudoun County, Virginia, was built in 1771. It was of brick, and was similar to the Upton Scott House, except that the pitch of the roof was steeper and the central pavilion in front was only one bay wide. A wing on the right was added to the house at one time, but now the whole building is demolished.

The other house was Strawberry Hill, just outside Annapolis. This was built around 1766 high on a hill. It was a frame house with brick ends, and was obviously intended to belong to the same family of design as the Paca House and the later Brice House, but of the group it was the poorest, if we can believe an existing watercolor. It had no dependencies, but a wing was added to the right side of the house.

Among other houses in which Buckland did some joinery were Rockledge, near Colchester, Virginia, on the Potomac, the Ringgold House at Chestertown, Maryland, which is now the residence of the President of Washington College (the woodwork has been removed and is now in a museum), Whitehall, near Annapolis, and the State House in Annapolis. Rosamond Beirne thinks that there is a possibility of Buckland's having designed the Caroline County Courthouse at Denton; this was a handsome brick building, judging from an old newspaper photograph, with a good door, a pediment with bull's-eye window, a modillioned cornice, and matching two-storey wings. Buckland put an advertisement in the newspaper in 1775 for builders to help him erect it, but before any work could be done the war intervened, and the Courthouse was not built until 1795; whether Buckland's design was used at that time or not is purely conjecture. In any case, the building is now destroyed.

## Joseph Horatio Anderson   (?-1781)

ANDERSON was roughly a contemporary of Buckland; the two worked together on the same building on occasions, as we shall see. He also worked in partnership with Robert Key, another contemporary. Not much is known of Anderson, but he was imaginative in his designs, and up-to-date to the extent that he may have had his training in England, especially since he appears not to have used any builders' handbooks.

Anderson's biggest surviving building is the State House in Annapolis. It has an academic façade eleven bays long, with the center three bays enclosed in a pedimented pavilion. It is two storeys high with an ungainly deck-on-hip roof; this roof is now surmounted by an even

*State House    Annapolis    1772*                         *now altered*       *Attribution:  certain*

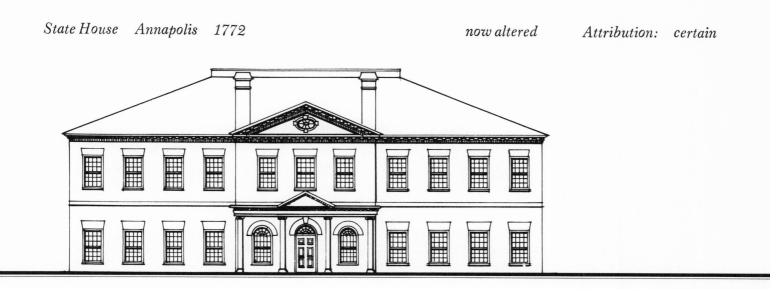

more ungainly enormous multi-layer cupola and dome, but fortunately we cannot blame Anderson for that. The brick is laid in Flemish bond, and the only exterior trim is a rich modillioned cornice, and a one-storey porch (probably by Buckland) in front of the pavilion. The windows and door of the pavilion are round-headed, but all the rest of the windows are rectangular. A chimney stands on either side of the pediment of the pavilion.

Inside, Buckland was employed to execute the beautiful Senate Chamber, which has now been restored after years of use and abuse. The Annapolis State House is the only one still regularly used since Colonial times. It was once the scene of the meeting of the United States Congress. The Treaty of Paris, which marked the end of the Revolution, was ratified here.

*Whitehall    Anne Arundel County   1765*              *slightly altered    Attribution:  probable*

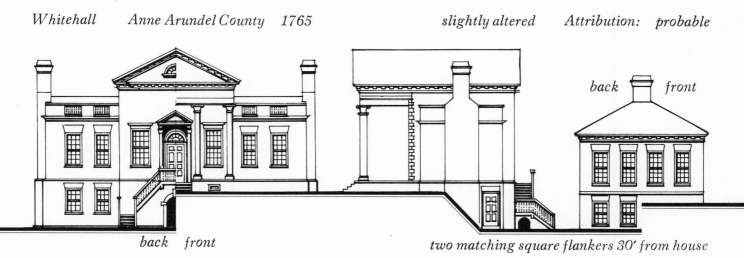

back   front

*back    front*                              *two matching square flankers 30' from house*

Outside Annapolis on the edge of a steep hillock is Whitehall, built for the popular Governor Horatio Sharpe in 1765. It is seven bays wide, with the center three bays enclosed by a pedimented pavilion, which is fronted by a Corinthian portico of giant order. This is the first time a giant-order portico was built for a house in the Colonies, although the motif was first used on St. Philip's Church in Charleston, South Carolina, and later on the Redwood Library in Newport, Rhode Island. There is a chimney at each end of the house. The back of the mansion is two storeys high because of the slope of the hill on which the house is perched; there is an elegant stairway leading up to the door at the back, which is placed at the same level as the door in the front. At each side of the building at some distance is a square dependency with hip roof and central chimney. These are actually bedrooms, for there is no room in the house proper for anything but reception rooms. This ambitious layout is part of an even larger scheme that was never carried out; this would have had, among others things, bathrooms with running water. The bedroom buildings are at present linked to the house, but originally they were detached, which must have been a hardship during the winter. Further alterations, were also carried out at one time, but now the body of the house has been well restored. Inside is more of Buckland's excellent woodwork.

*Mulberry Fields    St. Mary's County    1760*                     *Attribution:    possible*

*two matching three-bay forecourt dependencies*

Mulberry Fields, built in St. Mary's County in 1760 for Captain William Somerville, may not be by Anderson, but is closer to his style and period than it is to anyone else's, and so it is included here for lack of a better place to include it. Basically, it is a typical plantation house, with hip roof and forecourt dependencies. The brickwork is good, laid in Flemish bond with some glazing. The entrance porch is supported by Doric columns, and has a low pediment over it.

Among Anderson's other designs was one for Joseph Gallaway, Speaker of the House, which disappeared before anyone drew a picture of it, so we have no idea what it looked like. Anderson also sent designs to Providence, Rhode Island, for University Hall at Brown University, but they were rejected in favor of designs by Robert Smith of Philadelphia (*q.v.*); curiously enough, the man who made the choice was another of the Colonial architects, Joseph Brown (*q.v.*).

Anderson's last building was St. Anne's Church in Annapolis. Work was begun in 1776, but stopped almost immediately on account of the war. The church was not finished until 1792, eleven years after the death of Anderson. The work was continued by Robert Key, who made a few changes to the design, mostly internal and structural. The church burned down in 1858.

St. Anne's was an enormous building with no artistic merit to speak of, although it was called handsome by the people of the day. It was nine bays long and two storeys high with a gable roof. There was a tall thin tower at the west end with a hip roof of low pitch; it was this feature more than any other that reminded the viewer of an Italian Renaissance church, although the similarity was most likely unintentional.

The two tiers of windows were rectangular, the upper ones smaller than the lower ones. Between each of the lower windows was a pilaster, on which sat a row of arches that were engaged with the wall; this was slightly reminiscent of the inside of an Italian church. Nothing is known of the inside of St. Anne's.

It is puzzling indeed how Anderson, who designed such an exciting mansion as Whitehall, could create an uninspiring monster like St. Anne's, especially since the commissioning vestry was bound to be critical in view of the large amount of money involved. Even if Anderson could produce such a poor design as St. Anne's, there was still Robert Key who could have altered it for the better, but did not. This is another of those mysteries of the eighteenth century that will probably never be solved.

Anderson appears to have been quite cocky, for he claimed that there was no other architect in all the Colonies beside himself. Actually, one might almost believe him on the strength of some of his beautiful unexecuted designs, but his executed work does not necessarily confirm his claim.

*St. Anne's Church   Annapolis   1776-1792*                    *burnt 1858, reconstruction*

*Attribution:   certain*

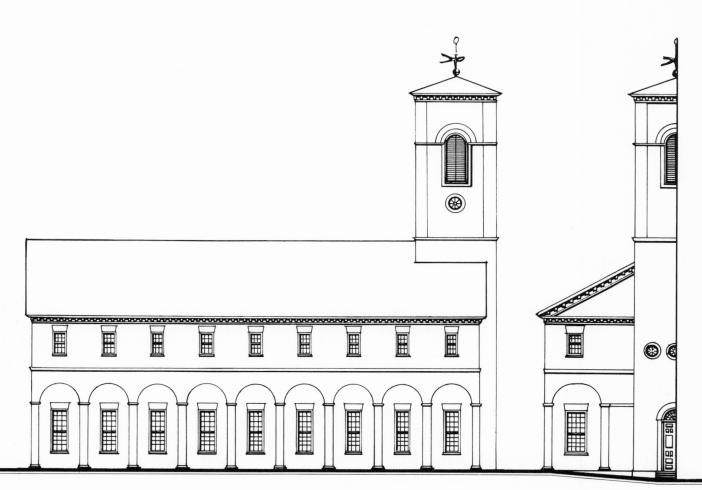

*Robert Key   (c.1740-c.1802)*

ROBERT KEY was also a contemporary of Buckland and Anderson, and like them he worked in Annapolis. Apart from collaborating with Anderson on St. Anne's Church he must have been responsible for many other buildings, but we have little information about him or his activities. He is known to have built additions to Governor Eden's mansion—a semioctagonal wing at the back, and a fine entrance porch from James Gibbs' book—and a ballroom on Duke of Gloucester Street in 1765, and a theater in 1771, but beyond that his life is a blank.

*Cokesbury Methodist College   Abingdon   1785*                    *burnt 1795, reconstruction*

*Attribution:   Possible*

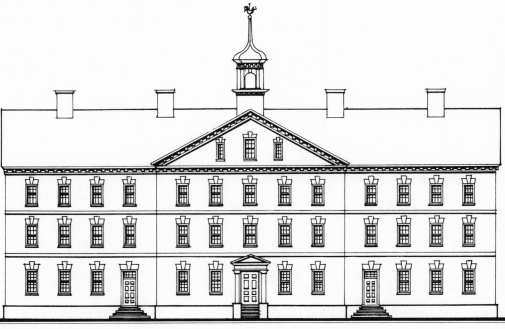

Completely on speculation, however, Cokesbury Methodist College has been included among these drawings. Since it only stood for ten years after its construction in 1785, practically nothing about it can be certain. It was thirteen bays long and three storeys high with a gable roof and a small cupola on top. The central pavilion was five bays wide. It seems to have been built of brick with stone lintels and keystones over the windows and doors. The loss of this by fire, the first Methodist college in the world, is greatly to be regretted; there is a picture of it in Clark's *An Album of Methodist History*.

ORTH CAROLINA is almost destitute of buildings designed by architects, in sharp contrast to the wealth in this department of her neighbors, Virginia and South Carolina. We have already seen Chowan County Courthouse at Edenton; that was attributed to the Virginia architect John Ariss. No other architect did work in or for North Carolina until Governor William Tryon imported John Hawks *(q.v.)* in 1764 to build the Palace at New Bern, except for the designer of St. Philip's Church in Brunswick.

*St. Philip's Church   Brunswick, North Carolina   1741-1768*　　　　　　*burnt 1776, reconstruction*

*Attribution:   possible*

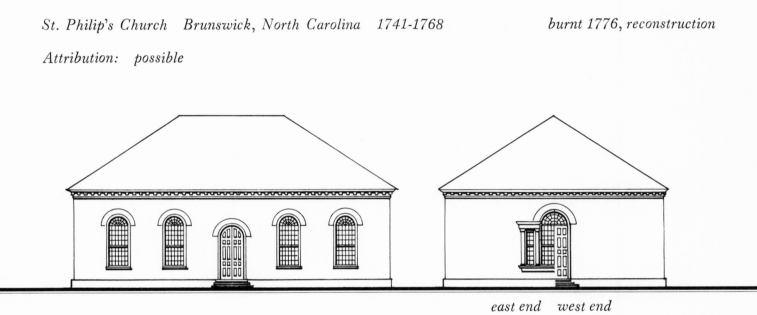

*east end   west end*

Brunswick is a ghost town across the river and downstream from Wilmington; it was once the capital, but mosquitoes and disease forced the inhabitants to abandon it. While it was the capital, it was decided to erect a church that would, as one writer put it, rival Boston's King's Chapel, although the King's Chapel in Boston that was worth rivalling was not built until 1754. An act was passed providing for the building of the new church in 1741, but it was not completed until 1768. The best guess as to who designed St. Philip's would have to be the Governor, Arthur Dobbs, who held his post from before the conception of the church until 1765 when he died and was buried inside the church. The building was finished under Governor Tryon, but by then it was too late to alter the design even if he or Hawks wanted to do so. The construction delays were chiefly due to lack of money and the damage of the new church by lightning in 1760 when it was all but finished. Therefore, the design must have been provided somewhere between 1741 and 1750 when we know that construction was under way.

St. Philip's, of which all that remains is the four walls, was a rectangular building with a hip roof. It was five bays of round-headed windows and a central door in length. The west end was pierced only by one very tall door, and the east end was lit by a Palladian window over the altar. The church was destroyed by the British in 1776 and again in the Civil War.

*John Hawks   1731-1790*

JOHN HAWKS was imported from England in 1764 by Governor Tryon for the express purpose of building a Palace for the Governor. With the exception of the Palace and its outbuildings, there seem to be only two other buildings designed by Hawks in North Carolina. Both of them are dated about 1770, and since Tryon departed in that year to become Governor of New York one must presume that he took Hawks with him in 1770 to New York. Records show that Hawks returned to New Bern after the Revolution and served in the legislature.

*John Wright Stanley House   New Bern   about 1770*          *now slightly altered*

*Attribution:   certain*

The public library in the center of New Bern was once the house of John Wright Stanly. It is a dignified Georgian house five bays long and two storeys high. It is a frame building, with the walls of wood smoothed to resemble masonry or stucco, and with wooden quoins at the corners. The ground floor windows are covered by pediments, and there is a fine front doorway. Inside, the staircase is excellent, as is the drawing room. The house has necessarily been altered inside and outside to accommodate the library; the wing at the back is in good taste, but the dormers are not.

*Bellair   near New Bern   about 1770*          *now slightly altered*

*Attribution:   certain*

A short distance south of New Bern is the Palladian plantation house known as Bellair. It looks like a smaller and simpler version of the Palace. It is seven bays long and two storeys high set on a high foundation; the center three bays are enclosed by a pedimented pavilion with a bull's-eye window in the pediment. The brick is laid in Flemish bond, and the hip roof rises from a plain cornice. One of the most striking things about the house is that it is only one room deep, although a frame lean-to has been added at the back; also added is a porch in front of the pavilion. Inside all detail has been removed except a Palladian mantel, similar to the one in the Stanly House, in the left room.

*Governor's Palace    New Bern    1767*                    *burnt 1798    reconstructed 1952-1959*

*Attribution:    certain*

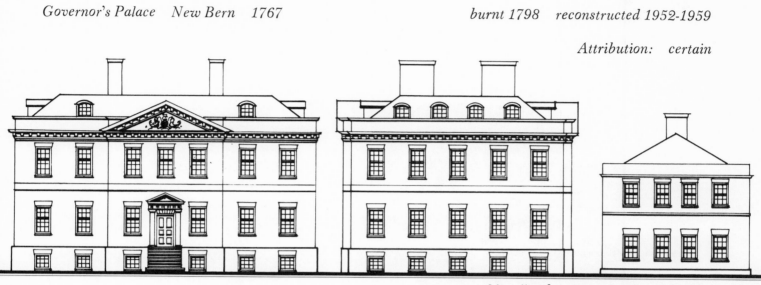

*two matching five-bay forecourt dependencies*

The Governor's Palace in New Bern was begun in 1767, and finished enough so that the Governor and his family could move in in 1770 just before they left for New York. After the Revolution, George Washington, who attended a ball there, remarked that it was fast falling to ruin. Only a few years later, in 1798, it burned to the ground, and soon after other buildings were erected on the site. In 1958 work was begun on its reconstruction with nothing original remaining except the west advance building, which was much altered. As soon as the new look of the bricks wears off the mansion will probably become one of the showplaces of America, thanks to the generosity of the late Mrs. J. E. Latham.

The front elevation is seven bays wide and two storeys high. The roof, surrounded by a parapet, is a deck-on-hip, and it is pierced by a few dormers. The center three bays constitute a pavilion with a dignified pediment on top. The house is five bays deep. A pair of large (four bays by five) dependencies mark off a spacious forecourt, the whole looking very English. The brick of the main house is laid in Flemish bond, but the brick of the dependencies is laid in English bond.

Inside the reconstructed mansion are mantels, panelling, furniture, etc., from English eighteenth-century houses; it was impossible to install copies of the original decorations because the plans for them do not exist. The only plans that have come down to us are the elevation and floor plan drawings preserved in the archives of the British Public Records Office. Verbal descriptions of the furnishings enabled the restorers to locate pieces that could not have been very different from the originals.

It is indeed a pity that Hawks did not design more than the three houses at New Bern; nothing else quite like his buildings was built during the Colonial period.

*Unknown Early South Carolinian(s)*

ONCE more owing to a lack of records, or perhaps only to a lack of research in the records, we have to rely on architectural evidence to piece together the story of the early architecture of this Colony. This statement could well apply to any one of many Colonies, but this time it is about South Carolina in the first forty years of the eighteenth century. Three names present themselves as being claimants to the title of architect(s) of a group of eight early buildings. They are John Wood, who was called both architect and joiner, and who died in 1744; Mr. Johns, who arrived in Charleston in 1698; the third is John Rich, who died in 1745, and who owned five pattern books. Rich sounds the most likely. In fact, we might really go out on a limb and say that Rich was the architect and Wood the joiner responsible for the excellent woodwork, especially that at Drayton Hall.

*Drayton Hall    near Charleston    1738*                               *formerly had two flankers*

*front*        *back*                               *side*

Easily the most impressive mansion built in this period is Drayton Hall. It is two storeys high on a high basement, seven bays wide and six bays deep. The roof is a hip-on-hip with a chimney on each side above the break. In the front the center three bays are recessed behind a two-storey portico which is surmounted by a pediment. The lower order of the portico is Tuscan or Doric and the upper order is Ionic; there are four columns to each floor of the portico. At the back, there is a pediment that matches the one in the front, only here it is not supported by any pavilion or portico; usually this looks unbalanced, but here it is carried off well. The divided steps to the back door are very attractive, and like the front portico are typical of the Palladian manner. The brick is laid in Flemish bond. The exterior of the house suffers now from two changes: the original front of the house faced the river, for that was the only way to travel in those days, while now the river front is the back. The other misfortune is the loss of the dependencies, about which we know nothing. The house, situated on the Ashley River, was built in 1738 for the Drayton family. A garden once stretched between the mansion and the river, which the Duc de la Rochefoucauld preferred to those of Middleton Place.

Inside, the extremely rich ornamentation is absolutely intact with the exception of pieces of two mantels that were replaced around 1800. It was fortunate that the owners in the Federal period did not replace any more than this, and that the Victorians did not touch it at all. During the Civil War, the mansion was in the path of a savage Union army, and the quick-thinking owner turned the house into a hospital for Negroes suffering from a severe form of smallpox and so saved the house. There is a splendid divided main staircase, and many heavy and rich overmantels from William Kent's book, *Designs of Inigo Jones.*

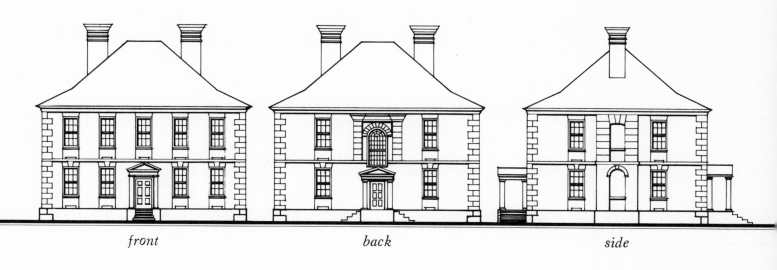

*front*                    *back*                    *side*

Brick House on Edisto Island was built in 1725 for the Hamilton family. The brick was imported from Boston as ballast; it is said to be a denser sort than any obtainable locally. The bricks are laid in Flemish bond, with a wealth of stone trim, including quoins and window dressing. The house is five bays wide and two storeys high with a tall hip roof. Massive baroque chimneys stand high above the hip. Inside was some high quality panelling and woodwork, although nothing approaching the rich detail of Drayton Hall. The house was gutted by fire a few years ago, but the owners announced their intention of rebuilding. Some writers have described the outside of this house as in the French taste; certainly the feeling inspired by it is French, but in many ways it is at least as much English as French. The house used to have two flankers of unknown shape.

*Archdale Hall   on the Ashley River   1706*                    *destroyed 1887, reconstruction*

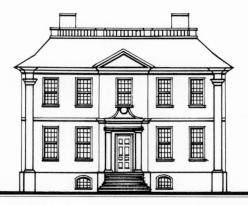

The first South Carolina house of architectural character was Archdale Hall on the Ashley River. Little is known of this building. It was built in 1706 for the Baker family and destroyed in 1887 by earthquake. It was five bays wide and two storeys high with a steep deck-on-hip roof. The center bay composed a pedimented pavilion, and there was a large pilaster at each end of the façade. Two chimneys stood on the roof deck, which was surrounded by a balustrade. The house was of brick covered in stucco.

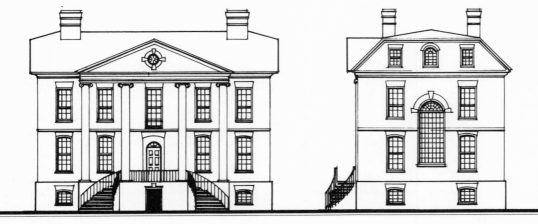

Rich's last building, if indeed he was the architect, was the Charles Pinckney House in Charleston; it was built in 1745 and burned during the Civil War. It was a monumental building with a jerkin-head roof, which however did not appear unacademic because of the arrangement of the four chimneys. The façade which was five bays long was interrupted by a three-bay pedimented pavilion. Under the pediment was an entablature supported by four Ionic pilasters the full two-storey height of the house. The front door was reached by an impressive divided flight of steps. On the end, a large round-headed window lit the stairs between two other bays of windows. The house was of brick.

In 1730 Fenwick Hall was built on John's Island for the Fenwick family. It is a typical brick house with brick quoins, a deck-on-hip roof and end-chimneys. Dependencies were built in about 1750, and are shown in an old watercolor; this same picture shows the house as having a high hip roof rather than the present deck-on-hip. In the Federal era, a wing with semioctagonal front was added to the left of the house. Inside, the walls are fully panelled.

*Fenwick Hall    Johns Island    about 1730*                    *slightly altered*

*had two two-story flankers,*
*but they were 1750 additions*

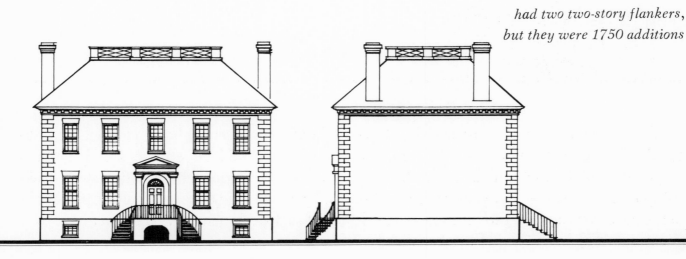

*two matching three-bay flanking dependencies*

The house was the headquarters of the British during the Revolution, and fell into disrepair after the Civil War; it has happily been restored in recent years. At the back are window arrangements in the shape of informal Venetian windows.

Crowfield, built in 1730 for the Middleton family, closely resembled Fenwick Hall, except that it had two chimneys to the latter's four, and some stone trim. Crowfield, which is now destroyed, was most famous for its water gardens which rivalled those of another Middleton family estate, Middleton Place.

Another watercolor painting in the collection of views of old South Carolina shows an unidentified plantation house along the Ashley River. This house, covered in stucco, looks a bit like Drayton Hall with its central porch and divided entrance steps. It was one storey high over a high basement, with a tall hip roof above. The entrance porch was three bays wide, and consisted of a pediment supported by four columns.

*Unidentified Plantation on the Ashley River*                      *demolished, reconstruction*

The only house still standing in Charleston that can claim to have been designed by an architect in this period is the Thomas Rose House, built in 1735. It is a square two-storey building with hip roof. It is covered in stucco, but the corner quoins show through. The street front, like so many Charleston houses, has no door; the door is around to the left inside a more recent portico. The back of the house, or right side, has a round-headed window to light the stairs.

Inside, the house is well supplied with handsome woodwork, which has been ably restored. The rooms, which are fully panelled, are grouped around a single chimney. The house is said to possess a romantic young ghost.

In 1735 a fine plantation was built on Wambaw Creek near Santee by a Huguenot named Noë Serré. The house is called Hampton, but it has been so much altered and enlarged that the original appearance is too doubtful to draw. Even so, it is almost certain from the scale of the building and from surviving interior decoration that this house belongs in the group under discussion. There were undoubtedly many other plantations along the various rivers of South Carolina that would belong in this group, but they have all been lost without trace or record. More is the pity, for here would be a group to rival the large number of early Virginia mansions.

*Thomas Rose House   Charleston   1735*                                        *slightly altered*

*side (street front)*                              *back*

*front is now obscured by
porches (garden side)*

*Samuel Cardy (?-1774) & William Rigby Naylor (?-1773)*

THE next phase of South Carolina's architecture was dominated by Samuel Cardy and his son-in-law William Rigby Naylor, although they were probably not responsible for all the buildings that are grouped together under their names in this book; the grouping is merely convenient in some cases.

The first record of Cardy in South Carolina is his witnessing a will in 1752, so he probably had been there several years before in order to be established enough to be counted as a witness to a will. He seems to have come from Dublin, since his own will mentions that his family was there. He called himself by the title of Architect many times, and although that did not necessarily mean in those days what it means now it was probably accurate in his case. Only two buildings are certainly designed by Cardy; these are St. Michael's Church in Charleston, and the lighthouse on Middle (now part of Morris) Island, which has long been destroyed. He may safely be assumed to have designed other buildings to which he is not connected by any documents that have come down to us.

William Rigby Naylor, who married Cardy's daughter Margaret, was another Irishman. Naylor is mentioned in H. M. Colvin's *Biographical Dictionary of English Architects* as having submitted designs for the new Royal Exchange in Dublin in 1769. The designs were rejected. At that time Naylor was listed as living in London; presumably, he was only in London on a short trip from Charleston. In Charleston, two buildings are definitely known to have been designed by Naylor: these are the Exchange or Custom House, and the Guard House. The Exchange has been altered, but it is still there; the Guard House was torn down in 1838 after it had been severely mutilated. When first built, it was two storeys high on a high basement, with a pediment supported by four massive Tuscan columns. Since the columns jutted out into the street, they were later removed, and a third storey was added to provide more room for offices, leaving the building rather nondescript. The fine cornice and entablature were also removed at that time. Not enough information exists about the Guard House to enable a picture to be drawn.

*Branford-Horry House    Charleston    1751*

*now altered slightly*

*Attribution:   possible*

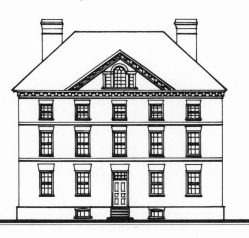

The Branford-Horry House in Charleston was built in 1751. There is no other house in South Carolina of this period with this degree of academic detail, although the house seems to be a companion architecturally speaking to many of the public buildings. Therefore, I am ascribing it to Cardy. It is a large three-storey house five bays wide with a hip roof. A three-bay pediment in the center of the roof contains a Palladian window; this pediment is not supported by any pavilion of pilasters. The exterior of the house has been altered somewhat by the addition of a two-storey porch on the front in 1830, and by the removal of what must have once been a modillioned cornice. Inside, the rooms are fully panelled; there are a number of fine mantels and overmantels in the style of the period.

Soaring 186 feet above the city of Charleston is the heavy white steeple of St. Michael's Church, built between 1751 and 1761. This was definitely designed by Cardy, although much

*St. Michael's Church    Charleston    1751-1761*                              *Attribution:    certain*

*side*

inside as it was being built, from a basilical church with rows of columns to an auditorium-confusion has been caused by the statement in the South-Carolina Gazette in 1752 that the 'Church will be built on the Plan of one of Mr. Gibson's Designs.' This has variously been interpreted, but the most likely explanation is that Cardy used one of James Gibbs' pattern books to help him; in one of Gibbs' books are the plans for rejected designs for St. Martin's-in-the-Fields in London, but they do not resemble St. Michael's. St. Michael's was radically changed

*formerly had roof parapet*

*as late addition*

*front*          *back*

like nave without any vertical support for the cove ceiling. Probably the original arrangement inside was going to look like one of Gibbs' designs (these designs by Gibbs were later used for St. Paul's Chapel in New York City and for the First Baptist Meeting House in Providence, q.v.). Certainly the steeple on St. Michael's does not remotely resemble any of Gibbs' slender spires.

Because St. Michael's has a portico of four giant Tuscan columns in front of the entrance, Carl Bridenbaugh attributes the church to Peter Harrison of Newport, Rhode Island; Bridenbaugh believed that Harrison's Redwood Library in Newport was the first building in the Colonies to have a portico with columns of a giant order, and since Harrison was also a sea captain who probably called at Charleston, Bridenbaugh naturally assumed that Harrison was the architect of St. Michael's. Actually, Bridenbaugh was not aware that St. Philip's Church, also in Charleston, had antedated the Redwood Library with a giant-order portico by some 25 years (q.v.), and so the inspiration for the portico would have come from only a few blocks away from St. Michael's.

St. Michael's is seven bays long on the outside. Each bay is separated from the next by a giant Tuscan pilaster. There are two tiers of round-headed windows, the lower tier being considerably taller than the upper tier. The heavy tower and steeple sit awkwardly on the edge of the gable roof at the west end, just to the east of the rather lower roof of the entrance portico. At the east end, a semi-oval apse is enclosed in a rectangular pavilion with a gable roof. Inside, a large number of people can be accommodated in the high box pews and the gallery which surrounds the church on three sides. Notable features are the tall two-decker pulpit and sounding board which stands on, but not in, the center aisle, and the Snetzler organ case at the back, which unfortunately has been enlarged without taste. St. Michael's has had a hard time surviving; it was hit by artillery in the Civil War, and has been partially wrecked by tornados and earthquakes. The church, which is built of brick covered in stucco, has been restored and remains in good shape. A parapet was once placed around the roof, but this has been removed.

*Prince William's Church   Sheldon   1753*          *in ruins since 1865    Attribution:   probable*

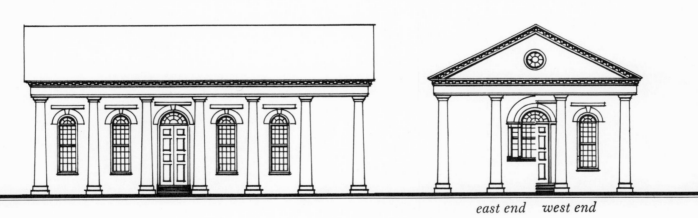

*east end    west end*

Two churches were built outside Charleston not long after St. Michael's, and their design was influenced by that of St. Michael's to a certain extent. The first of these was Prince William's Church, built in Sheldon in 1753. This church was the first conscious attempt in America to imitate a Greek temple. Viewed from the side, the church seems to be built along a row of seven columns, five of the bays between the columns being filled up with wall and the other bay left open for a portico. In the wall between the engaged columns there is a single tier of tall round-headed windows. The original appearance of the interior of the church is in doubt, because the building was set on fire by British troops during the Revolution, and was repaired only to be ruined again in the Civil War. Today most of the four walls still stand, a picturesque ruin overgrown with vines. The brick is laid in Flemish bond, except in the columns where it is laid in an all-header bond. Over the altar was a Palladian window. This church was very likely designed by Cardy.

*St. James' Church    Santee    1768*                                    *Attribution:    probable*

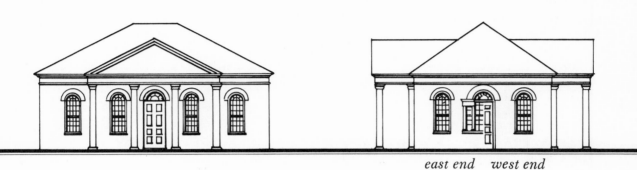

*east end    west end*

St. James' Church in Santee was built in 1768. It is a typical brick rectangular country church, five bays long with a hip roof, except that it has a massive portico of four columns on each side. The porticos were no doubt inspired by those at St. Philip's, St. Michael's and Prince William's Churches. The columns are of brick, like the ones at Sheldon, but they are of a more graceful design. There was a small Palladian window over the altar, but the internal arrangement of the church has been changed, and the altar reoriented to the side. The original arrangement is most unusual, for in churches with cross-aisle plans the main door is at the west end. Here, however, the main door is at least encouraged to be under whichever of the two porticos faces the road, and both porticos are on the sides, not the end. Naylor may have been the architect, but he probably was not.

*Exchange and Custom House    Charleston    1767-1771        now altered        Attribution:    certain*

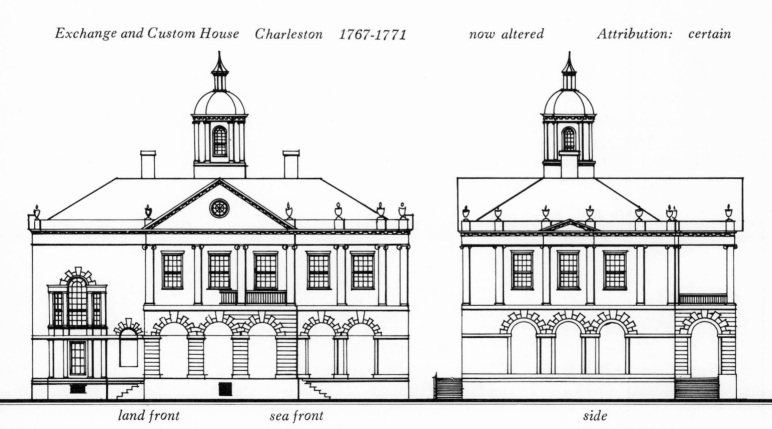

*land front        sea front                                                    side*

Naylor's greatest surviving work is the Exchange or Custom House. This is a large building built between 1767 and 1771. The ground floor on the sea front and on the two ends consisted of a series of open arches, similar to a traditional English market building. On the land front only the center three bays, which compose a pedimented pavilion marked off on the upper storey by Ionic pilasters, have the open arches; on either side of the pavilion are large Palladian windows, behind which rise the stairs to the upper floor. The upper floor has a row of rectangular windows interspersed with pilasters. The roof, which is a deck-on-hip, was surrounded by a parapet, but it has been removed. There used to be a handsome cupola on top, but this too has been removed. Another feature now removed was a majestic portico that once jutted out on the seaward side of the Exchange. The building is covered in stucco.

*State House    Charleston    1752-1756*                    *burnt 1788    Attribution:    probable*

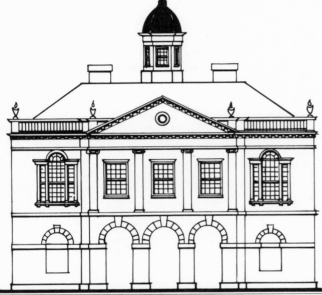

A building that apparently bore quite a resemblance to the Exchange, and by which the latter was probably influenced, was the State House. This was built at the same time as St. Michael's, from 1752 to 1756. There is only one picture of it, and even that is a crude one. As far as can be reconstructed, the State House was smaller than the Exchange and had different proportions, but had essentially the same composition, including arches, some of the windows, pilasters and a cupola. It was almost certainly designed by Naylor, although possibly with the help of Cardy, for Cardy would have been too involved with St. Michael's to be able to tackle another major building at the same time. The State House burned down in 1788, but part of it was incorporated, we are told, in the County Courthouse of 1792.

*Pompion Hill Chapel    on the Cooper River    1763*                    *Attribution:    possible*

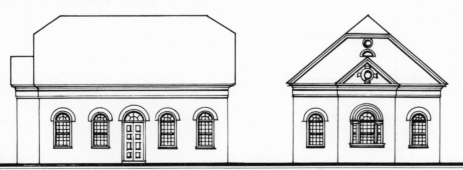

Pompion Hill Chapel, on the Cooper River, was built in 1763. At first glance it is another typical brick country church, five bays long and one storey high. Further inspection, however, reveals that it was definitely inspired by St. Michael's, though in a different way than the other churches we have discussed. It has a high jerkin-head roof, as is the custom for small churches in South Carolina, and a small gable-roofed rectangular addition to the east end, in which is an oval apse. In spite of the simplicity of the church as far as concept is concerned, the execution is of high quality; the roof is supported on a deep architrave, the apse contains a Palladian window and the bricks are well laid in Flemish bond. Inside, there are many details copied from St. Michael's, such as the apse, the coved tray ceiling and the design of the pulpit and sounding board, which is at the extreme west end of the church. The architect is unknown, although many names have been proposed.

*St. Stephen's Church    St. Stephen's Berkeley County 1767*        *Attribution:    possible*

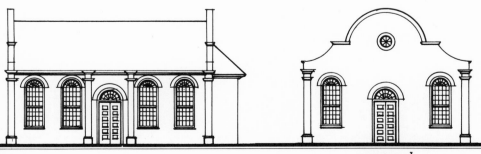

*east end    west end*

About the same size as Pompion Hill Chapel is another country church; St. Stephen's Church was built in Berkeley County in 1767. It is an attractive little church at first glance, but the individual elements that go into its composition are almost incredible. It is rectangular, five bays long, and three bays wide. A Doric pilaster stands between each pair of round-headed windows and supports a deep architrave. The window in the center of the east end is Palladian. On top of the architrave is the most enormous roof imaginable for such a small building; it is a high gambrel in order to give enough room for the coved tray ceiling inside. The gable ends are of rubbed and moulded brick and are shaped in the most elaborate and fantastic form of Jacobean gable. Critics say that all this gives the church a top-heavy appearance, but that is not unpleasant in a composition such as this.

*Prince George's Church    Georgetown    about 1741*        *now altered    Attribution:    possible*

*west end*

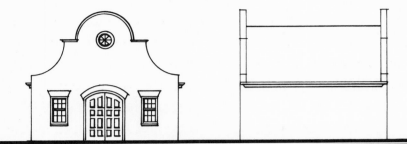

There were earlier attempts at Jacobean gables in South Carolina, including Middleton Place, but the only two noteworthy examples that remain are Prince George's Church in Georgetown, built in 1741, and the stable at North Chacan Plantation, built in 1760. The church has been altered considerably, among other things by the addition of a tower, but it used to look like an unpolished version of the later St. Stephen's Church; it has not as many nor as fine pilasters as St. Stephen's, and the gable ends are not so high, well proportioned or well detailed. At the east end is a semicircular apse. The stable at North Chacan is a simple building with no windows in the sides; the high Jacobean gable hides a gable roof.

As far as can be determined from the evidence at hand, the last four buildings discussed here were designed by the same man, but who he was, nobody knows; in view of the similar motifs in the two later churches and St. Michael's it would seem that this architect was a mason or builder employed by Cardy to work at St. Michael's. The man probably was not Cardy himself, although this possibility can not be ruled out.

*Ezra Waite   (?-1769)*

EZRA WAITE was imported from England around 1765 by the Brewton family to build them an elegant house in Charleston. He was well qualified to do this, for he was not only an architect but also an excellent joiner and wood-carver. In fact, his abilities were rather like those of William Buckland towards the end of the latter's career in Annapolis. While he was in Charleston, Waite only built this one house, and its stable block. After that, we have no further word of his life, and he is presumed to have died shortly after the completion of the house in 1769, for his will was probated late in that year. Other men apparently helped Waite with work on the mansion, for he felt obliged to advertise that he was the architect of the building, and not any of his helpers.

*Miles Brenton House   Charleston   1765-1769*      *slightly altered   Attribution:   certain*

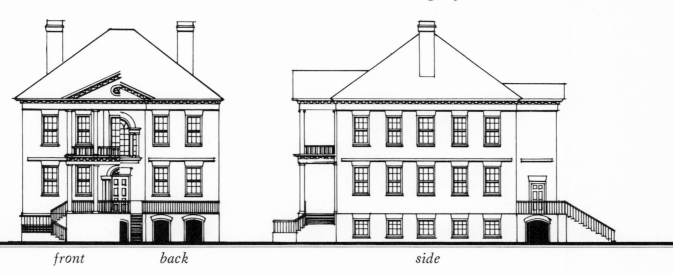

*front          back                        side*

The body of the Brewton House is square, five bays in each direction, and two stories high on a high basement. The roof is a tall hip with a chimney on each side. In the front is a pedimented portico two storeys high, like the one at Drayton Hall. The portico, which is three bays wide, is composed of Tuscan columns for the lower order and Ionic columns for the upper level. In this case, the upper columns are not separated from the lower ones by the balustrade that separates them at Drayton Hall, although there is a balustrade on the intervening porch. At the back, a one-bay pedimented pavilion juts out far into the garden; this encloses the interior staircase. In recent years, enclosed porches have been built out level with the pavilion. The steps up to both the front door and the back door are divided in the best tradition of Palladio.

Inside, the woodwork and decoration is superb, and reminiscent of the work of Buckland. Across the front of the house upstairs is a large ballroom with a high coved ceiling. Although the house was occupied by the British during the Revolution and by Federal troops during the Civil War it has suffered remarkably little damage and is in excellent condition.

At about the time the Miles Brewton House was built, a number of houses appeared around Charleston in a style that can only be called Jeffersonian, although Jefferson obviously was not their architect. These buildings quite properly belong in a discussion of post-Revolutionary architecture, although by date they are placed before the Revolution. For this reason, they are not illustrated in this book. Among them are the Ferguson House, the John Edwards House, the Charles Elliott House, the Colonel John Stuart House, the Colonel Charles Pinckney House, the William Gibbes House, the General William Washington House, and probably others.

# Architects of the American Colonies: North

*James Porteus   c.1660-1737*

IN 1682, William Penn brought a young builder or architect from Dumfries in Scotland to Pennsylvania. Penn's purpose was to build himself a country mansion and a town house suitable for the Proprietor of the Colony, which he was.

Porteus immediately set about building Pennsbury Manor, near Bristol, and finished it eight years later. It was a curious mixture of a fine late Stuart brick front and a medieval wooden back. It was five bays wide and 2½ storeys high, with two chimneys standing on the deck of the high deck-on-hip roof. There were three hipped dormers on the front of the roof. All the windows were naturally casements, since sash had not yet been invented. A large kitchen wing with a massive chimney stuck out to the right. In the center of the back the placement of some of the windows indicates the progression of the staircase against the back wall. On either side of the staircase windows, two small windows on the ground floor stand underneath a large one on the upper floor. This medieval effect is in sharp contrast to the learned appearance of the late Stuart front façade, but it may have had something to do with a scarcity of materials or good workmen.

*Pennsbury Manor   near Bristol   1682-1690*          *demolished about 1750, reconstructed 1932-1939*

*Attribution:   probable*

Penn was absent from the Colony most of the time, and while he was away the house was allowed to fall into ruin. It had completely disappeared by the middle of the century, and by 1800 another house had been built partly on the old foundations. In 1932 work began on a reconstruction of the house, which was finished in 1939.

In the city of Philadelphia, Penn caused a town house to be built for him. This was built of brick somewhere between 1687 and 1699. The roof was of slate, and since slate was rare in the Colonies the house was commonly known as the Slate Roof House. In plan it was U-shaped, five bays wide, and 2½ storeys high. The tall hip roof had a chimney at each end, and there was another chimney in one of the wings. A few hipped dormers sprouted from the roof. A pronounced belt course that was not the same level all around the building divided the two floors of the house. Although all old pictures show sash windows in the house, it must originally have had casements. The lower ones were arched on the soffit. This building was quite up-to-date with contemporary work in England, although there it would be more likely to be found out in the country rather than in the city. The Slate Roof House was soon sold by Penn, and successive owners included Isaac Norris, and Samuel Carpenter, after whom the house is sometimes called. It was demolished in 1867.

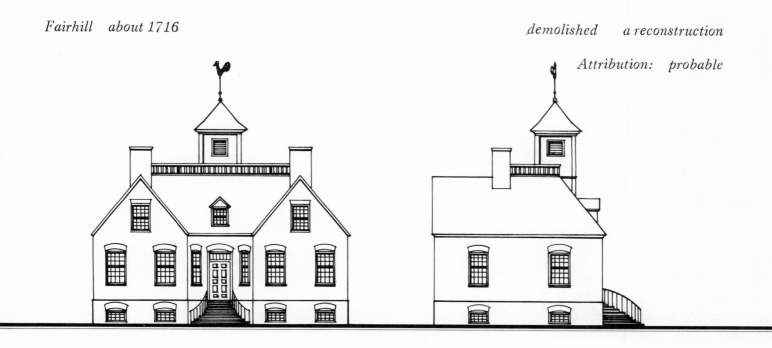

Isaac Norris who bought the Slate Roof House for his town house liked it so much that he commissioned Porteus to build him a country mansion, which he called Fairhill. Fairhill was built of brick in about 1716. It too was U-shaped, but it was only 1½ storeys high. The wings to the front ended in gables rather than hips; the dormers similarly were gabled. The hip roof was topped by a balustraded deck, and at the rear of the deck stood an attractive square tower with a hip roof. The lower windows were arched on the soffit. The front door, standing in the hollow between the two wings, was flanked by a pair of narrow windows, which motif was repeated at Stenton a few years later. The house burned down.

In 1718, Porteus built a small but dignified brick house in Trenton, New Jersey, called the Trent House. It is five bays wide and two storeys high. It has a pair of end-chimneys and a low hip roof on which stands a hexagonal cupola. The exterior brickwork is like Fairhill and Stenton, and the interior detail like Stenton and Hope Lodge.

Hope Lodge, a seven-bay 2½-storey brick house, was built in 1723 in Whitemarsh Valley. It has a high gable-on-hip roof, to which dormers were later added. Over the front door is a round-headed panel that looks like a window that has been bricked in, and may even be one; this motif is found at Readbourne, a contemporary in Maryland.

Stenton, in Germantown, was built between 1728 and 1734. It is easily the finest house in Pennsylvania of those built up to its time, and so it is interesting to compare it with Westover, contemporary in Virginia. Beside Westover, Stenton looks more masculine, but not so polished. The upper storey in front is six bays wide—a mistake by classical standards, which require odd numbers of bays; the lower storey fills the space of the middle two windows upstairs with a door and a pair of narrow flanking lights, as at Fairhill. The lower windows are arched on the soffit. The dormers have gable roofs. The roof of the house is a deck-on-hip with power-ful chimneys at the break. At the back, windows mark the progress of the stairs, as at Penns-bury. The interior woodwork is very good, and is related to that at the Trent House and at Hope Lodge. Stenton was the residence of the Logan family.

*Pemberton's Plantation   about 1735*                                    *demolished     a reconstruction*

*Attribution:   possible*

Pemberton's Plantation, built around 1735, has a roof similar to Stenton's. It is, however, a much smaller building than Stenton, since it is only 1½ storeys high, but it represents a change in Porteus' thinking, for he first uses a central projecting pavilion in this house; this pedimented pavilion, only one bay wide, encloses the front door. The house, which was five bays wide, has been demolished.

Porteus must have been pleased with the effect of the pavilion, for he built his next two houses with central pavilions. The first was Walnut Grove, in Philadelphia, built around 1735. This was 2½ storeys high and seven bays wide with a three-bay pedimented pavilion. The roof was a hip-on-hip or Mansard with a pair of chimneys just inside the break. Windows mark the staircase at the side of the house this time. Walnut Grove was destroyed many years ago.

Bush Hill was built in Philadelphia around 1737. It resembled Walnut Grove, except that it was three storeys high and had a deck-on-hip roof and chimneys just outside the break; the front door had a pediment. The house burned down in 1808.

Porteus' masterpiece is undoubtedly Christ Church in Philadelphia. Construction began in 1727 as part of a project to replace the old church piece by piece. Consequently, it was not finished until 1744, which was seven years after Porteus' death, and even then it lacked a steeple; the steeple was added in 1754 to designs of two carpenters, John Harrison and Robert Smith, who based their design on one by James Gibbs.

The outside of the church, which is of brick with stone dressings, is eight bays long, but inside it is only seven bays long, for the eighth is taken up by the chancel. The outside is lavishly decorated, so much so that some complain of its being too 'busy.' The side of the nave has two tiers of round-headed windows separated by an architrave, and each window is separated from its neighbor by a brick pilaster. Above these is a balustrade. Behind this is a form of clerestory without windows, and above that the gabled roof. The balustrade and the pediment at the end of the gable are covered in flaming urns.

*Christ Church   Philadelphia   1727-1744*          *Tower and steeple by Harrison and Smith   1754*

*Attribution:   probable*

At the east end the focal point is the large Palladian window that lights the altar. On either side of it heavy pilasters support an entablature that carries the clerestory and the pediment on top. On either side of the clerestory is a large stone volute. The outside of the east end is a bit like some of Wren's London churches, most notably St. Bride's Fleet Street and St. Andrew's Holborn; in fact, the exterior looks like the work of Wren, while the interior is more characteristic of Gibbs; both exterior and interior were actually by Porteus, although the church is commonly attributed to one of its vestrymen, Dr. John Kearsley, who was appointed to oversee its construction.

Inside, the church is basilical. Giant Doric columns, whose position bears little relation to the position of the windows, support flying entablatures underneath longitudinal arches; from an architrave above these arches rises the clerestory to the coved ceiling. A gallery runs around three sides of the church, and supports itself by abutting against the columns, after the manner of Gibbs; the giant order supporting a flying entablature is also a feature of Gibbs' work.

Without a doubt, the Colonies started off on the right foot with four such architects during the first quarter of the eighteenth century as James Porteus, John Prince of Virginia, Robert Twelves of Boston, and the anonymous man in South Carolina. Porteus was the first architect of the Colonies, all claims for Peter Harrison to the contrary. Perhaps even more significant were Porteus' steps toward planning for the future. While Prince groomed Taliaferro as his successor, Porteus founded the Carpenters' Company in 1724. This was more than the guild company it appeared to be, for in it young architects received their training. The supreme achievement of this training was Robert Smith (*q.v.*), who was more of a contemporary of Ariss than of Taliaferro.

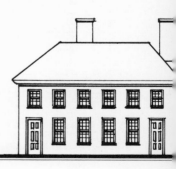

*Edmund Woolley   1696-1771*

O F all the public buildings in the Colonies, one of the most impressive is Independence Hall in Philadelphia. This is partly on account of its prodigious size, and partly because of its elaborate conception of five parts. Presumably since Philadelphia was the second largest city of the British Empire, the seat of government there needed to be larger than that of any of the other Colonies. Edmund Woolley, about whom little is known beyond his dates and that he was a member of the Carpenters' Company, seems to have been the architect. The construction took many years, from 1732 to about 1755, and the design probably changed as time went by, especially since the tower was not begun until 1750.

The main building is two storeys high and nine bays wide. It is of brick with white stone quoins and dressing. The shallow gabled roof has a balustraded roof-deck on top, and a battery of chimneys at each end. Jutting out behind the main building is a tower of colossal girth, decorated with brick pilasters on its upper stages; atop the tower stands a charming steeple

*Independence Hall*　　　　*Philadelphia   1732-1755   tower begun 1750*

*Attribution:  probable*

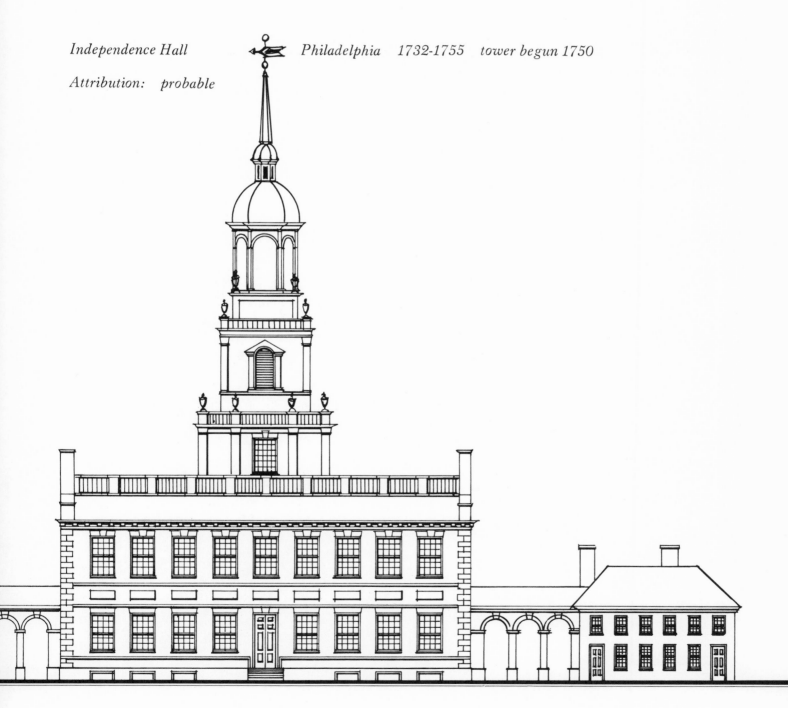

roughly based on that of Wren's St. Mary-le-Bow in London. This steeple has become one of the many symbols of American freedom, for from its bell stage rang the celebrated Liberty Bell, which is now on view inside the base of the tower.

The main building is connected to a pair of smaller flankers by an arcade of three arches. Each flanker is six bays long and two storeys high with a hip roof, but their scale is vastly diminished from that of the main building. Independence Hall is presently undergoing restoration on the inside, and it is hoped that the restorers will eventually get around to the steeple; the original steeple was found decayed early in its life and was taken down. After the tower had stood bareheaded like a dead tree stump for a number of years, another steeple was built almost like the first one, but it substituted a clock face for the original curious louvred opening of the bell stage.

It is a pity we know no more of Woolley, for a man who had enough imagination and skill to design such a fine building as Independence Hall could surely have succeeded with other buildings; perhaps he did, but none of them has turned up.

*Independence Hall    views of tower*

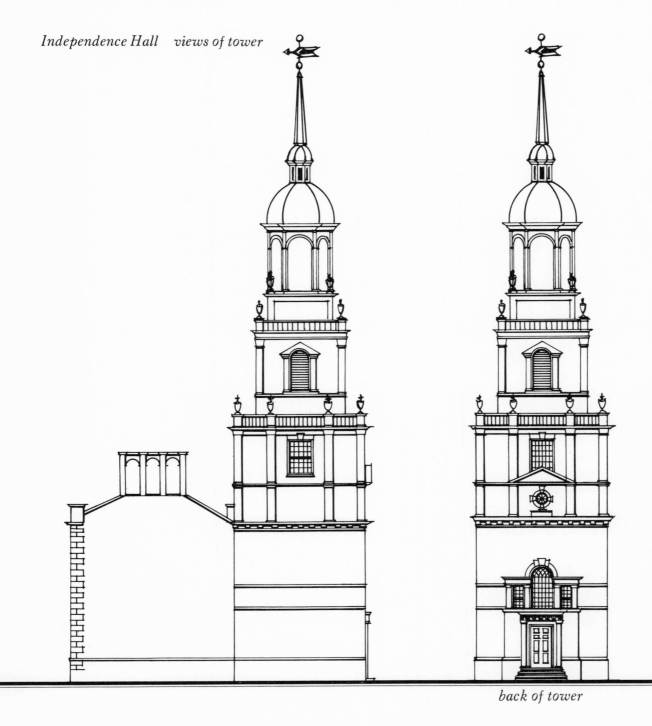

*back of tower*

*Unidentified Philadelphian*

ANUMBER of buildings built in the Philadelphia area from 1707 to 1729 have certain characteristics about them that suggest that they were the work of one man. The man's name is not known, but probably could be found with some good research. He almost certainly did more buildings, but I have only found four. That he was in favor with the authorities, is obvious, because of these four buildings three are governmental or church buildings. The identifying characteristic that I have used is their gable ends; all the gables have an angle of about ninety degrees at the apex, and the cornices are deep white coves. Now, cove cornices are hard to handle successfully, and this man has made some really heavy ones look light. The overall effect is charming. Some of the features on these buildings are Scandinavian in origin, and yet some of the fundamentals are British, so little of value can be learned about the past history of the architect from that kind of analysis.

*Town Hall    Philadelphia    1707-1710*                    *demolished 1837*

Between 1707 and 1710 this man built the Philadelphia Town Hall. This was constructed in brick after the old English custom of an arcaded market underneath the council chamber. The building was three arches long, and one arch wide. Over the arch on one end was an elegant pedimented doorway leading out onto a balcony. On either side of the door was a small window, and there were two in the gable end above the door. On the sides, the upper storey contained one window for every arch below, and there was a similar number of dormers above. On top of the roof in the center stood a wooden cupola, square in plan. This building became the head house at one end of the long market until it was torn down in 1837.

About 1720 in League Island Park, Philadelphia, was built a house called Belair. It is of brick laid in Flemish bond with glazed headers, and is five bays long and 2½ storeys high. Apart from the cove cornice, the only decoration is provided by the center bay of the façade; this has a balcony over the front door, and a shell hood set into the cornice above the French window that leads out to the balcony. Shell hoods, although common in England, were rare in the Colonies, or at least few survive today. A pair of chimneys are well spaced along the ridgepole.

One of the most delightful kinds of buildings built in England between 1670 and 1720 is the Almshouse. These were, in effect, housing for the elderly and the poor. Therefore, as long as the architect of an Almshouse kept it down to one or two storeys he could have free rein to design one of his most imaginative buildings; a community of buildings is almost always more attractive than the single statement of a single one, and the sprawling Almshouses can well be called a community of buildings. Usually they were built around a green or garden, and had a focal point at one end. Some of the most perfect in that way are the Trinity Almshouses at Mile End Gate in London, designed by Wren. In all the Colonies there was but one Almshouse; of course it was in Philadelphia, for of all the Colonists the Quakers were the most interested in such philanthropy. This was the Friends' Almshouse, built in 1729 of brick laid in Flemish bond. It consisted of a long building, 1½ storeys high, surrounding a large rectangle of garden, and a large opening placed asymmetrically in one side. Close to the opening was a short stretch three bays long and 2½ storeys high. In the center of this block was an arched doorway leading into the courtyard and surmounted by a pediment. There was a tall chimney for each occupant, which meant that there was a veritable forest of chimneys, but this is a charming characteristic of most Almshouses. The brickwork was laid in Flemish bond with glazed headers. The Friends' Almshouse was demolished in 1840. The country could now well do with more such communities for housing its elderly citizens.

*Friends' Almshouse   Philadelphia   1729*                    *demolished 1840, reconstruction*

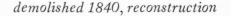

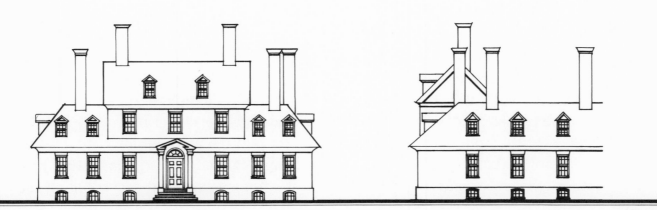

The Presbyterian Church at New Castle, Delaware, was built in 1707. It has the same cove cornice as the other buildings, but instead of a gable roof it has a high jerkin-head roof; hipping the top portion of each gable end in this manner was a clever idea, for if that had not been done the roof would have looked awkward. The church is five bays long with one tier of round-headed sash windows; this is one of the earliest instances of the use of this kind of window in the northern Colonies. On the top of the roof, slightly offset to one end, is a small hexagonal cupola. The ceiling is a simple barrel vault. The brick is laid in Flemish bond.

Possibly connected with this style was Immanuel Church as originally built in New Castle, Delaware around 1705. However, old pictures of the church are not clear enough to confirm this, and the building was substantially altered and enlarged by Strickland in the nineteenth century.

*Presbyterian Church    New Castle, Delaware    1707*

*back        front*

## Samuel Rhoads    1711-1784

**S**AMUEL RHOADS, a member of the Carpenters' Company, is only recorded to have designed one building. This was the Pennsylvania Hospital in Philadelphia. It was to have been built in three stages; the first stage, the right-hand wing, was built to his design from 1755 to 1756, but so much time elapsed before the building of the central block and the left-hand wing that different architects were hired for each. On account of this, we will describe the right-hand wing by itself.

*Pennsylvania Hospital    Philadelphia    1751-1756*        *Attribution:    certain*

*front of wing*

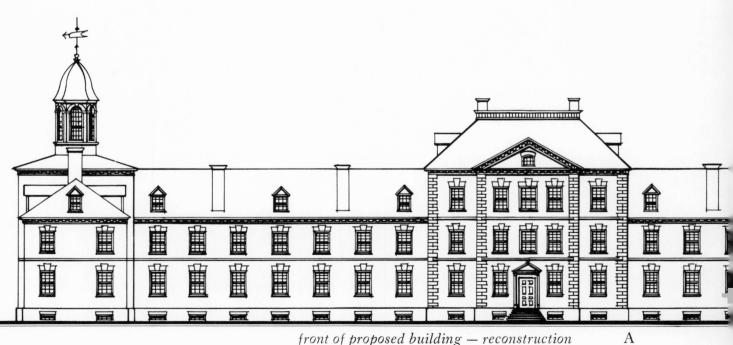

*front of proposed building — reconstruction*        A

126

From the side, it is seven bays long and 2½ storeys high, but the central three bays are enclosed in a pavilion that rises three storeys. On top of the pavilion is a large octagonal cupola of unusual design. The dormers on the hip roof are gable-roofed.

Because the Rhoads wing by itself is obviously ugly, we have drawn the whole building as Rhoads designed it. The section marked A-A on our drawing is the wing that was built. The Pennsylvania Hospital shows a mature grasp of the principles of design, so it is indeed unfortunate that Rhoads' plans were not executed in their entirety, and that we know of no further buildings by this talented hand.

*side of wing*

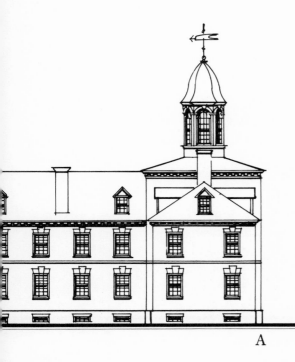

A

*Robert Smith    1722-1777*

**R**OBERT SMITH, a contemporary of John Ariss and Peter Harrison, was a member of the Carpenters' Company, and in fact was the supreme achievement of Porteus' informal school of architecture set up inside the Company. Smith worked with other carpenters on various projects in and around Philadelphia, and seems to have begun work on his own about 1750. The majority of his commissions were for public buildings of one sort or another, and so he must have been held in high esteem to continue to be given these valuable commissions.

There have been many theories over the years about how to plan a college dormitory. The 'entry' system, in which students' rooms are grouped around a series of entries or staircases, was often used by Smith in his college buildings; while it can not be said that he invented it, yet he was responsible for its popularity during and after his time. In 1761, he designed a dormitory for Pennsylvania College—now University of Pennsylvania—on the entry system. The building was not a success because it and the rooms inside it were so small. It was twelve bays long in three entries, three bays wide and three storeys high. The gable roof ended in an heroic pediment, a characteristic feature of Smith's architecture. The dormitory was demolished in 1845.

*Pennsylvania College Dormitory    Philadelphia    1761-1763*

*demolished 1845, reconstruction*

*Attribution:    certain*

*Pennsylvania College Provost's House    Philadelphia    1761*

*demolished 1845, reconstruction*

*Attribution:    certain*

Many years after he had built the dormitory, Smith was asked to design the house for the Provost of the College in 1774. Although this was only four bays long, three wide and 3½ high, it was much more than half the size of the dormitory. Either Smith was learning from the past or he had more respect for the comfort of the Provost than he had for the students. This building also had an heroic pediment; these brick pediments on brick buildings are not only peculiar to Smith but to Philadelphia as a whole.

Smith built a large number of churches. All were variations on the basic shape of a Roman temple, some elaborate, and some nearly as plain as a barn. About half way between these two extremes was St. Paul's Church in Philadelphia, built in 1761. The congregation of St. Paul's had broken away from Christ Church and St. Peter's because it thought they were too dependent upon ceremony; this seems to be the first evidence of a Low Church—High Church controversy in the Colonies. St. Paul's is five bays long and three wide. It had two tiers of round-headed windows interspaced with giant pilasters; the church and the pilasters are both of brick. The building was altered around 1840 by the architect William Strickland; he changed the window and interior arrangements. The church is now partly covered by a layer of gray cement.

*St. Paul's Church    Philadelphia 1761*                    *altered about 1820*

*Attribution:    certain*

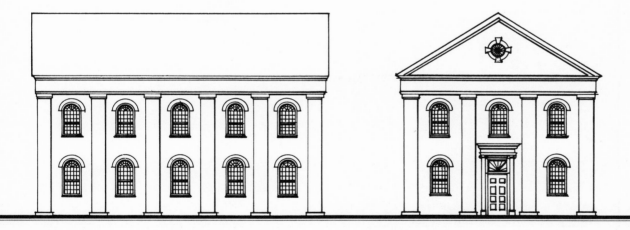

In 1770 Smith handsomely repaid the Carpenters' Company for all he had learned from it by designing them the Carpenters' Hall. This lovely building is of brick with white stone trim, and is cruciform in plan. Each leg of the cross is three bays wide and protrudes one bay from the body of the building. It is two storeys high, and each leg is capped with a pediment. The entrance front is the most elaborate, having round-headed windows on the upper floor and more trim than on the other sides of the building. On the roof is a charming octagonal cupola.

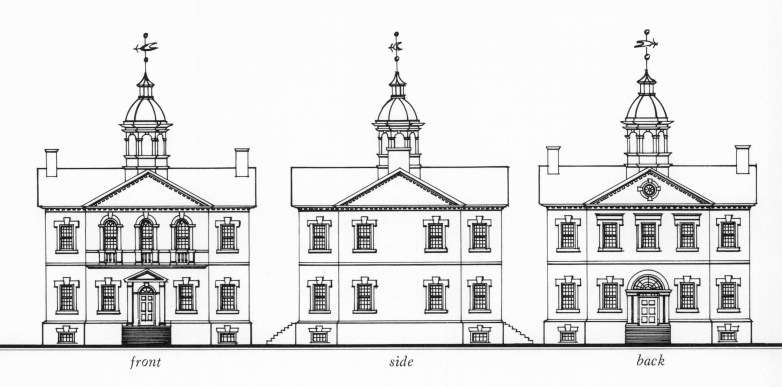

*front*                           *side*                           *back*

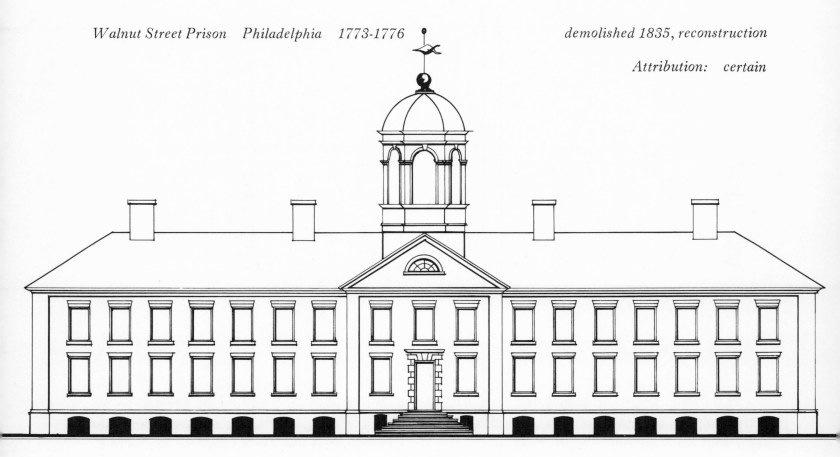

As we have seen from a look at the Carpenters' Hall, Smith was well suited to designing small buildings to a small scale. He was just as adept, however, at larger buildings done to a large scale. One of these was the Walnut Street Prison in Philadelphia. It was erected from

1773 to 1776, no doubt partly as a deterrent to those acts of civil disobedience that began to take place at about that time. It was seventeen bays long and two storeys high. The central three bays were enclosed in a pedimented pavilion of stone, while the rest of the building was of brick. The only decoration to this suitably grim building was a quoined doorway in the center, from one of James Gibbs' books, and a large sturdy cupola over the middle of the roof. The prison was torn down in 1835, but the underpinnings were so strongly built that they were left behind and have been used as foundations for a number of successive buildings on the site.

*Woodford   Philadelphia   1756*                                    *Attribution:   probable*

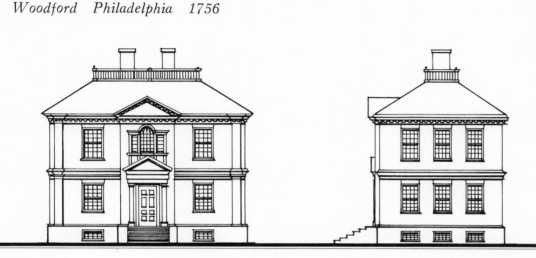

Five houses in the Philadelphia area, built over a period of six years, almost certainly were designed by Smith, and even if not by Smith they were obviously all by the same man. These are Woodford, built in Philadelphia in 1756, Mount Pleasant, built in Philadelphia in 1761, Cliveden, built in Philadelphia in 1764, Laurel Hill, built in Philadelphia in 1762, and Port Royal, built in Frankford in 1762. Apart from many interior similarities, all of these houses have the same motif on the outside: a one-bay pedimented central pavilion in the front.

The main part of Woodford is brick, three bays wide and two storeys high. The deck-on-hip roof has a balustrade around the deck and a pair of chimneys close to the middle of the deck. Above the rather large front door in the central pavilion is a Venetian window. The level of the upper floor is prominently marked by a course that looks like an abortive roof; this a common feature of Philadelphia houses, but not really expected on a formal house such as this. There is a large wing on the back, which is just as well, for the formal part of the house for all its pretentious proportions is really rather small.

Mount Pleasant is the grandest of the five houses; it is the only one with a pair of formal dependencies. In fact, dependencies are practically non-existent north of Maryland. The house, which was built for a Scottish *nouveau riche*, shows all the marks of its ostentatious owner's tastes. For instance, although there is a superb view from the house's location, it is not used to advantage because the wall facing in that direction completely lacks windows; in order to preserve Georgian symmetry there are fake doors to balance real doors on the other side of a room or hall. Even the material of the house's façade is unusual: it is stucco with brick quoin trim at all the corners. In spite of all these eccentricities, Mount Pleasant is with-

131

out doubt a very fine house. It is five bays wide and 2½ storeys tall on a high basement. There is a balustrade around the top of the deck-on-hip roof, and a massive chimney of unusual design stands over the slope of the roof at each end; this unusual design consists of a cluster of four flues on a square base, with the flues being joined together at the top by arches and a chimney cap. The only two dormers on the front are of the so-called Chippendale style. The front door in the central pavilion is round-headed with a pair of Tuscan half-round engaged columns supporting a pediment; above the doorway is a Palladian window. The attractive dependencies are two bays square and 2½ storeys high; each has a hip roof with splayed eaves.

Cliveden, built for Chief Justice Benjamin Chew, is 2½ storeys high and five bays wide. The roof is unusual for this kind of house because it is a gable with an heroic pediment at each end. The roof is decorated with a pair of wide chimneys along the ridgepole, a pair of dormers quite like the Chippendale ones at Mount Pleasant, and an array of flaming urns such as Smith also designed on the Zion Lutheran Church a few years later. Cliveden is fronted with ashlar masonry, but the sides revert to the less expensive stucco with brick quoins found at Mount Pleasant. Cliveden was occupied by the British during the Revolution, but the Ameri-

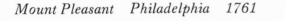

*Mount Pleasant   Philadelphia   1761*                    *Attribution:   probable*

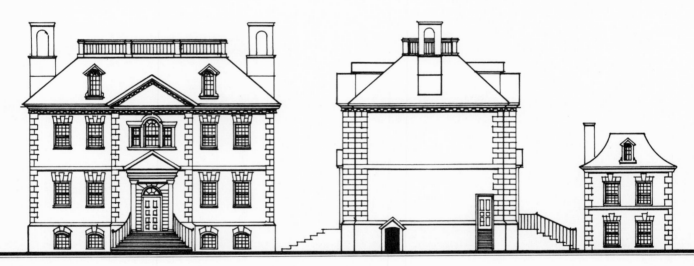

*Clivedon   Philadelphia   1761*                    *Attribution:   probable*

can troops, seeing that the house was the property of their own general, were reluctant to fire on it. General Chew, however, ordered them to fire regardless. The British eventually left the house, which fortunately was only slightly damaged by the American cannons. It has remained in the same family to this day.

Laurel Hill, also in Fairmount Park along with Woodford and Mount Pleasant, is the smallest of this group of houses. It is only three bays wide and two storeys high with a low hip roof. It is of stucco with stone trim. Wings have since been added to each end of the house.

Port Royal is the only one of this group to have been demolished. Parts of it survive, however, among the rooms at the Henry F. duPont Winterthur Museum in Delaware, the graveyard of many fine houses that had to be demolished for one reason or another. Port Royal, built of brick, might almost be described as a poor man's version of Mount Pleasant. It was almost exactly the same as the latter, except that it lacked Mount Pleasant's most ostentatious details. Inside, on the other hand, the decorations were every bit as lavish. The roof was a hip-on-hip with a pair of thin end-chimneys and a pair of Chippendale dormers. Stone quoins at the corners gave relief from the rather severe brick of the rest of the house.

*Laurel Hill  Philadelphia  1762*                                                    *Attribution:  probable*

*Port Royal  Frankford, Pennsylvania  1762*          *demolished*     *reconstruction, pieces at Winterthur*

*Attribution:  probable*

*Whitby Hall   Philadelphia   1754*                    *demolished    reconstruction, pieces in Detroit*

*Attribution:   probable*

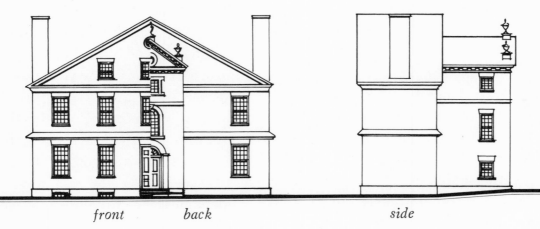

front          back                    side

Another house that almost belongs in the previous group of houses was Whitby Hall in Philadelphia, built in 1754. Inside, the details could well be a part of any of the foregoing houses. The outside, however, was most odd. The main part of the house consisted of a two-storey fieldstone face five bays wide crowned by an heroic pediment; this was only one room deep, and at the back was a formal wing or pavilion in the center housing the staircase; the staircase was lit by a round-headed window. A chimney stood at each end of the gable. Like Woodford, a heavy ledge ran around the house to mark the level of the upper floor, and like Woodford there was a wing at one side, suitably camouflaged, for the formal part of the house was too small for comfortable living. Whitby Hall has been demolished, but the interior has been reerected at a museum in Detroit.

Smith built a less imaginative house the same year as Whitby Hall; this was the President's House at Princeton University. It is five bays long and two storeys high with a gable roof and two chimneys along the ridgepole. It is now the residence of the Dean of the Faculty.

*President's House   Princeton   1754*                    *Attribution:   certain*

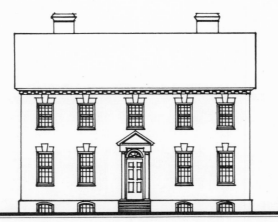

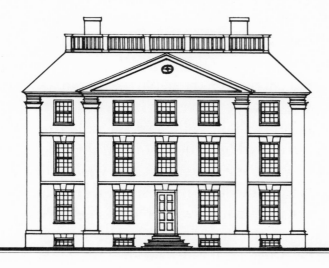

The last of Smith's mansions was Chalkley Hall in Frankford, built in 1776. It was three storeys tall with a balustrade surrounding the top of the deck-on-hip roof; a pair of chimneys protruded through the deck. The front was five bays wide, and the central pavilion took up three of those bays. The corners of the pavilion and of the house were emphasized by giant Tuscan pilasters. Chalkley Hall was actually the rebuilding of a much earlier house. A large wing was added at the left-hand side. The house has been demolished.

*St. Peter's Church Philadelphia    1761*                                    *now slightly altered*

*Attribution:    certain*

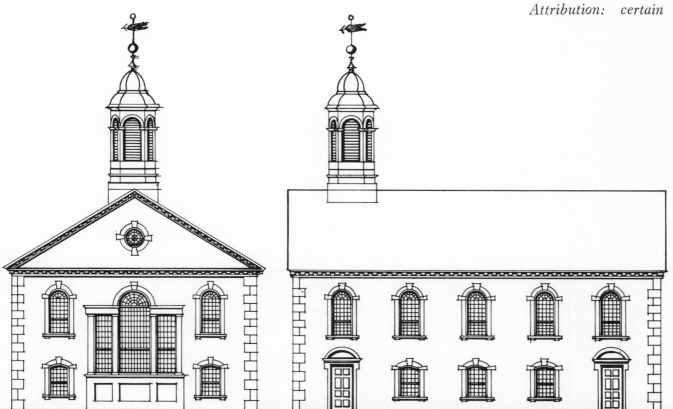

In the same year that St. Paul's Church broke away from the mother Christ Church in Philadelphia, another group founded St. Peter's Church close by to relieve the crowded conditions at Christ Church. Smith built for these people quite a simple building in his usual style. It is five bays long with two tiers of windows. The upper tier of windows are round-headed, while the lower windows have segmental arches. At the east end is an enormous Palladian window to light the altar, and perched on the gable roof at the west end was an interesting octagonal cupola, since removed; a heavy tower was built at the west end around 1843 by William Strickland, and on top of that is a tall white spire of rather uninspired design. The brick of the body of the church is decorated by white quoins at the corners. Inside, the design is not so satisfactory. A low barrel vault stretches from one wall to the other, having absolutely no relation with the galleries that surround three sides of the church. The pulpit is at the west end, being part of the structure that once supported the cupola. The organ, which was originally placed in a side gallery, is now squashed in above the altar, neither of which places is satisfactory, especially the latter, for it hides the great east window.

A few years later, in 1766, Smith began construction of another church about the same size as St. Peter's. This was the Zion Lutheran Church, and it was completed after three years. It was much more elaborate than St. Peter's, having giant pilasters between the windows and corresponding flaming urns above the eaves of the roof. The interior, of which we know little, was hailed as the finest in the Colonies; if the speaker was correct, it really must have been superb. A tower jutting out of the middle of the far side of the church—an unusual place for a tower—had a beautiful tall white steeple on top, but this burned down in 1794 and was not rebuilt, and since no pictures survive of the church before the fire, we have no idea of the appearance of the steeple, which is a pity. The church was repaired otherwise after the fire, but was torn down in 1869, a macabre way to celebrate the hundredth anniversary of the building's completion.

*Zion Lutheran Church    Philadelphia    1766-1769*

*demolished 1869, reconstruction*

*Attribution:    certain*

Smith, who seems to have been ecumenical in his outlook, also did some churches for the Presbyterians. The first one he worked on was the Second Presbyterian Meeting House at the corner of Third and Arch Streets in Philadelphia. This was built shortly after 1750, and was demolished in 1803. We know little of the church itself, but it is possible to reconstruct the appearance of the steeple from an old painting of the city from across the river. Therefore, although we have no record of the fine steeple atop the Zion Lutheran Church, we at least have an idea of one steeple by Smith. This one was in the Wren tradition of graduated steps of squares and octagons, but not so polished as the actual works of Wren, which is to be expected for this was one of Smith's first works. About this prominent steeple some Philadelphia wag wrote this rhyme:

> The Presbyterians build a church
> And fain would have a steeple;
> We think it may become the church,
> But certainly not the people!

*Steeple of the Second Presbyterian Meeting House    Philadelphia*

*built after 1750    destroyed 1803    reconstruction    Attribution:    certain*

The Third Presbyterian Church at the corner of Pine Street and Fourth Street obviously was more conservative, or perhaps just poorer than the Second Church. When Smith built the Church in 1768 it was quite plain and had no steeple. The only decoration this brick building had was a white giant pilaster at each corner. At one end, over the door, was a Palladian window. The church was five bays long with two tiers of round-headed windows. The church building is still there, although it has been so altered from time to time as to be completely unrecognizable.

Even plainer was the First Presbyterian Meeting House in Carlisle, Pennsylvania, built of stone between 1757 and 1770. It was basically the same as the one in Philadelphia, but it was slightly smaller, and lacked the pilasters and Palladian window. It has since been altered and enlarged.

*Third Presbyterian Church   Pine Street, Philadelphia   1768*          *now much altered, reconstruction*

*Attribution:   certain*

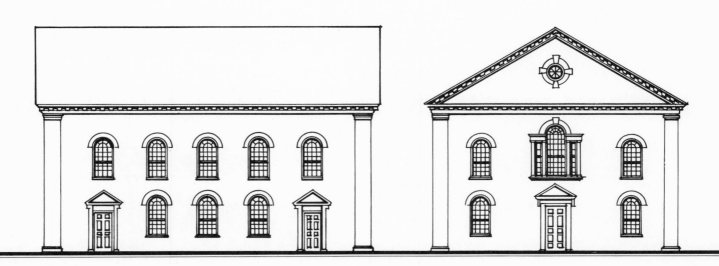

*First Presbyterian Meeting House   Carlisle   1757-1770*          *now altered*

*Attribution:   probable*

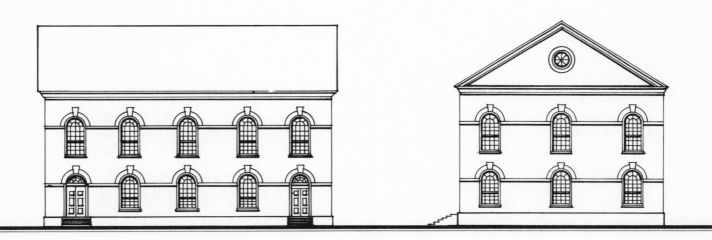

One of Smith's most successful buildings was Nassau Hall at Princeton University, built between 1754 and 1756. In fact, it was such a successful design that one wonders why it has suffered such ghastly alterations over the years. It was of stone, twenty-five bays long, with a central pavilion five bays wide. One door in each wing supplemented the central door; Smith had not yet arrived at his idea of the entry system for college buildings. It was three storeys tall on a high basement. The hip roof was studded with a large number of heavy white chimneys; the pediment of the pavilion was decorated with three flaming urns, and a fine powerful octagonal cupola stood in the center of the roof. With the great importance of higher education these days, colleges have little or no funds available for work on old buildings, but it is to be hoped that Princeton University might some day find the money to right the grievous harm done to Nassau Hall.

*Nassau Hall   Princeton   1754-1756*                                   *Attribution:   certain*

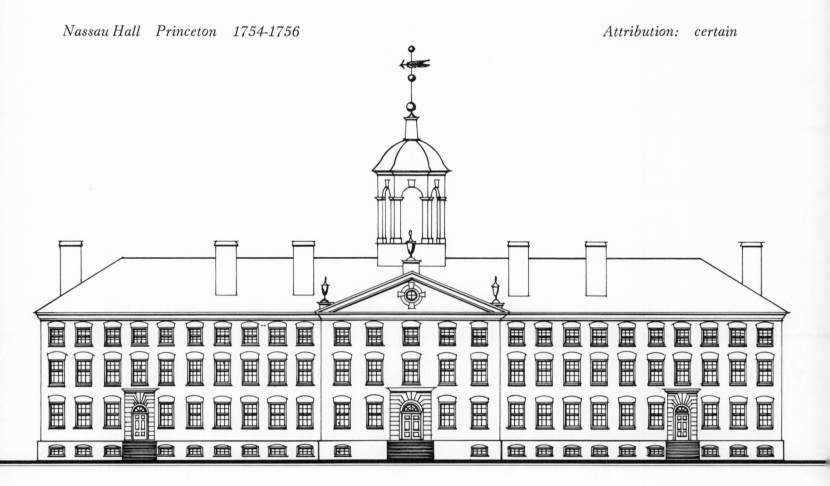

Some fifteen years after the building of Nassau Hall, Smith was invited to take part in a competition to design a building for Rhode Island College, or Brown University as it was later called. Smith won the competition; one of the men he defeated was Joseph Horatio Anderson of Annapolis (*q.v.*), and Joseph Brown (*q.v.*) was on the committee judging the competition. This commission helped Smith to be the architect in the Colonies with buildings spread the farthest apart, for he also designed two buildings in Williamsburg; this is a significant development, for most of the architects of the Colonies confined themselves to their own Colonies, or at least to their own immediate area.

Architecturally speaking, University Hall at Brown University is not as good as Princeton's Nassau Hall, but this may be due to alterations by the Rhode Island workmen, because the biggest fault is the rather weak cupola in the center of the roof, and the cupola is one of the likeliest things to be altered under these circumstances. The building is seventeen bays long with three bays enclosed in the central pedimented pavilion. The brick structure is 4½ storeys high, and has but three entries like Nassau Hall. The front of the deck-on-hip roof has four massive chimneys, behind which is a balustrade around the roof deck. In contrast to Nassau Hall, University Hall looks on the outside the way it originally did in the eighteenth century. Similar to both of these is Hollis Hall at Harvard University (1767), but it is not as good.

As was mentioned above, Smith designed two buildings in Williamsburg, as if they needed his talent, for at the time Virginia had a large number of architects available, including Richard Taliaferro, John Ariss, James Wren and Thomas Jefferson. However, it was decided that since Smith came from Philadelphia he would be inclined to know more than anyone else about building a mental hospital in Williamsburg, for the Quakers ran many hospitals and similar institutions in Philadelphia. The Mental Hospital was built in 1769. It was nine bays wide, with a three-bay pedimented pavilion in the center. A one-storey porch supported on four Tuscan columns projected from the pavilion in front of the entrance. The two-storey brick building had an attractive octagonal cupola sandwiched between two small chimneys along the ridge of the hip roof. The building has long since been demolished, but Williamsburg officials are cautiously optimistic about the possibility of reconstructing this interesting building in the near future.

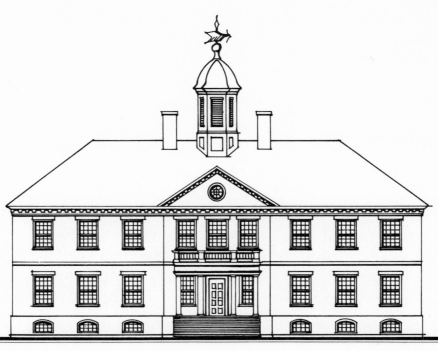

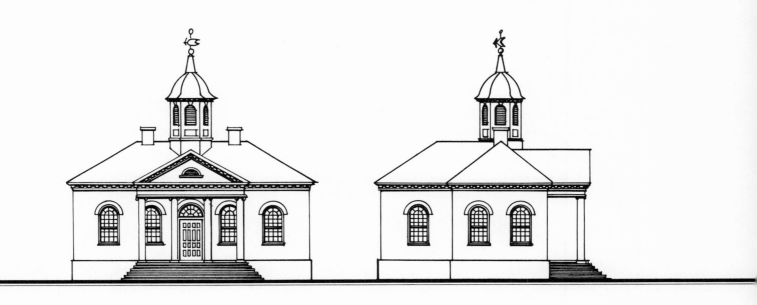

While there is documentary proof of Smith's having designed the Mental Hospital, a strong attribution can be made to him of another building in Williamsburg, although researchers say that Smith probably never actually came to Williamsburg; furthermore, he certainly had nothing to do with the steeple of Bruton Parish Church, built about this time; it is simply not in his style. The Williamsburg Court House, begun in 1770, is cruciform. It is of brick laid in Flemish bond, one storey high with a hip roof. An Ionic pediment in the front forms the shortest leg of the cross, but it was never completed; the pediment was cantilevered out to await the arrival of the columns from England, but because of the troubled times the columns never arrived. Colonial Williamsburg has kept the Court House unfinished, although in this book the columns have been drawn in for the sake of completeness. The building is five bays wide with one tier of round-headed windows. A large octagonal cupola stands on the center of the roof with a small chimney on either side. The building is now used to house archaeological exhibitions.

In 1766, Smith began work on the largest building constructed in the Colonies. This was the Philadelphia Bettering House, a noble institution founded by the Quakers to take care of the poor and the elderly; one part was a workhouse, and the other part an almshouse. It was built of brick with a ground plan in the shape of a U. At the angles and ends of the U were blocks four storeys high, joined together by wings 2½ storeys high. In the center of the layout was a three-storey pedimented pavilion, five bays wide, with an octagonal cupola on top. The façade was 27 bays long. The wings linking the taller blocks were arcaded on the sides that faced the courtyard. The whole was a most ambitious and imaginative scheme, and it is a pity it was demolished, piece by piece, until it completely disappeared by 1834.

Smith also built a number of nondescript town houses. The earliest recorded ones were a pair of three-storey brick houses on Third Street, 21 feet wide apiece, built in 1763. Soon after in 1764 came a house for Benjamin Franklin on High Street; this was brick, three storeys high and 34 feet square with the kitchen in the basement. In 1771 the Vestry of Christ Church commissioned four houses on Spruce Street; these were to be at least two storeys high with a basement underneath and to be worth 200 pounds apiece. In 1776, one of his last works, Smith constructed barracks and other buildings at Fort Billingsport in New Jersey. Smith almost certainly worked on the inside of the Steadman-Powel townhouse in Philadelphia, some of which can now be seen at the Metropolitan Museum in New York. Probably none of these less important buildings survives, but it was worth mentioning them to finish this too brief account of a busy and talented life.

*Bettering House    Philadelphia    1767*

*Attribution:    certain*

*demolished 1834, reconstruction*

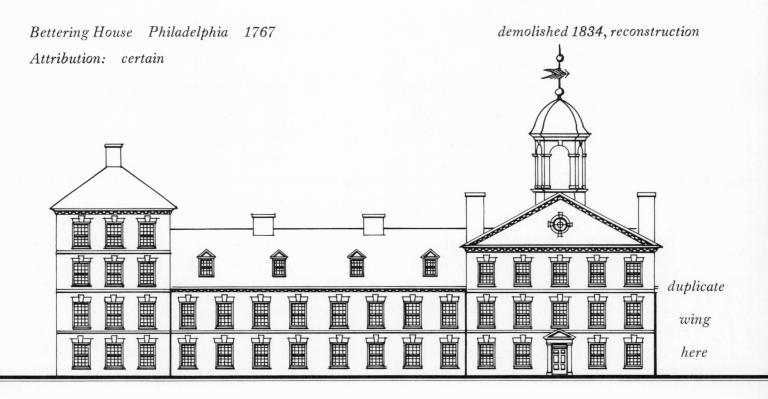

*duplicate*

*wing*

*here*

*Thomas McBean*

ARCHITECTURALLY speaking, the most important building erected in New York during the Colonial period was St. Paul's Chapel, begun in 1764 as a chapel of ease to Trinity Church. The architect, about whom little is known beyond the fact of his Scottish ancestry, used almost no imagination, for the building is virtually copied stone by stone from James Gibbs' book, in which it was inserted as one of the rejected designs for St. Martin's-in-the-Fields in London. The material of St. Paul's, however, being Manhattan micaschist brown stone, has given the building a totally different appearance than St. Martin's would have had if this design had been accepted in London. The inside of St. Paul's is a simplified version of the way St. Martin's was actually built.

The church is seven bays long with windows arranged in two tiers; the upper windows are round-headed and the lower ones have segmental arches. At the east end, a large Palladian window sheds light on the altar. There are quoins at all the corners of the building and a balustrade around the eaves of the gable roof. An Ionic portico was added to the east end in 1794, but this was not part of the original design; the tower and steeple, which were not added to the west end until that same year, were part of the original design. The steeple was the tallest in the land.

Inside the church, the nave is basilical. A series of Corinthian columns each support a flying entablature, which in turn supports an elliptical barrel vault. Over each bay, the barrel vault is crossed by a transverse barrel vault, which also crosses a similar ceiling that runs the length of each side aisle. Over the side aisles, partway up the columns, is a gallery that runs around three sides of the church. The church is lit by a large number of splendid Waterford crystal chandeliers.

It is not known whether McBean was responsible for any other buildings in the Colonies, but there are a few buildings in and around New York built about the same time as St. Paul's that are of the quality of those buildings usually ascribed to architects. While we will not go so far as to ascribe any of them to McBean, they are included here for the reader to draw his own conclusions.

*Van Rensselaer Manor    New York    1765*        *conjectural restoration    Attribution:    possible*

*much altered in 1840-1843 by Richard Upjohn*

*now moved to Williamstown, Massachusetts*

*St. Paul's Chapel   New York   1764-1766*                    *copy from James Gibbs*

*Attribution:   certain*

*Spire added in 1794, also a portico (not shown)*

side

*back*　　　*front*

In 1765 a Manor was built in New York for the Van Rensselaer family, who were of Dutch descent and who owned large estates throughout the Colony. It is a large brick house, seven bays long and 2½ storeys high; the center three bays are enclosed in a pedimented pavilion. There are stone quoins at all the angles, and the windows are lavishly trimmed with stone; those of the upper floor are crowned with pediments. The dormers are in the Chippendale style. Massive end-chimneys grow out of the gable ends. The Van Rensselaer Manor was pulled down and re-erected as the Sigma Phi fraternity house at Williams College in Williamstown, Massachusetts.

Another is the Ford Mansion, built in Morristown, New Jersey, in 1772. This is a two-storey building, five bays long, with a deck-on-hip roof. The main feature of the house is the doorway, which is composed like a Palladian window; above it is a corresponding window in three sections with a low pediment on top of the center section.

Fairly like the Ford Mansion is Johnson Hall in Johnstown, New York, built in 1762. This house has a hip-on-hip roof, and the doorway and corresponding windows above are not as academically composed as the Ford Mansion. Neither house is particularly outstanding for its day and could easily be the work of mere housewrights.

*Ford Mansion, Morristown, New Jersey, 1772*                                    *Attribution:    possible*

*Johnson Hall    Johnstown, New York    1762*                                    *Attribution:    possible*

The next two houses are definitely of more architectural merit. The first, an unidentified house from an engraving of the New York fire brigade in action around 1750, seems to have been built of brick with stone trim shortly before the engraving was made. It was two storeys high and five bays long with the center three bays enclosed in a pedimented pavilion. The roof was a steep deck-on-hip with a balustrade around the deck. In the pediment of the pavilion was a curious arrangement of three oval windows. A stone course marked the level of the upper floor, and the doorway was trimmed with quoins after a plate in one of James Gibbs' books.

The other house, the Roger Morris or Jumel Mansion, was built in 1765 in New York and still survives. The architect again is unknown, but it was certainly not Peter Harrison, in spite of the fact that in various details the house bears a superficial resemblance to works by Harrison and that Harrison was in fact living in the area at that time. The most immediately noticeable parallels with Harrison (*q.v.*) are the use of wood cut to resemble ashlar masonry and the giant portico. The fake ashlar, although a trade mark of Harrison, was also used elsewhere, as at Mount Vernon and houses in Williamsburg. The portico, also used almost exclusively by Harrison in the North, is in this case most un-Harrisonian in scale; its tall, thin columns more look forward to the era of Jefferson and the Federal style than backward to the heavier Baroque and Palladian of Gibbs and Harrison. The house is five bays wide and two storeys tall on a high basement. The portico covers the central three bays. The roof is a deck-on-hip with an asymmetrical arrangement of chimneys. A quasi-Chippendale balustrade surrounds the roof deck. The inside of the house was altered during the early Republic and again during the reign of Queen Victoria. It is possible, but not probable, that the slim columns of the portico are a Federal replacement of earlier more robust columns.

*Unidentified House    New York    about 1750*      *demolished    reconstructed drawing*

*Attribution:    possible*

*Roger Morris (Jumel) Mansion    New York    1765*      *now slightly altered*

*Attribution:    possible*

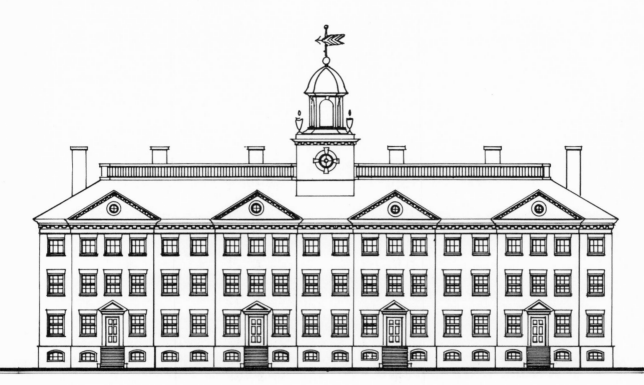

From an engraving made about 1790 we know the general appearance of the main building of King's College (now Columbia University), built about 1760 in New York. This was brick, three storeys tall on a high basement, and twenty bays long. It was a peculiar building, in that the man who designed it was well acquainted with correct architectural details, such as the shape of cornices, pediments, etc., but awkwardly disregarded basic principles of architectural composition; he did this by having an even number of bays instead of an odd number, and by grouping the windows into an even number of pavilions, leaving the center rather weak. There were four pedimented pavilions, each with three bays, and two bays between each pavilion. A tower and cupola stood on top of the deck-on-hip roof above the center two bays; a balustrade surrounded the roof deck. The designer of this building did, however, make one important contribution to college design in New York: he adopted the entry system, which we have also seen used by Robert Smith (*q.v.*) in Philadelphia. In spite of the broken architectural rules, King's College was an attractive and almost quaint building; its loss is to be regretted.

Not too long before the Revolution, an unidentified public building was erected in New York City. It formed the background for a scene showing a mob pulling down a statue of the king in a contemporary painting. It was built of brick with white stone trim, and was two storeys high and five bays wide. The focus of the front was a pedimented pavilion that included the front door on the ground floor and a large Palladian window above the door; in fact, the Palladian window was so large in scale that it projected above the cornice-line of the hip roof, and so the pediment of the pavilion had no horizontal member. The doorway itself had a semicircular light immediately above it, and the windows of the ground floor also had semicircular heads. In spite of the lavishness of the stone trim, including a belt course and keystones, the building had no quoins to define its corners.

After Philadelphia, four Colonial cities were roughly equal in size; of the four, it is odd to note that Charleston and Newport were extremely wealthy in the architecture of the period —and still are—while New York and Boston were nearly barren. Some of this bareness in the case of New York can probably be attributed to a scarcity of evidence and records, but it remains astonishing how poorly endowed in architectural treasure was such a large city as Colonial New York.

*Unidentified Public Building    New York    before 1776                    demolished            reconstruction*

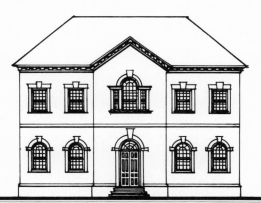

*Richard Munday    c.1685(?)-1739*

OCCASIONALLY it is difficult to distinguish between the work done by an architect and that done by an ordinary builder, carpenter or mason. Usually the work of an architect is more advanced and often more daring than the work of the others, but what happens if the man is a shade of both types of man? Such is the case of Richard Munday of Newport, Rhode Island. He was an excellent house carpenter, and yet there is more than just a glimmer of architectural quality in his work; this quality is partly hidden by the fact that the majority of his buildings were built of wood, and a frame construction usually points overpoweringly to a carpenter as its author. There is, of course, no good reason why we tend to confine in our minds the work of architects to stone or brick buildings; it just happens that most of the Colonial architects or first-rate builders did not use frame construction very much. Richard Munday was the exception to this rule, and, as we shall see, New England architecture in general followed his lead.

The first years of Richard Munday in the Colonies are obscure. The first references to him tell us that he married a Newport girl in 1713, and arrived in Newport in 1714. It is my belief, however, based entirely on speculation, that he was in the Colonies as early as 1707, when I think he built St. Paul's Church Narragansett. He did not rely entirely on architecture for his livelihood, for he kept an inn in 1719. He also must have been more than a simple carpenter, for his second wife, Elizabeth Hubbard, was a woman of high station.

*Jahleel Brenton House    Newport    1720*                    *demolished 1920    Attribution:    certain*

*panelling at Rhode Island School of Design*

One factor making study of the life of Richard Munday difficult is that the majority of the buildings he designed have been demolished, although fortunately not without record in most cases. The first house he did in Newport was the Jahleel Brenton House, built in 1720, and demolished not long ago. Detailed measured drawings were made before demolition, and the excellent flying staircase and panelling from the parlor have been saved in storage. The house was 2½ storeys high and five bays long with a gable-on-hip roof, with a chimney at the outside of each gable end. There were three pedimented dormers.

Like the Brenton House, only smaller, was the John Gidley House, built in 1724. When it was demolished, the stair-hall arch and some fine panelling were incorporated in a Victorian house, and the panelling has since been removed and installed at Winterthur. All the panelling in Munday's houses was of the bolection moulding type, and the Gidley panelling was of quite an unusual and original shape in outline, having ogee tops to each panel.

*Governor Joseph Wanton House    Newport    1738*          *rebuilding of earlier house, much altered*

*Attribution:    probable*                                        *about to be demolished*

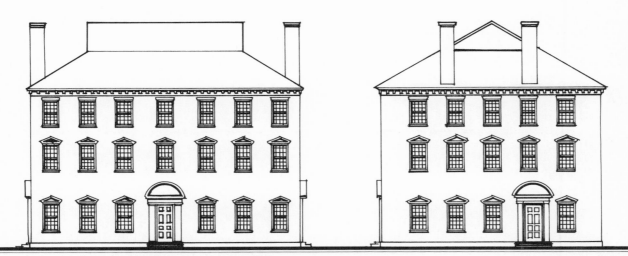

*back same, without pediments*

Across the street from the Brenton House stood the Governor Joseph Wanton House; at the time of writing, it still stands, but unrecognizably altered so that it is doubtful whether more than the corner posts remain. It was most recently a department store, and is to be demolished shortly for an Urban Renewal project. Old photographs show it to have been an ambitious attempt at grandeur that failed miserably. It was seven bays wide and three storeys high with a gable-on-hip roof and four end-chimneys. The windows on the lower two storeys on front and sides were capped with pediments. The composition suffered most from overcrowding and repetition; it probably would have been far more effective if it had only been five bays wide. It was built at the end of Munday's life, in 1738, and actually may not have been designed by him, because there is no documentary evidence, but there are certain features of trim and construction that link it to some of Munday's other houses; the semicircular front door steps were among these features.

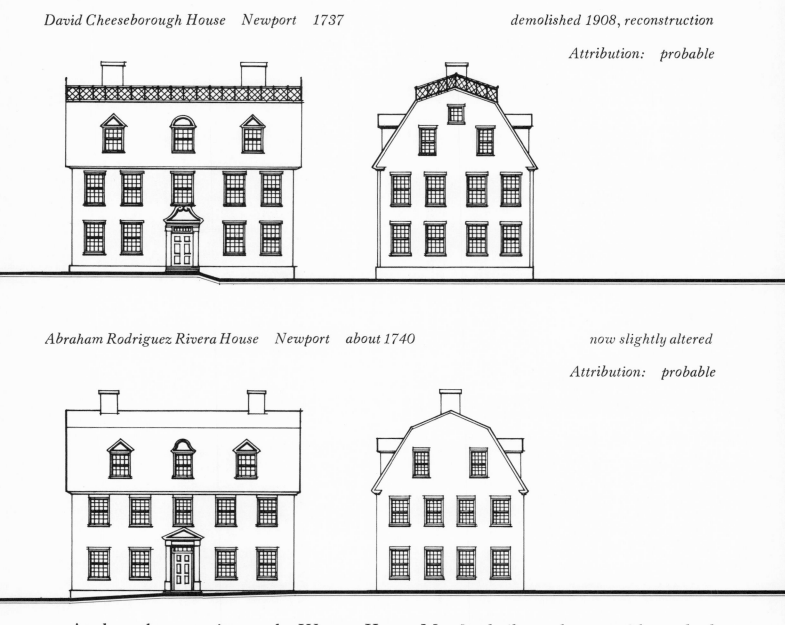

*David Cheeseborough House    Newport    1737*      *demolished 1908, reconstruction*

*Attribution:    probable*

*Abraham Rodriguez Rivera House    Newport    about 1740*      *now slightly altered*

*Attribution:    probable*

At about the same time as the Wanton House, Munday built two houses with gambrel roofs that were almost identical to each other. These were the David Cheeseborough House and the Abraham Rivera House. They were five bays wide and 2½ storeys high. The Cheeseborough House had a Chippendale-style roof-top balustrade. Each had three dormers, the outside ones being capped by normal pediments, and the center one with a high ogival pediment with a cartouche inside. The Cheeseborough House, which had a magnificent staircase with twisted balusters and excellent panelling in its parlor, was demolished early in this century to make way for a YMCA. The Rivera House has been substantially altered, but is in good condition; it now has its north end refaced in brick (all of Munday's houses so far mentioned were frame houses) and the inside has been gutted to make room for the offices of a bank.

At about the same time, Munday also built a smaller house with a gambrel roof and a central chimney. The most notable feature of this house, the Daniel Ayrault House, was the shell-hood doorway, now fortunately preserved at the Newport Historical Society. The Ayrault House is one of the earliest buildings for which an actual plan, drawn by the architect, survives; it is not very detailed, leaving much to the imagination of the builders, but there were obviously other drawings on other pieces of paper now lost to us.

Munday was not limited to frame buildings. In 1728 he built a brick town house for Godfrey Malbone on the site of the present Post Office Building. This had a gambrel roof, and

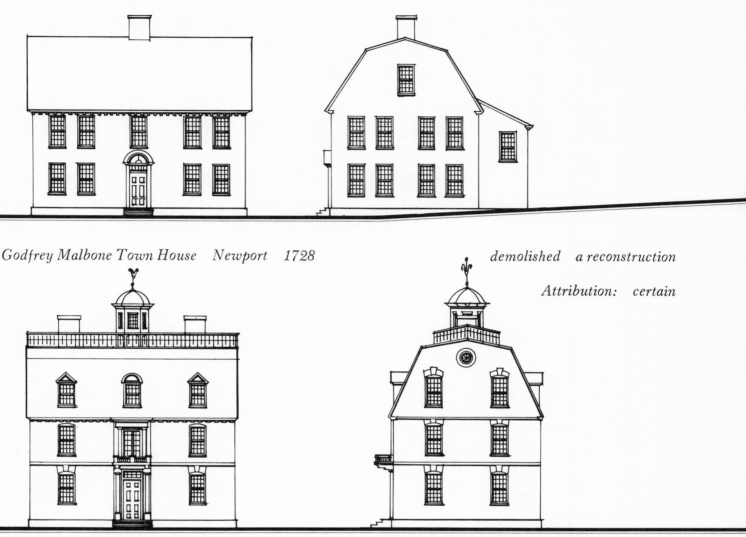

*Daniel Ayrault House    Newport    1739*    *demolished, reconstruction*

*Attribution:    certain*

*Godfrey Malbone Town House    Newport    1728*    *demolished    a reconstruction*

*Attribution:    certain*

was three bays wide and 2½ storeys high. The central bay was elaborately carved with a balcony over the door; a capital from this arrangement survives at the Newport Historical Society. This capital, although archaic, shows great imagination; among the details carved on it are a pair of birds at the angles. Also at the Historical Society is one of the marble fireplaces ordered by Malbone from France. The two outside dormers were capped with triangular pediments and the middle one with a segmental pediment. In the center of the roof, behind a balustrade, stood an octagonal cupola.

A house very similar to the Malbone House, and to other Munday buildings, was the John Hancock House, built in 1737 in Boston. It was slightly more elaborate, was built of stone, and lacked a cupola. It was five bays wide, and was decorated with quoins. Measured drawings were made before the house was destroyed in 1863, and a reconstruction was made in 1926 at Ticonderoga, New York; this is now the headquarters for the New York State Historical Association. Various interior trim from the old house has been incorporated in scattered houses in Massachusetts. This includes the fine staircase with twisted balusters, which incidentally is another key to Munday's authorship, for the detail of the twisted balusters and newel post is clearly the same as some examples he did in Newport. The outside too, as we noted above, is typical of Munday, especially the large round-headed window at the back to light the stairs, and the balcony over the front door; the French window leading to the bal-

*Hancock House   Boston   1737*

*demolished*

*Attribution:   probable*

*round-headed
window
at back*

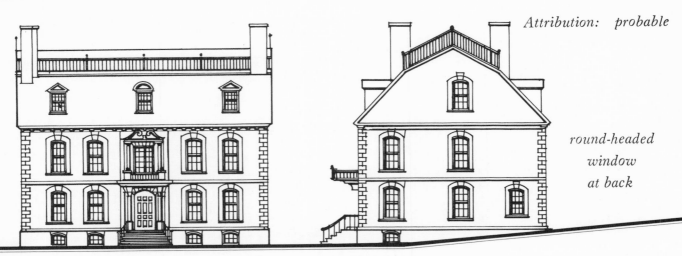

cony is crowned with a split ogival pediment, while Munday used a split segmental pediment in a similar position in other buildings. Some historians argue that all these similarities of the Hancock House with Munday's other work is pure coincidence, and that there were many designers in Boston capable of the house without having to call in a stranger—especially one who belonged to the Church of England—but lack of historical records has prevented us from knowing the actual prowess of the Boston builders; what evidence we have indicates that they were not very advanced. Furthermore, Hancock was a member of the Church of England. I shall let the reader draw his own conclusions.

It may seem surprising to the reader that a drawing is offered here of the next house, for there are no photographs nor prints or pictorial evidence of any kind to base our drawing on, but in this case verbal descriptions were so detailed that a drawing was able to be made. Godfrey Malbone, whose town house we have already seen, began his country house, known as Malbone Hall, in 1739, the year of Munday's death. This house closely resembled the Colony House which was being built at the same time. It was built of brown stone, and trimmed with wooden quoins that were painted to look like marble. The back door is said to be the one that was later put on the Hunter House, but this is a speculation. Over this back door was a large round-headed window to light the grand circular stairway.

*Malbone Hall   Newport   1739-1741*

*burnt down about 1766      a reconstruction*

*Attribution:   certain*

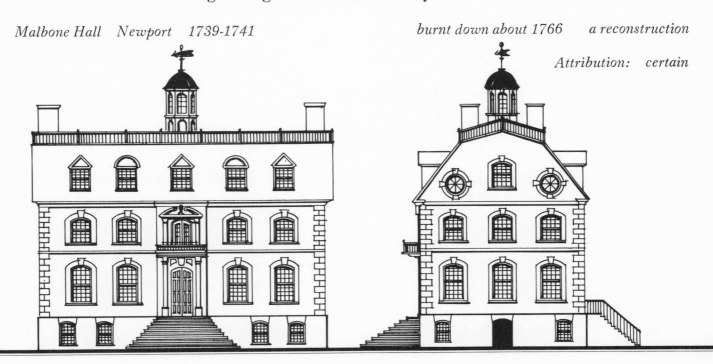

Around 1766, when Malbone was giving a sumptuous dinner party, the story is told that the house caught fire. The fire brigade at length arrived and dragged all their equipment up the front stairs. Malbone arose from his dinner and insisted that the firemen use the back stairs, and when they had therefore dragged their equipment around and up the back stairs the fire was out of control. Malbone, being informed of this, exclaimed that he could not allow a fire to interrupt his dinner party, and so he instructed that the tables be taken out onto the lawn!

For many years visitors were escorted around the ruins and the splendid gardens. Around 1845 a new house was erected partly on the old foundations, and using the original stonework; this is a typical Victorian house of the period, and gives no clue to the appearance of the original house. The location of the original foundations is quite clear, however; they were high foundations, and so there is a high mound there now, covered in grass.

The greatest achievement of Munday's designs is the Colony House in Newport. It is built of brick, and is trimmed with the same kind of brown stones as were used for the construction of Malbone Hall. It is 2½ storeys high, and seven bays wide in front, although only four bays in the rear. The roof, almost a gambrel, is actually a curious deck-on-gable with a balustrade around the deck; a cupola stands in the middle. The dormers have segmental pediments. Over the center of the front stands a large brick pediment of the same configuration as the gable ends; it is not supported by any pavilion. This pediment is pierced by a pair of circular windows, one on either side of a large clock. Under the pediment, which is three bays wide, is the elaborate central bay that we have seen on the Hancock House and both Malbone Houses. It consists of a balcony above the door, and a split segmental pediment over the French windows that lead out onto the balcony; the split pediment is beautifully carved. The ends of the building are three bays wide, and each has a door, simpler than the front door, but still well composed and executed. Inside, the large hall on the lower floor is fully panelled, and contains a row of Doric columns with flying entablatures supporting the floor above; these are said to have been added later, and since Munday died before the building was completed it is difficult to say whether the columns were part of his design or not.

*Colony House   Newport   1739*                                    *Attribution:   certain*

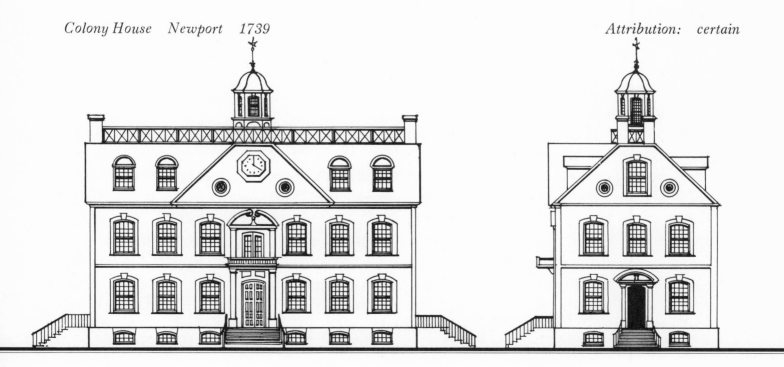

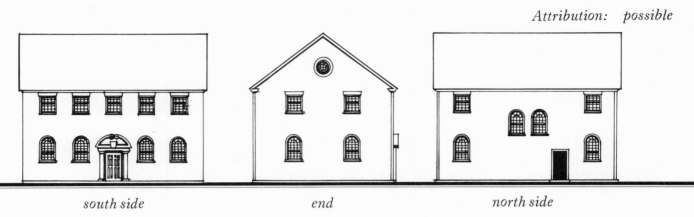

*St. Paul's Church   Narragansett   1707*

*moved to Wickford, Rhode Island, 1800*

*Attribution:   possible*

south side                            end                            north side

Munday's first design was for St. Paul's Church Narragansett, built in 1707. The church was moved to Wickford in 1800, and has been well restored. It is five bays long and two storeys high with a gable roof. The lower tier of windows is round-headed and the upper rectangular; this is about the first use of round-headed sash windows in the northern Colonies. The central bay contains the door, which has a split segmental pediment, unrefined, but still the shape of more of Munday's work to come. Galleries were added in 1721. The general layout of St. Paul's is similar to that of the first Trinity Church in Newport, built in 1701; doubtless Munday had seen it.

In 1729 a plain and small meetinghouse was erected for the Sabbatarians or Seventh Day Adventists. If one saw only the severe exterior one would never guess the extent of the rich interior. Many architectural historians have examined and measured this building and compared details of its panelling to that in other Newport buildings, particularly Trinity Church; they are not in agreement about whether Munday was the architect or not. Without wishing to become involved in this controversy, it does seem to me that Munday's hand is quite obviously the one that shaped the interior of this little meetinghouse. The panelling, although similar to that in Trinity Church, is naturally not identical with it; for one thing, Munday did not design Trinity, but only built it, and for another, four years had elapsed since the erection of Trinity—plenty of time for Munday to invent another section for the panelling in his next building. The ceiling is quite like that at St. Paul's Narragansett, although it lacked the latter's cross-tie beams; this omission was structurally a mistake, but aesthetically it was an attempt to lighten the whole effect.

The meetinghouse has a gallery around three sides and a splendid pulpit on the fourth side. The pulpit, which is crowned by a sounding board, has fine carving, particularly in the twisted balusters and newel posts, and in the sounding board; a motif on the bottom of the sounding board is almost the same as one on the ceiling of the back pews at Trinity Church. The Sabbatarian Meeting House, whose congregation was disbanded long ago, has been encased in brick and incorporated in the building of the Newport Historical Society.

In 1729 the Dean of Derry in Ireland, the noted philosopher George Berkeley, came to live in Newport while he was awaiting in vain the arrival of some funds from England to build a college in Bermuda. He preached often from the lovely central three-decker pulpit in Trinity Church, and when he returned to Ireland and was made Bishop of Cloyne he sent over Trinity's first organ. While he was living in Newport he decided to build a house, which he called Whitehall. It was built in 1729 in record time, and evidence indicates that Richard Munday

was the architect. The front of the house, which is of frame construction, is formal in appearance, having a hip roof and central chimney. In the side view, however, the formal façade blends into a long salt-box roof that gives it a charming, informal, rustic air. The front is five bays wide and two storeys high. The doorway is very academic; it is a double doorway, except that one of the two doors is a dummy. It is surrounded by Ionic pilasters which support a cushion frieze and a triangular pediment. The house is now owned by Yale University and is open to the public.

Munday built a number of other buildings; some of these are so obscure that we know practically nothing of their appearance, and there were likely some not recorded at all. As has been mentioned before, Munday built, but did not design, Trinity Church; this was definitely designed by Sir Christopher Wren (*q.v.*), and although it is a credit to Munday that he was able to execute Wren's elaborate design so well, he probably made few innovations of his own in the design; one innovation is the shape of the pediments over the north doors. They are segmental with a reversed segment cut out of the top. Munday also built St. Michael's Church in Bristol, Rhode Island, but little is known of its appearance. Sometime between 1720 and 1730 a large house was built for Captain John Potter in South County; parts of this house survive, including the staircase and two rooms with their panelling, but the original exterior appearance is doubtful. The interior details link this house with the Brenton House in Newport. From Munday's death in 1739 until 1746 Newport was without an architect, but those seven lean years were repaid in full with the next architect.

*Peter Harrison   1716-1775*

IN about 1738 a young Yorkshire lad called Peter Harrison sailed as a member of the crew of his elder brother's ship to Newport. He showed promise and was soon promoted to being captain of his own ship. In 1745 he was captured by the French and taken to Louisburg and later released. While he was there he acquired a sufficient knowledge of the place so as to be able to draw an accurate map of the French fortifications and to direct an English expedition against Louisburg under Governor William Shirley of Massachusetts and William Pepperell of Kittery, Maine. This map is preserved at the Public Record Office in London, and is the earliest preserved specimen of Harrison's drawing. The expedition against the French was successful, and Governor Shirley was so pleased about the part that Harrison had played in it that he gave him the commission to design his new mansion. Shirley Place was built in Roxbury, just outside of Boston, in 1746, and it survives today on different foundations and in dilapidated condition; a movement is under way to restore it.

It was a massive building, five bays wide and two storeys tall on a high basement. On top of the high deck-on-hip roof were a balustrade, two thick chimneys and a heavy cupola. The front of the house was dressed with ten Doric pilasters with flying entablature, and the back had four. The house was of frame construction, but the exterior surface was covered in wood carved into blocks, so as to give the appearance of ashlar masonry; this was the first time this technique was used in the Colonies, and Harrison was to use it many times again. There were heavy keystones over the windows and the front door; the back door, all glazed, was an elaborate Palladian window. The divided steps leading up to the front door were also typical of the English Palladian school, although the general appearance of the house was not. Harrison must have seen a future in designing buildings and probably began collecting his library of architectural pattern books soon after building Shirley Place.

*Shirley Place   Roxbury, Massachusetts   1746*                    *to be restored*

*Attribution:   certain*

Harrison was a Quaker, but quickly changed to the Church of England when he saw that it was the thing to do in Newport. He had become involved in a lawsuit concerning the Pelham family soon after his arrival in Newport, and fell in love with Elizabeth Pelham. The Pelhams and their cousins the Banisters objected strongly to the match because although they liked Peter he was not of gentle birth. Nature found a way, and Elizabeth, expecting a child, eloped with Peter to New Hampshire. They returned to Newport and built a house called Leamington Farm in 1747.

Leamington Farm, which survives today, is so altered as to be unrecognizable except for its two chimneys. Therefore this book contains no drawing of the house, but it probably was a simple house without much architectural detail or quality.

Harrison's next building was the Redwood Library, built in Newport in 1748. This is the most Palladian of Harrison's designs, and is derived from drawings in three of his pattern books: Edward Hoppus' *Palladio*, Isaac Ware's *Designs from Inigo Jones and others* (1735) and William Kent's *Designs of Inigo Jones* (1727). The Redwood Library has the first giant portico designed by a resident architect in the Colonies, although St. Philip's Church in Charleston, designed by James Gibbs (*q.v.*), had the first giant portico in the Colonies. The Library is five bays wide, with the center three bays enclosed by the giant Doric portico. Under the portico it is two storeys high, but the wings are only one storey high; the configuration of the front is as a double pediment. The building is constructed of wood, again rusticated to resemble ashlar masonry. The building has been much enlarged to accommodate the large collection of books of a modern library. On the grounds of the present library is a charming gazebo or summerhouse built by Harrison for the founder of the Library, Abraham Redwood. When Redwood's house was torn down, the gazebo was moved to the garden of the Library. The gazebo, which is based on a design by Gibbs, is also constructed of rusticated wood. It is octagonal, and has a domed roof.

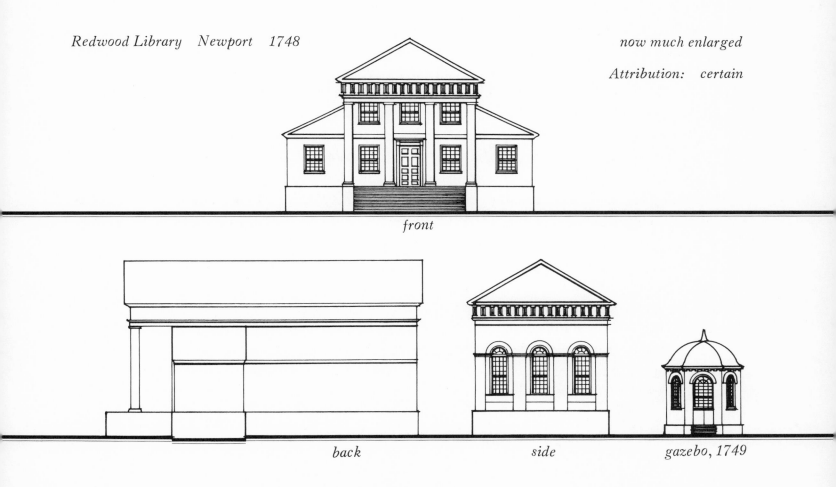

*Redwood Library   Newport   1748*                    *now much enlarged*

*Attribution:   certain*

*front*

*back*                                    *side*                    *gazebo, 1749*

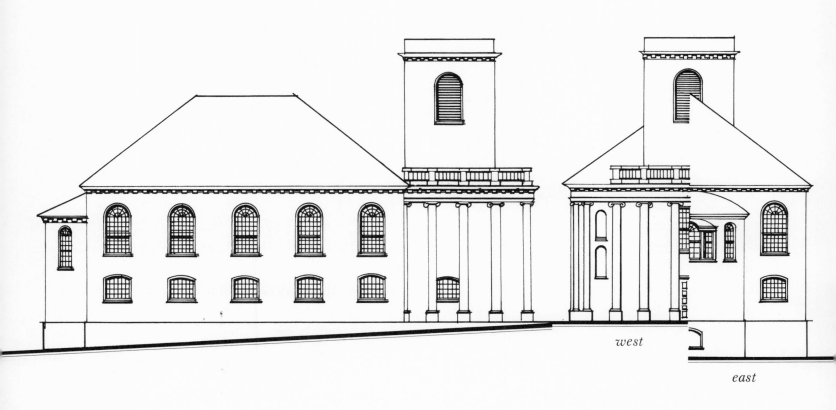

*west*

*east*

Soon afterwards, Harrison produced a design for a new building for King's Chapel in Boston. Inside a plain exterior with an ambitious steeple was to be the most sumptuous church interior in the Colonies. However, although the interior splendor was realized, the exterior never was finished. A parapet and balustrade with urns around the roof and the tall stone steeple were never built, and the giant Ionic portico around the tower at the west end was added later using the original design. Interesting concepts of the steeple design have been drawn by A. L. Kocher and John Coolidge, but no one knows for sure what it was to have looked like. The church is five bays long with a shallow apse at the east end. The windows are arranged in two tiers, the upper ones being round-headed, and the lower ones having segmental arches. The apse is pierced with a Palladian window. The roof is a high hip, which gives the church somewhat the appearance from the side of a kneeling camel. Inside, the cove ceiling is supported by pairs of giant Corinthian columns with joint flying entablatures. The barrel-vaults over each aisle are linked with the center ceiling by cross barrel-vaults at each bay. A gallery around three sides of the church abuts on the backs of the columns. The whole arrangement is a variation on a theme by Gibbs, the same theme, in fact, that was used without modification a few years later in St. Paul's Chapel in New York. The organ in the rear gallery incorporates part of the first organ in the Colonies. The fabric of the church is in good condition and is well restored, but the congregation slipped out of the Anglican Church to become the first Unitarian Church in America; ordinarily the Anglican Church's parish system is so set up that this could not happen, but in this case the switch was made in the one year that the Anglican Church was most disorganized: immediately after the Revolution.

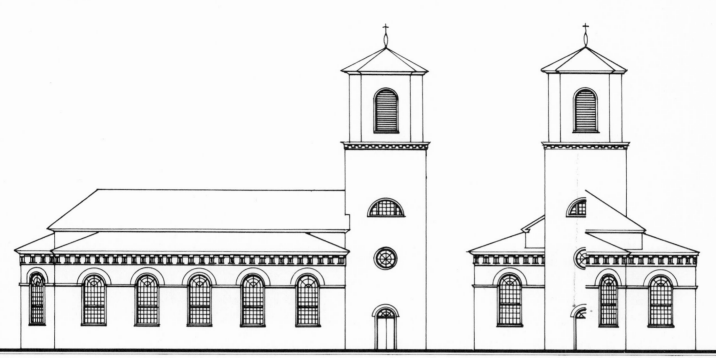

Harrison designed another fine church in the Boston area. This was Christ Church, Cambridge, built between 1759 and 1761. Like King's Chapel, Christ Church was never finished on the outside. Harrison intended to build a tall steeple on top of the tower, to cover the outside of the church with 'roughcast' (a form of stucco) and to place Doric pilasters along the nave between the windows.

Christ Church is built of wood, and was five bays long, although it has since been lengthened. It has one tier of round-headed windows. The church is not oriented; that is to say, the apse and altar, usually at the east end, this time are at the west end. The tower, which is at the east end over the entrance, has a large semicircular window on each of its three exposed faces; this kind of window, common in this country after 1800, is unique in Colonial architecture. A bishop's mitre crowns the tower.

Inside, a row of giant Ionic columns with flying entablatures support a cove ceiling over the nave and flat ceilings over the aisles. The rear gallery, which once contained the organ, is an adaptation of an arch in one of James Gibbs' books. The once high pulpit has been cut down, moved to the side and deprived of its sounding board. The box pews have been replaced in the interest of accommodating a larger congregation. The Palladian window in the apse is modern, but not out of place; originally the apse had a round-headed window at each side, and a Palladian altarpiece after a design by William Kent.

Harrison received the invitation to design Christ Church partly as a result of his impressive design for King's Chapel, and partly because the senior warden of the vestry, Mr. Vassall, knew Harrison from a visit he made to Newport. While Harrison was engaged on Christ

Church, Mr. Vassall asked him to design him a house in Cambridge. This house, known as the Longfellow House because it was once the property of the poet Longfellow, was built in 1759. It is five bays wide and 2½ storeys tall. A balustrade surrounds the deck of the deck-on-hip roof. The central bay is projected in a pedimented pavilion, the edges of which are marked by a pair of Ionic pilasters; pilasters also mark the ends of the front. An addition to the back with porches has spoiled the unity of the house, but much of the original interior remains.

*Vassall-Longfellow House   Cambridge   1760*                              *Attribution:   certain*

*Apthorp House   Cambridge   1760*                                        *now slightly altered*

                                                                          *Attribution:   certain*

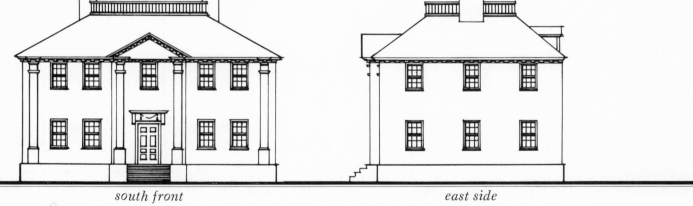

*south front*                                    *east side*

When he saw what the senior warden of his vestry was getting, the Rector of Christ Church, Rev. East Apthorp, asked Harrison to design him a house like it. Apthorp was allegedly convinced that he was soon to be made the first bishop in the Colonies, and he wanted a house like a bishop's palace. He got the house with little trouble beyond the snide remarks of his puritan neighbors, but a letter arrived from England informing him that there was to be no bishop in the Colonies, to prevent an uprising on the part of the nonconformists, and that even if there were to be a bishop in the Colonies it would certainly not be Apthorp. The main difference between the two houses was that the chimneys were placed outside the roof-deck balustrade on Apthorp House, and inside on the Longfellow House. Apthorp House, which is now the Master's residence for Adams House at Harvard, has been substantially altered on the outside, notably by the addition of a third storey, and of some small wings.

After a while, the word went around to Apthorp's relatives that he had built a splendid new house in the wilderness, and that the architect was Peter Harrison. Harrison was commissioned to design a house for Apthorp's father in Brighton, Massachusetts, and for his brother in New York. The Apthorp House in New York, which was built in 1767, was far more academic than the Cambridge houses. It had the shape of a modified Greek or Roman temple. It was five bays long and 2½ storeys high. Four giant Ionic pilasters on each face of the house, which was built of wood rusticated to look like ashlar, supported an entablature

*Apthorp House    New York    1767*                                         *now demolished*

*Attribution:    certain*

*Apthorp  House    Brighton, Massachusetts    about 1717-63*        *demolished    a reconstruction*

*Attribution:    probable*

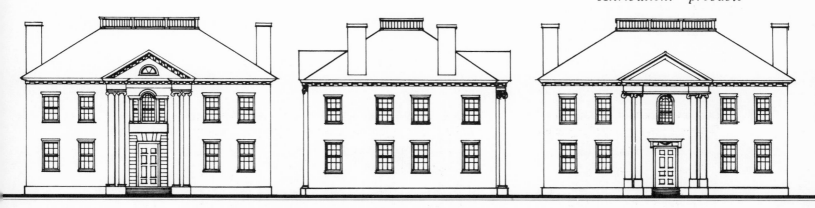

that ran all the way around the house. The center two pilasters of the front supported a pediment to form an unusual type of pavilion: the inside of the pavilion was cut away so that the space between the pilasters was actually a recessed porch. The doorway leading out to this porch was a Palladian window. The rest of the windows on the ground floor were capped with pediments. At each end, looking rather incongruous above an heroic pediment, were a pair of chimneys, one for each slope of the gable.

The Apthorp House in Brighton, built about 1763, was also demolished, but a mansion was built in Nahant, Massachusetts, whose design was based on this one. Our drawing in this book is an attempt to trace the design back from the Nahant mansion to its original state, and may not be entirely accurate. It seems to have been quite like the Cambridge houses, with a few exceptions: the chimneys, of which there were four, were set in the end walls, and the four Ionic pilasters were grouped in twos to mark the central pavilion.

Another house rather like the Cambridge houses by Harrison is the Lady Pepperell Mansion at Kittery Point, Maine. This was built the same year as the Cambridge houses, in 1760, and is probably the result of the Pepperell family's having remembered Harrison's part in the capture of Louisburg many years before. It only has two pilasters in the front, both to mark the pavilion, and it also has its chimneys set in the end walls; the Pepperell House is a little smaller than the Cambridge houses. While some of the house is finished in clapboards, part of it is in wood treated to look like ashlar, and it even has wooden quoins at the corners of the house. It has been well restored after a serious fire.

*Lady Pepperrell House   Kittery Point, Maine   1760*                    *Attribution:   certain*

*Brick Market   Newport   1761-1772*                    *Attribution:   certain*

Apart from the Redwood Library, Harrison built two other public buildings in Newport. The larger was the Brick Market, built between 1761 and 1772. It is seven bays long and three bays wide, and three storeys tall with a hip roof. The ground floor was built of brick in the tradition of an open arcaded market, such as we have seen in the Exchange at Charleston and the Town Hall in Philadelphia. The arcade has now been glazed in, and is used as a shop selling eighteenth-century reproductions. Above the market are rooms that have been used as the City Council chamber and as a theater and for a variety of other purposes. The outside of the upper part shows rectangular windows capped alternately with triangular and segmental pediments, and square windows above; separating each bay from the next is a giant Ionic pilaster, with two of them at the corners. These pilasters support a full entablature that runs around the building. The whole configuration was borrowed from Inigo Jones' Somerset House in London, a design often copied both in Britain and America.

Harrison's other public building was the Touro Synagogue, built between 1759 and 1763. It is the oldest synagogue in America, and was founded by a group of Spanish and Portuguese Sephardic Jews. Newport was one of the only places in the Colonies where the Jews could live as any other citizen could; in fact, they established a plutocracy jointly with the Anglicans and Quakers that was the envy of nearly everyone. On the outside, the Synagogue is small and austere, built of brick painted beige with brown trim. The building is rectangular, three bays wide and four bays long, with an ugly wing to the north that Harrison did not want to incorporate into the building; this wing was originally the Jewish school. The windows of the Synagogue proper are arranged in two tiers, both round-headed. The fine entrance porch with arches and Ionic columns was derived from a design by James Gibbs. The cornice under the hip roof is a replacement for an elaborate one removed in the nineteenth century.

Inside, there are two orders of columns. Ionic columns support the gallery that goes around three sides of the building, and above them Corinthian columns support the fine cove ceiling. At the east end, the Ark is enclosed in a fine design, which is a clever combination of chimney breasts by William Kent and Batty Langley. The whole is a surprisingly good result, considering that Harrison was brought up in the Quaker and Anglican faiths with little knowledge of Jewish tastes and requirements.

*Touro Synagogue   Newport   1759-1763*                    *Attribution:   certain*

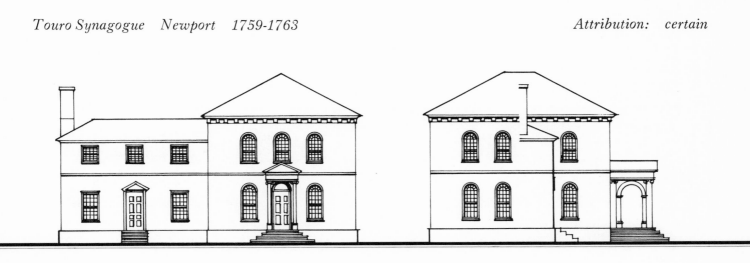

Although Carl Bridenbaugh in his book *Peter Harrison, First American Architect*, tends to ignore it or even to try to refute it, Harrison did design a number of private houses, including some in Newport. Two of these are three storeys high with hip roofs. The Peter Buliod House was built around 1756 out of rusticated wood; it was tastefully trimmed with quoins, window keystones and a pedimented doorway. The ground floor has now been completely altered, and the house is the headquarters of the Salvation Army.

*Peter Buliod House   Newport   1756*                                *now slightly altered*

*Attribution:   probable*

*Francis Malbone House   Newport   1760*                              *now slightly altered*

*Attribution:   certain*

The other house, built of brick in 1760, is the Francis Malbone House. Francis Malbone belonged to the same family as Godfrey Malbone (*q.v.*). The exterior was well decorated with belt courses, wooden moulded heads over the windows, and a pedimented doorway. Most of this decoration has either been removed or hidden under a coat of yellow paint. The house is now a nursing home run by the Sisters of St. Clare. Some of the interior trim remains, including a lovely staircase with twisted balusters.

The Wentworth-Gardner House, built in Portsmouth, New Hampshire, seems to have had some connection with Harrison, although the extent to which he was involved as the designer of this house is uncertain. While the shape of the house is typical of the finer mansions of Portsmouth, the technique and details are not, and they are more like Harrison's work. It is pure speculation, but what may have happened is this: the Wentworth family, who were friends of Harrison's, and who later commissioned him to build them a country house at Wolfeborough, were having a house built by a local builder, perhaps the same man who carried out Harrison's designs across the river that same year at the Pepperell Mansion. Since Harrison was in the area, he was asked to inspect the Wentworth House as it was going up,

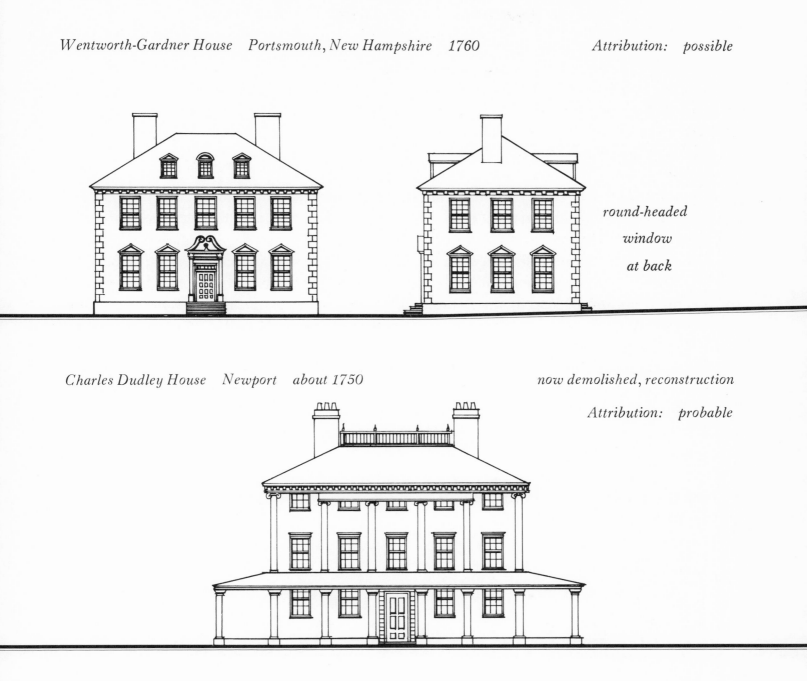

*round-headed*
*window*
*at back*

*Charles Dudley House   Newport   about 1750*          *now demolished, reconstruction*

*Attribution:   probable*

and he made some suggestions. The finish of the outside is rusticated wood with quoins at the corners, and pediments over the windows of the lower floor. The splendid doorway, derived from a plate in William Salmon's *Palladio Londinensis*, is similar to the one at Westover in Virginia; this is not surprising, since a member of the Wentworth family is quoted as having been tremendously impressed by Westover on his visit to Virginia. Two Corinthian pilasters support a split ogee pediment with a pineapple in the center. The entablature under the pediment contains a cushion frieze. Inside the house there is some splendid panelling, interspersed with Ionic pilasters. The lower stair-hall contains an elliptical arch over the stairs, which has twisted balusters; the upper stair-hall has a cove ceiling, and a round-headed window at the back. The pediments of the dormers on the high hip roof are alternately triangular and segmental.

Three more houses in Newport can be attributed to Harrison. The earliest was the Customs Collector Charles Dudley House, built around 1750. It was three storeys high with a hip roof, and five bays wide. The most unusual feature about it was the pavilion comprising the center three bays of the front that was marked by four Ionic pilasters; these pilasters, however, only stretched over the upper two storeys, in the manner of the Brick Market which was built several years later. Old photographs show a porch of heavy Tuscan columns that surrounded the whole of the house at the ground-floor level; while this porch was certainly most uncharacteristic of Colonial architecture, yet it cannot be denied that something had to have been there just to stand under the pilasters above. Whether the porch in the photographs was the original one or not is impossible to say. The fabric of the exterior was rusticated wood. The house was torn down not many years ago.

Close to the Dudley House was the John Banister House; John Banister was the head of the shipping firm in which Harrison received his start as a captain, and had been the relative of Elizabeth Pelham who had most disapproved of her marriage to Harrison. Consequently there had been considerable animosity between Banister and Harrison, and most historians believe that Harrison would therefore not have designed a house for Banister. Whatever his reasons for designing the house—perhaps as an attempt to patch up their quarrel—it is obvious from architectural evidence that Harrison was the architect of the building. In spite of its unacademic gable-on-hip roof, the rest of the house is very academic in proportion and detail, and is finished in Harrison's favorite material: rusticated wood. Both inside and outside the Banister House bears more than a superficial resemblance to the Bowler-Vernon House in Newport. The Banister House, which was built in 1756, was taken down recently and parts of both the inside and outside have been re-erected at Winterthur.

*John Banister Country House    Newport    1756*          *now demolished*          *Attribution:   certain*

*reconstruction, part is at Winterthur*

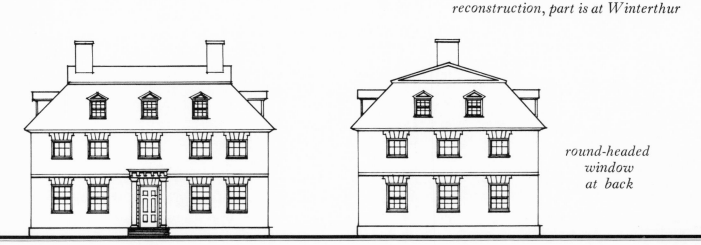

*round-headed window at back*

The Bowler-Vernon House was built somewhere between 1756 and 1758. It differs from the Banister House in that it has a deck-on-hip roof with a balustrade surrounding the deck, dormers with triangular and segmental pediments, and a taller upper storey than Banister's house. The stair-halls and staircases of the two houses are almost identical, to the last twist of a baluster; both have large round-headed windows at the back to light the stairs. The doorways of both houses consisted of a pair of Doric pilasters supporting an entablature without pediment. During the Revolution, the Vernon House was the headquarters of the Comte de Rochambeau, the French Commander in Chief, and was the scene of his famous meeting with Washington. In one of the front rooms can be seen traces of a seventeenth-century house on the site that Harrison incorporated into his design.

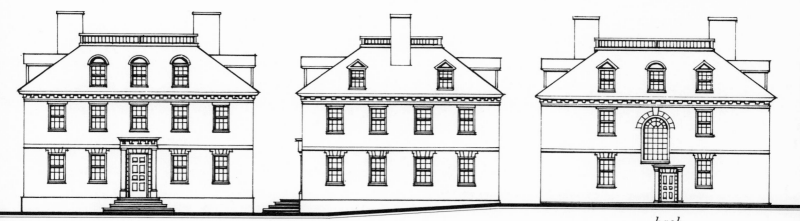

*back*

*Winthrop House    New London, Connecticut    1754*          *demolished 1892, reconstruction*

*Attribution:    certain*

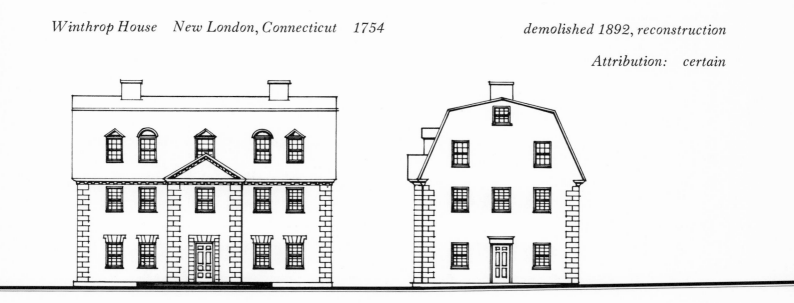

After the publication of Carl Bridenbaugh's book on Harrison, documentary evidence turned up that ascribed another house to Harrison; this was the Winthrop House, built in 1754 in New London, Connecticut. It was demolished in 1892, and there are few pictures of it. Even so, from what evidence there is it has been possible to piece together a reasonable drawing of the house. It was five bays long and 2½ storeys high with a gambrel roof; this is admittedly a shape of roof totally unexpected from the academic Harrison. The pediments of the dormers are alternately triangular and segmental. A pedimented pavilion enclosed the central bay of the front, and a round-headed window at the back lit the stairs. The fabric of the house was rusticated wood, trimmed with quoins at the corners of both house and pavilion.

A most unusual similarity exists between the Winthrop House and The Lindens, built in

Danvers, Massachusetts the same year, in 1754. The outsides of the two houses are almost identical, the chief differences being the placement of the chimneys and the treatment of the pavilion in the front. The pavilion of The Lindens has a steep pediment, like the one on the Wren building at Williamsburg, the pediment being supported on a pair of half-round giant Corinthian columns with flying entablatures. The material of construction is again rusticated wood. The interior, which has been carefully restored, is typical of the buildings we have ascribed to Harrison, and so we must conclude that he designed The Lindens as well. The Lindens was moved to Washington, D. C., during the Depression.

*The Lindens   Danvers, Massachusetts   1754*                    *moved to Washington, D.C.*

*Attribution:   probable*

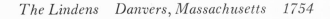

There remains one final speculation to make: the James Gardner House was built in Boston in 1762 and is now long since demolished. It was a five-bay row-house, three storeys high. The doorway was similar to that on the Vernon House, and façade was broken by four giant Ionic pilasters with flying entablatures set on high bases. It was built of brick, and had a course to mark each floor level; the windows of the lower two floors were arched on the soffit. Except for its appearance there is no reason to attribute it to Harrison.

*James Gardner House   Boston   1762*                    *now demolished, reconstruction*

*Attribution:   possible*

Harrison is known to have worked on other buildings; some of these have disappeared without a trace, and on others Harrison was only responsible for details. He built the Wentworth Mansion in Wolfeborough, New Hampshire in 1767, but it was never finished, and was later demolished. In 1755 he built Fort George on Goat Island at Newport, but this has been demolished, although detailed plans of it still exist. Harrison also worked on the Beavertail Lighthouse across Narragansett Bay at the southern tip of Jamestown or Conanicut Island. The foundations of Harrison's lighthouse still remain. Around 1763, he designed a Masonic Hall in Newport, and work was begun on it; it may never have progressed beyond the foundations, but we are told that it was to have been a splendid building. Harrison also made alterations to the Pitts Head Tavern in Newport, including the addition of a fine doorway, a modillioned cornice and dormers with alternately triangular and segmental pediments.

Harrison's only flaw in the eyes of the historian was that he was a Tory. At the end of his life he moved to New Haven, Connecticut, where he was made Customs Collector. He was as fair a Collector as there ever was, but in those days any officer of the Crown was unpopular in certain circles in the Colonies. Fortunately, he died before the Revolution broke out; otherwise he would have been torn between fighting for his King and for the country where he had poured out so much of himself. Whatever he would have done had he lived scarcely interests us; the great tragedy is that after his death a mob of so-called patriots burned all Harrison's books and the designs he had drawn. This shameful act, of course, did not aid the cause of the Colonists; in fact, if the Patriot Thomas Jefferson had only known about Harrison, he would have taken drastic action to save the books and certainly the drawings. Harrison was the first Colonist to experiment with Palladian ideas, and Jefferson after the Revolution popularized the same style so that it became for a time the national style. Jefferson believed himself to be the first. If only he had known!

*Unknown Massachusetts Housewright*

ONE of the most outstanding mansions of New England seems not to have been the work of an architect as we have loosely defined the term; however, this house deserves to be included in this book just on the grounds of its design. It is the Lee Mansion, built in Marblehead, Massachusetts, in 1768. There are various stylistic hints about it that suggest the hand of Peter Harrison (*q.v.*), but it is wise not to rush into a conclusion that Harrison was the architect. The points against his authorship are that he was nowhere near Marblehead at the time, and that the few buildings he designed this late in his career were more academic; he probably would not have included an archaic gable-on-hip roof in the design at the same time as he was experimenting with the Greco-Roman gable roof of the Apthorp House in New York, and he also would almost certainly have included some giant pilasters on the façade of such a grand building. On the other hand, it is entirely conceivable that if Harrison was the architect he designed the house with a deck-on-hip roof, and the local builder substituted the gable for the deck; it is also quite possible that Harrison designed this house for the Lee family ten years before, and they kept the design until they were ready to build. In favor of an attribution to Harrison are the three-bay pedimented pavilion in the center of the façade, the use of rusticated wood and corner quoins on the exterior, and the fact that certain interior panelling is almost identical to that found at other Harrison houses, including The Lindens; the staircase, too, is related to that at The Lindens. The only problem is that Harrison designed all these other buildings ten to fifteen years before the Lee Mansion was built.

*Lee Mansion    Marblehead    1768*                                          *Attribution:    possible*

The house is seven bays long, three bays wide and three storeys high. An attractive octagonal cupola and a pair of massive chimneys form an interesting group on the top of the roof. At the back, an off-center round-headed window provides light for the staircase. Inside, the woodwork is exquisite. The fully panelled parlor in particular is very important in the history of Colonial architecture: while on the one hand it has archaic bolection mouldings around the panels, on the other hand the frieze and cornice at the top of the walls is delicately carved, and the overmantel, in the manner of the great English woodcarver Grinling Gibbons, is probably the finest in the Colonies. Similar details in the drawing room and dining room are also of high quality. The staircase is extremely wide, and ascends in a long, shallow run to the landing that is lit by the large round-headed window at the back. The balusters and newel post on the stairs are twisted, and the step-ends are panelled with elaborate carving beneath each panel. A careful look at the house itself confirms the suspicion in the reader's mind that the Lee Mansion is too good to have been designed by the carpenter who built it, and yet the historian would balk at an attribution to any particular architect based on the scanty evidence so far presented. My guess is that Peter Harrison was the architect, but it would serve no purpose to go out on a limb to defend my guess.

*Godfrey Malbone    fl. 1770*

THE reader may remember two houses built in Newport by Richard Munday for Godfrey Malbone; one of these houses burned down under unusual and embarrassing circumstances. Godfrey Malbone became the laughingstock of Newport, and so his son, also named Godfrey, decided to take advantage of a piece of property recently willed to him in Brooklyn, Connecticut, and to leave Newport before he died of shame. However, he soon found out that Brooklyn was not exactly an easy place to live; Malbone was an Anglican, and the rest of Connecticut was Congregationalist. Malbone resented a tax imposed on him to build a new Congregational meetinghouse at Brooklyn, and so organized his own Anglican parish in opposition. He himself made the designs for Trinity Church in Brooklyn (named after his mother parish in Newport), and the building was actually finished before the rather drab Congregational building, although they were both started at the same time.

The origins of the design of the church are unmistakable; Trinity is really a mixture of the two ecclesiastical buildings that Malbone knew best, Trinity Church and Touro Synagogue in Newport. It has the pew patterns and gallery structure of old Trinity and the hip roof and cove ceiling of the Synagogue; the doorway is also based on the entrance porch of the Synagogue. While the ideas behind the design were extremely commendable, the execution is not particularly outstanding, but this is understandable in view of the great haste in which the church was built and of the unskilled labor in that part of Connecticut. Outside, the church is rectangular, five bays long and three bays wide with a hip roof. The windows are arranged in two tiers, the lower ones having segmental arches and the upper ones being round-headed; this treatment, which is different from the Newport churches, was probably the result of Malbone's trip to England, for many of Wren's and Gibbs' London churches have their windows arranged in this fashion.

*Trinity Church    Brooklyn, Connecticut    1770*

*now slightly altered*

*Attribution:    certain*

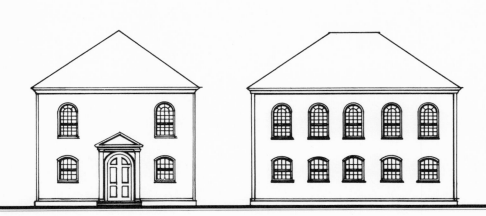

As far as we know Malbone never designed any other buildings; Trinity Church was a single attempt by a gentleman who rose to the occasion as a result of the standard discursive training given to the eighteenth-century gentleman. Incidentally, the reader might be interested to know of a happy ending to the feud between Anglican Malbone and his Congregationalist opponents, who were led by General Israel Putnam. Putnam's son Daniel married Malbone's niece. Their descendants are Episcopalians, and the graveyard at Trinity contains the tombstones of many Malbones and Putnams.

*Joseph Brown    1733-1786*

THE third of the architects from the Colony of Rhode Island was Joseph Brown. He worked exclusively in Providence, and stuck exclusively to pattern books by James Gibbs. He was the brother of the wealthy merchant, John Brown, for whom he built a mansion at the end of his life. It may seem incredible in a Colony the small size of Rhode Island, but it is highly unlikely that any of the three architects who worked there ever met each other; Munday, who died in 1739 when the other two were too young to be interested in architecture, obviously never met Harrison or Brown. If the latter two met, it certainly did not leave any mark on the younger Brown, for the buildings he designed were based on drawings in books that Harrison used some thirty years earlier. Presumably, if Harrison had met Brown he would have recommended to him some of the other more up-to-date pattern books. All this is not meant to disparage the designs of either Gibbs or Brown, for Brown produced some interesting and original adaptations of Gibbs' drawings.

As far as can be told from available evidence, Brown only designed five buildings, although he also participated in the selection of a design for University Hall at Brown University. The earliest building was the dignified three-storey mansion known as the Joseph Russell House, built in 1772. This house is the only one of Brown's designs that is not documented, but the details of the fine interior and of the front door are unmistakably by Brown's hand. The house is of brick, and the elegant doorway is either of stone or of wood rusticated to look like stone (it is hard to reach because of alterations to the building). The doorway is framed by a pair of half-round Corinthian pilasters on a rusticated background with a segmental pediment on top. The house, which is in poor condition, has been much altered by wings and by being raised up a storey on top of a department store. The best panelling has been removed and placed in a museum.

*Joseph Russell House    Providence    1772*                                        *now much altered*

*Attribution:    probable*

In 1774, Joseph Brown built an unusual brick house for himself. It is 2½ storeys tall on a high basement. The gable of the deck-on-gable roof faces the street, and is in the shape of a giant ogee. The pediment over the front door is also an ogee, or was, for it has been removed. A Chippendale balustrade around the roof-deck and a few urns strategically placed give the house a happy air. Inside, the front hall is lavishly decorated: the elliptical arch rests on two pairs of Ionic columns instead of the more usual brackets. The handrail on the open side of the stairs is supported by twisted balusters, while that on the wall side terminates at its bottom

175

end in a vertical scroll. Before the house was altered many fine fireplaces and overmantels graced its rooms, and a few yet remain. A story is told of a French officer during the Revolution who on a dare rode his horse up the high double flight of steps leading to the front door; the horse refused to go down the other side, and so had to be led through the house and out the back.

*Joseph Brown House    Providence    1774*                              *slightly altered*

*Attribution:    certain*

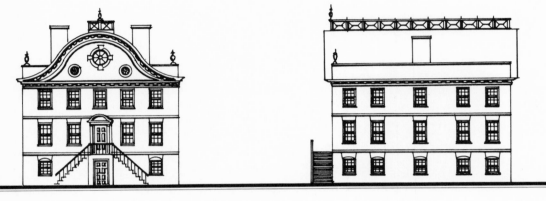

*John Brown House    Providence    1786*                              *slightly altered*

*Attribution:    certain*

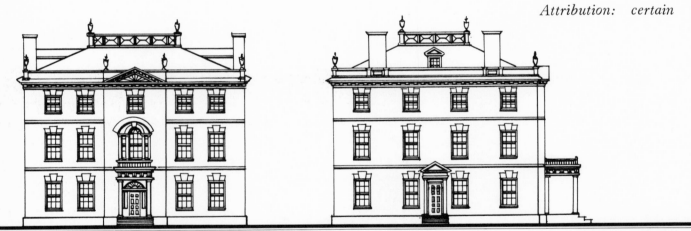

The last building designed by Joseph Brown was for his brother John Brown, and it was built in 1786. It was an almost square brick building before the Victorian wing was added to the back. The house stands 3½ storeys high, and is five bays wide with a one-bay central pedimented pavilion. The balustrade around the eaves and the Chippendale balustrade around the roof-deck are both profusely decorated with urns. A Doric entrance porch frames the front door, and above it is a Palladian window. The chimneys are set in the end walls. The interior, which was about the most lavish of its day, is beautifully decorated with overmantels, cornices, arches, doorways, etc., taken from Gibbs' books. The John Brown House is open to the public under the auspices of the Rhode Island Historical Society.

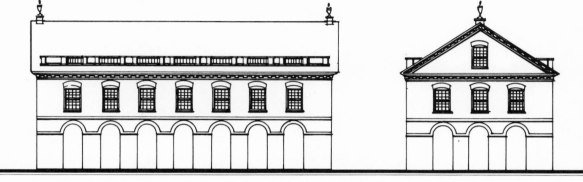

Joseph Brown was commissioned to design two public buildings; the first was the Market, built in 1773. The design was not particularly inspired, but it served its purpose for a time. It was of brick, seven bays long and three wide. The ground floor was a series of arches to form an open air market similar to that at the Brick Market in Newport. Above that was but one storey, whose rectangular windows were arched on the soffit. On top of that was the gable roof with a parapet along the eaves, and an urn at each end at the peak. The building, which was altered in 1793 by the addition of a third storey, is now used by the Rhode Island School of Design.

Brown's most monumental achievement was the First Baptist Church, built in 1774. For this, he freely adapted James Gibbs' rejected design for St. Martin's-in-the-Fields in London, which design we have seen before at St. Paul's Chapel in New York. The steeple is an exact copy in wood of Gibbs' drawing, but the rest of the church, also in wood, is slightly different. It is five bays long with two tiers of round-headed windows, and almost as wide as it is long, after the meetinghouse tradition. Decoration on the outside includes some fine doorways by Gibbs and quoins at all the corners of the building.

Inside, making allowances for the increased width of the Providence building, the arrangement of ceiling and columns is more like that at Gibbs' All Saints Cathedral at Derby than at St. Martin's. In this arrangement the main difference is that Doric columns are used instead of Corinthian columns. Galleries surround three sides of the church. This church was the last of several excellent houses of worship in the Colony of Rhode Island. It seems strange that such a small area is so well blessed with fine churches.

*Attribution:   certain*

*east*

*west*

*Robert Twelves, and possibly others*

ALTHOUGH Boston was one of the most important cities throughout the history of the Colonies, it had few important buildings attributable to architects and has precious little in the way of records to make up for the destruction of most of the Colonial city. In the early days the Puritans had no use for any ostentatious show of architecture, and so their most important buildings, such as the Province House and the various meetinghouses, were plain, if occasionally large. Even in the years immediately preceding the Revolution enough of the Puritan influence remained that formal architecture was discouraged. Nevertheless, a handful of buildings were designed by one or more local architects to add to the number built by outsiders such as Peter Harrison.

For the sake of convenience and as a result of certain similarities in detail six of these buildings have been arbitrarily attributed to Robert Twelves. The earliest of these buildings was known as the Foster-Hutchinson House. It was built around 1688 and demolished in 1833. It had a seven-bay façade interrupted by four elaborate Ionic pilasters; the capitals of the pilasters were festooned with garlands and swags, and one of the capitals is preserved in the Harrison Gray Otis House in Boston. The central bay contained the front·door, which was surmounted by a balcony; the window leading out to the balcony was round-headed under a segmental pediment which was supported on volute-shaped brackets. The top storey, above the pediment, had square windows under a heavy modillioned cornice. Above the cornice was a balustrade along the front of the roof. The roof was a deck-on-gable, apparently with no balustrade around the deck, although it may once have had one. On top of the deck in the center was an octagonal cupola, and although this seems to have looked quite natural, it may have been a later addition, especially since hexagonal, not octagonal cupolas were in vogue in the early days of Colonial architecture. The ends of the house were blank brick walls, each one culminating in a pair of chimneys.

The total composition of the Foster-Hutchinson House was such that if it had been built in London it would probably have been considered typical of Inigo Jones' row-houses or terraces. However, Inigo Jones could not possibly have designed this house, for he had been dead about thirty years when it was built. Jones had a number of pupils and imitators, such as John Webb, Sir Roger Pratt and Hugh May, but all these had died before the house was begun.

*Foster-Hutchinson House    Boston    about 1688*                                        *demolished 1833*

*Attribution:    possible*

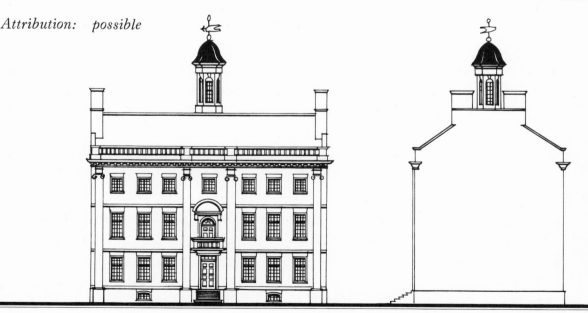

Therefore, the identity of the architect of this house would remain a mystery, even more so because the original appearance of the house is in doubt—it suffered damage by fire and at the hands of angry mobs at least twice in the middle of the eighteenth century, and the only picture we have of the house was rather crudely drawn late in its life—were it not for some stylistic similarities it has to certain other buildings in the area.

*William Clarke House   Boston   1712*                    *demolished      reconstruction*

*Attribution:   possible*

The Foster-Hutchinson House is the earliest house in New England included in this book. The two houses that are stylistically closest to it were not built for another twenty-five to thirty years, but their late date does not bar them from being by the same hand as the first. These are the William Clarke House, built in Boston in 1712, and the MacPhaedris-Warner House, built in Portsmouth, New Hampshire, from 1716 to 1723. Little is known of the former, except what can be determined from a contemporary picture; the house has long been demolished. It was apparently built of stone, seven bays wide and 3½ storeys tall; the first and seventh bays contained windows only half as wide as the rest. In the center was a fine doorway with split-ogee scroll pediment; the doorway is obviously from the same plate in Salmon's book as the famous one at Westover in Virginia. The deck-on-gable roof had a balustrade around the deck and a pair of chimneys in each end wall. The five dormers on the front of the roof had alternately gable and splayed-eaves semicircular pediments. The heights of the windows diminished at each storey.

In many ways, the Clarke House was just a larger version of the MacPhaedris-Warner House in Portsmouth. The Warner House is five bays and 2½ storeys high. It is built of brick laid in Flemish bond, with a strong belt course to mark the upper floor level. The lower windows are arched on the soffit—an elegant touch—but the upper windows have flat tops. The handsome doorway may be a later alteration, but if it is original it certainly fits our theory, for it again comes from Salmon's book, and is closely related to the doorway on the Clarke House. It has a segmental pediment supported by Corinthian entablature and pilasters. The steep roof holds a row of five dormers which are roofed alternately with segmental and triangular pediments. Above the dormers is a roof-deck balustrade in front of a hexagonal cupola. When it was first built, the roof did not have a deck, and some think that it did not have a cupola either, although I do not agree; the original roof, as outlined in dotted lines on the drawing, was a pair of gables, back to back, with a deep gully in between, running the length of the house. This is a typical arrangement for an English country house of the period, but since the Portsmouth house has its gable ends filled in, the effect of the Colonial house is a little more professional than its English counterparts. Some of the windows in the end walls of the house are narrow like the outside windows of the Clarke House. In the center of the back of the house, a large round-headed window lights the staircase. Although in most ways they are quite dif-

*MacPheadris-Warner House   Portsmouth, New Hampshire   1716-1723*          *Attribution:   possible*

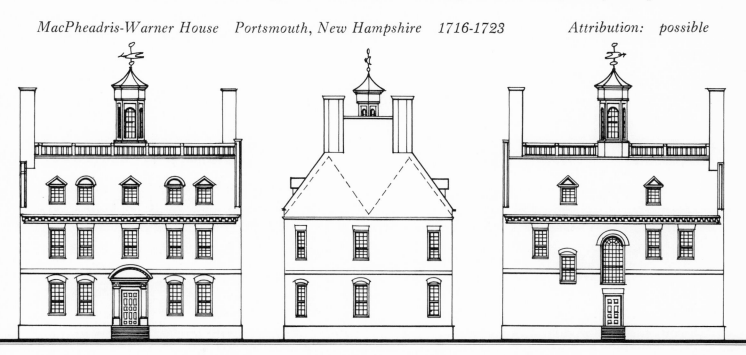

ferent, a front view of the Warner House is very similar to the same view of the Governor's Palace at Williamsburg; this is a result of the early date of both more than anything else, and is not indicative of their having the same designer.

If our theory is correct, a man with the architectural talent that this man appears to have had could not have escaped the notice of important men on committees that were responsible for erecting public buildings. The earliest public building that seems to be connected with our architect was Stoughton College at Harvard University, built in 1699. According to its appearance in old prints, it was probably never finished as designed, although it is not known how it would have looked if it had been completed. As built, it was a long, narrow, rectangular building, 3½ storeys high with a steep gable roof. The windows were arranged symmetri-

*Stoughton College, Harvard University   1699   demolished 1781, reconstruction   Attribution:   possible*

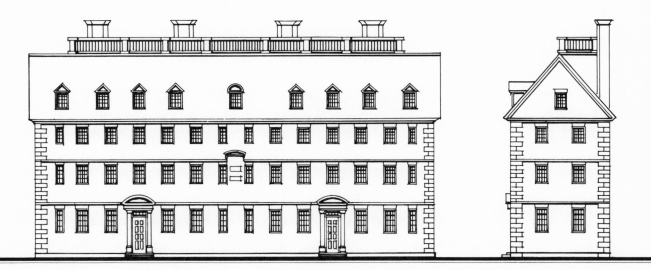

cally around the two doorways, each of which was crowned by an elegant segmental pediment, possibly related to plates in Salmon's book. A balustrade stretched along the top of most of the roof in front of the four heavy chimneys that sprouted from the back wall, which evidently would not have remained the back wall had the building been completed according to plan. There were sixteen windows across each storey of the façade, but only nine dormers on top of them; all the dormers had triangular pediments except the center one, which had a semicircular pediment. In the center of the front were plaques and crests of the Stoughton family, flanked by a set of windows narrower than the rest; more of these narrow windows occupied the outside bays of the building, as at the Clarke House. The building, which was two bays thick, had attractive white stone quoins at the corners; this was the first appearance of this academic motif in the Colonies.

Stoughton College formed the center of a U-shaped arrangement of buildings at the entrance of the Yard consisting of Stoughton, Harvard and Massachusetts Halls. It was used to house troops during the Revolution, and being in ruinous condition was pulled down in 1781. A new building was erected not long after on a different site and called Stoughton Hall.

In 1711 the citizens of Boston decided to build a new Town House (now known as the Old State House), to replace the old one that had just burned down. The result was an excellent building, far ahead of its time in New England. In end profile, it looks like a large version of the ends of Wren's charming Trinity Almshouses at Mile End Gate in London; the likeness is in the motif of a stepped and pedimented gable. The building is a long, narrow rectangle, 2½ storeys high on a steep hill, which causes the two ends to have completely different proportions. The ends are three bays wide, with the center bay of the upper floor decorated with a

*Colony House   Boston   1711-1713*                              *Attribution:   possible*

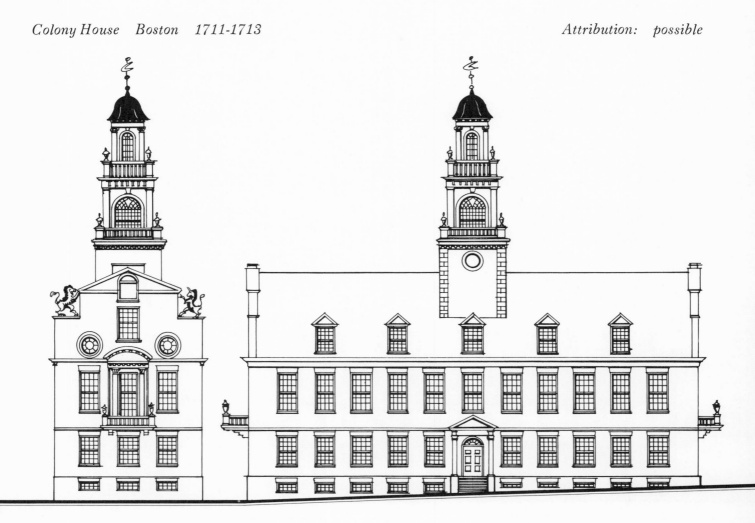

balcony and French window; this window is set in a doorway with elaborate segmental pediment from Salmon's book again. The sides of the Town House are eleven bays long with the center bay containing the door. The steep gable roof has five gabled dormers on each side and is crowned by a lofty tower of three stages. Some say the tower was not built until thirty years after the building, when the whole structure was rebuilt along the old lines after a fire; however, the tower appears crudely but clearly drawn on a map of Boston of 1717, so it is almost certainly part of the original design. It is an extremely close copy of the tower on the Royal Exchange, built in London in 1671 by Wren's friend Edward Jerman; Jerman died immediately after building the Exchange, so he certainly could not have designed the Town House. The Exchange appears in Colin Campbell's *Vitruvius Britannicus*, which however was not published until after the building of the Town House. Therefore, our architect must have been in London between 1671 and 1711. Whatever its origin, the tower has an annoying likeness to the steeples of Christ Church in Boston and Trinity Church in Newport, both built more than ten years after the Town House, but probably designed before it; I say 'annoying,' because apart from writing off the similarities in these buildings as coincidence there is no good explanation for this phenomenon, for it is impossible that the Town House was designed by the same man as the two churches.

The Town House has had a disturbed career. After it witnessed the Boston Massacre only a few yards from the downhill end of the building, it became known as the State House, until it was replaced by Bulfinch's great domed State House on the top of the hill. During the nineteenth century it suffered all sorts of alterations, both internal and external. Later, mistaken restorers who were trying to return it to its original appearance gave it the circular staircase and odd internal plan of the building as it was a hundred years after it was built. It also suffered the indignity of having a Subway station built in and under it. It is said that the building will soon be properly restored, but some say skeptically that the combination of its being undermined by the subway and weakened by the vibrations of neighborhood construction projects will cause it to collapse long before the restoration funds are available.

The last building of the six attributed to the same man is the Old South Congregational Meeting House on Milk Street in Boston. However, we know from the records that the architect of this building was called Robert Twelves; could this be the man for whom we were looking? Nothing at the moment is known about Twelves, according to the records, such as whether he was an old man in 1730 when the Meeting House was built, or whether he actually designed any other buildings. No more than an educated speculation, based on stylistic similarities, can presently link the name of Twelves with the other five buildings in this group.

Obviously, the Old South was an attempt on the part of the Congregationalists to build a more impressive church than Christ Church 'the Old North,' built by the Anglicans only a few years before. To the untrained eye, in fact, the Old South looks a good deal like Christ Church, if only a little bigger. However, while the Old South is by no means a poor building, yet it could never hope to equal Christ Church. The Old South is a rectangular building with a steeple on one end; at first glance one might suspect the interior to be basilical like Christ Church, but it is not. The inside is a large version of the typical New England meetinghouse plan, with the pulpit against the north wall as the focal point of the room. Galleries stand out from the opposite side wall and from both end walls. The Tuscan columns under the galleries have no relationship with the tray ceiling that spans the wide room unaided.

The Old South is built of brick laid in Flemish bond, and is seven bays long, excluding the tower, and five bays wide. Two tiers of round-headed windows ring the building, except for in the middle of the north wall where a single round-headed window half way up lights the pulpit. Since the building is so wide, the steep gable roof stands up very high; this forces the brick portion of the tower to be taller than perhaps it ought to have been. The tower is five storeys high. On top of the tower is a wooden steeple in two octagonal stages below the spire. The lower stage consists of a colonnade of eight arches standing outside a drum, a little like Wren's St. Mary-le-Bow in London. It is important to notice that this church was an attempt to draw a completely original design within the rules and traditions of the period, and is not a copy of anything, in the way that the Town House tower is a copy of the tower on the London Royal Exchange. Therefore, even if Twelves can not be conclusively connected with the other five fine buildings, it is to his credit that he tackled such an ambitious project as the Old South with such originality. It is a pity that more is not known about him.

*Old South Meeting House (Congregational)*       *Boston*     *1729*

*Attribution: certain*

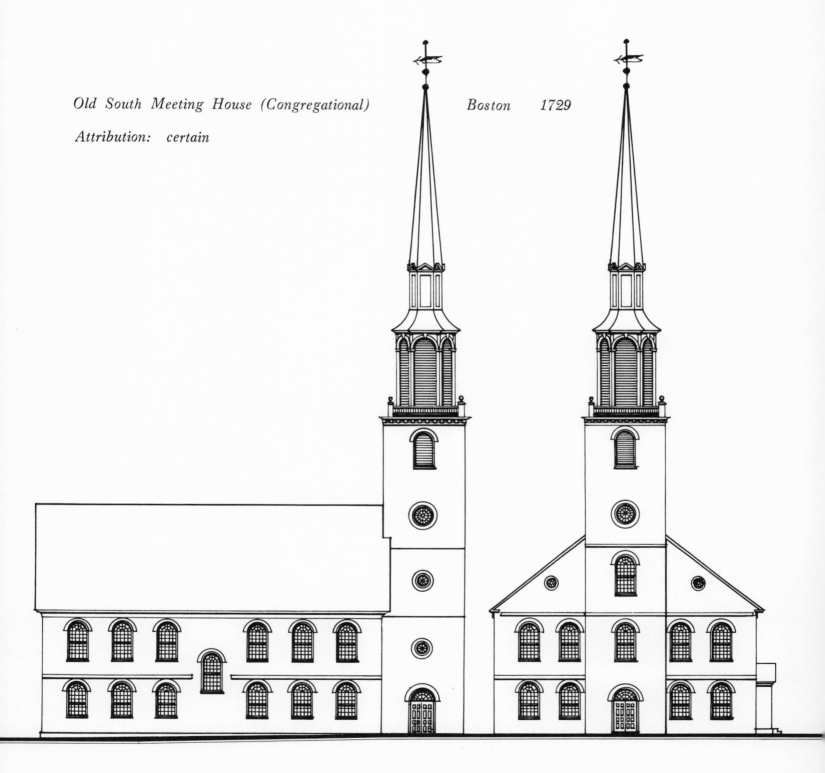

*John Smibert    c.1680-?*

THE renowned painter John Smibert, a native of Edinburgh, came to Boston in 1729 to paint portraits and teach art students. While he was there he was prevailed upon to design a market hall for the Boston merchant, Peter Faneuil, in 1740. The building was built during the next two years by Samuel Ruggles, the carpenter, and Joshua Blanchard, the master mason, and still stands today as altered by Bulfinch in 1805; these alterations increased the width and height each by a factor of two. As built it was nine bays long and three bays wide. It was two storeys high with a gable roof and tower and cupola on top. The lower storey was the traditional English open air market, such as was later built in Newport by Peter Harrison and called the Brick Market. Between the arches were Doric pilasters supporting an entablature that marked the level of the upper floor. The pilasters and entablature were repeated for the floor above, which contained a row of round-headed windows. The square tower, which stood in the center of the roof (and was moved by Bulfinch to one end), was capped by a heavy but attractive octagonal cupola. This cupola, if viewed as on an elevation drawing, looks extremely ungainly, but if viewed from any other direction looks just right because of the interplay of the different sides of the octagon.

Faneuil Hall burned down in 1762, but was immediately rebuilt along the original lines. It was in this building that so much activity was planned at the early stages of the Revolution. The present building would be considerably improved by restoration, as parts of it are in need of repair. Smibert is not known to have designed any other buildings.

*Faneuil Hall    Boston    1742    rebuilt 1762*                    *altered substantially 1805, reconstruction*

*Attribution:    certain*

*Governor Francis Bernard*

IN 1766 it was decided to replace the medieval building known as Harvard Hall in Cambridge. The Governor of Massachusetts offered to draw the plans, and so a fine Georgian building was erected as the third member of the quadrangle of Queen Anne style buildings, that included Stoughton College (*q.v.*) and Massachusetts Hall, built in 1722. Governor Bernard's design was strictly academic, as one might expect from the average eighteenth-century gentleman trained in all the arts and sciences. It was of brick, eleven bays long, three bays wide, and two storeys tall. The central three bays formed a pedimented pavilion. The windows of the lower floor were all round-headed, while those of the upper floor were rectangular. The roof was a hip, but apart from the central pediments over the pavilions it also has a pediment at each end, so that the whole just falls short of being a gable-roofed building. Above the middle of the roof stands an octagonal cupola that looks clumsy on the plan but which comes into its own when seen from an angle. Harvard Hall was the first college building in the Colonies to be built solely for the purpose of providing classroom space; in other words, no part of it was to serve as a dormitory. Today it stands much altered with wings protruding from it, while the original inside was lost through a fire many years ago. Since the present interior, though larger than the original, is not exactly functional nor attractive it is hoped that some attempt will be made to restore the building to its eighteenth-century appearance. Governor Bernard, about whom little is known, is not thought to have designed any other buildings.

*Harvard Hall   Cambridge   1776*

*now altered and enlarged*

*Attribution:   certain*

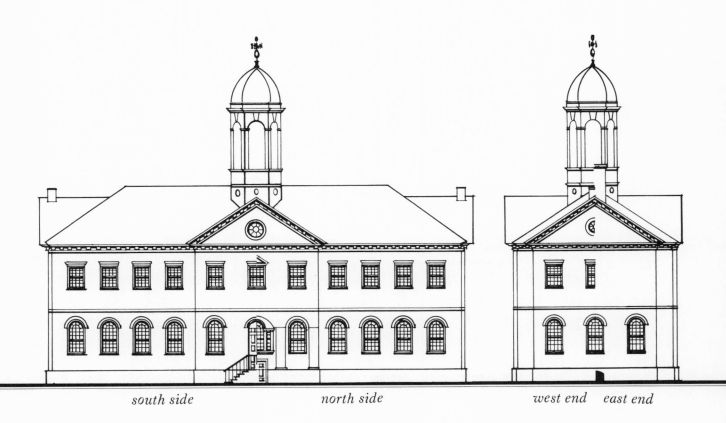

*south side*          *north side*          *west end    east end*

*Unknown New Hampshire Housewright*

AT the beginning of the second half of the eighteenth century, at least three attractive houses of fairly academic design were built in Portsmouth, New Hampshire. The name of their designer is unknown; furthermore, these houses have no relation to the two houses by Peter Harrison that were built in the area at about the same time. All have deck-on-hip roofs with a balustrade around the deck. All of them also have curious flimsy pediments over all the front windows except those of the top floor.

The most impressive of the three houses is the Moffat-Ladd House, built in 1763. This is three storeys tall and has end-chimneys. The pediments over the lower windows are segmental, and the windows on the floor above have split ogee pediments; the center window and pediment of the upper floor are enlarged and in better proportion with better detail. The front door is covered by a Tuscan entrance porch with pediment. The corners of the house are decorated with quoins, although the rest of the house is covered in clapboards, which look a trifle out of place beside quoins. Inside, the Moffat-Ladd House has two outstanding features, the grand staircase, which in this unusual plan takes up the whole right front quarter of the house, has some fine details, including panelled step-ends, well-carved balusters, and a large elaborate panel on the under side of the second run of steps. The house also has a lovely fireplace which is alleged to be the work of Grinling Gibbons; although it is of excellent workmanship, there is no proof that Gibbons carved it, and he probably did not.

*Moffat-Ladd House    Portsmouth    1763*

*Cutter-Langdon House    Portsmouth    about 1750-1760*          *demolished about 1950, reconstruction*

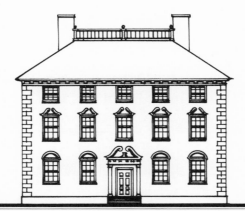

The Cutter-Langdon House was the same size as the Moffat-Ladd House with the same proportions. It was, however, built a few years earlier, and so its details were not so carefully worked out as those of the Ladd House. Instead of end-chimneys, it had one chimney on either side of the roof deck. The pediments over the windows were identical with those on the Ladd House, except for the doorway and the window above it; the door is surmounted by a split ogee pediment instead of the entrance porch of the later house, and the window above the door is identical with the windows on either side of it. Inside, the house was completely different in plan from the Ladd House. It had a central stair-hall with a massive elliptical arch resting on engaged Tuscan pillars at the bottom of the stairs. The parlor was fully panelled, and had a heavy modillioned cornice around the ceiling. This house was unfortunately torn down only a few years ago.

*Colonel Joseph Whipple House    Portsmouth    about 1760*                                            *now altered*

The Colonel Joseph Whipple House, built around 1760, although it has not been torn down, yet has been severely altered, especially inside. It is only 2½ storeys tall with a deck-on-hip roof; the chimney on one side is set in the end wall and that on the other side stands at the break of the hip. Weak triangular pediments are attached to the wall above each of the ground-floor windows; the fine doorway is crowned with a segmental pediment. The gables of the dormers end alternately in triangular and segmental pediments. Inside, although the house is much smaller than the Ladd House, it has almost the same floor plan as the Ladd House. To the left of the door is a large stair-hall. The staircase, which is similar in every way to that in the Ladd House, is lit by a round-headed window over the landing. The Whipple House is now a hotel.

There are a few other houses in Portsmouth that seem to be by the same hand, such as the John Paul Jones House, and possibly the State House, but they were not really sophisticated enough for their late dates to warrant being included in this book.

# GLOSSARY

APSE   *A projecting part of a building, usually semicircular in plan; it is most often found in churches, where it contains the altar and sanctuary.*

ARCHITRAVE   *The lowest of the three divisions of an entablature.*

ASHLAR   *A facing of squared stones, or sometimes of wood shaped to look like squared stones.*

BAY   *A subdivision of the façade of a building, such as one window's worth, or that space between two pilasters.*

BOLECTION MOULDING   *A moulding along the edge of a panel or fireplace, which projects beyond the level of the face of the panel.*

BRICK BONDS:   ENGLISH   *A method of laying brick whereby one course is laid with stretchers and the next with headers, so that the two thicknesses of brick are bonded together.*

FLEMISH   *Another method of laying brick, whereby headers and stretchers alternate in the same course, and headers in the course above are placed directly over the stretchers below. Flemish bond is considered to be a more academic way to lay brick, and is also usually more attractive than English bond, especially when the headers of the Flemish bond are glazed.*

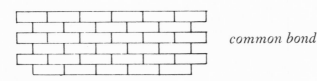

*common bond*

*English bond*

*Flemish bond*

BULL'S-EYE WINDOW   *A round window, usually set in a pediment, and sometimes surrounded by a cartouche.*

CARTOUCHE   *An ornament, part of which is scroll-shaped.*

CORNICE   *A decorative feature found under the eaves of a roof; also the uppermost of the three levels of an entablature.*

COURSE   *A continuous horizontal row of brick or stone in a wall;*
        *A* BELT COURSE *or* STRING COURSE *is such a row that projects from the face of the wall.*

COVE   *A concave shape, especially a type of ceiling.*

DENTILS   *Small oblong blocks spaced in a band to decorate a cornice.*

*cornice with dentils*

ENTABLATURE    *An assembly of the top three parts of a Classical order: architrave, frieze and cornice, usually seen on top of a column.*

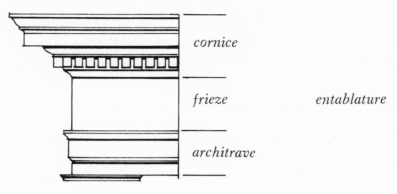

*cornice*

*frieze*          *entablature*

*architrave*

FAÇADE    *The front face of a building.*

FINIAL    *An ornament, often urn-shaped, used to decorate the top of a pediment, etc.*

*finial*

FORECOURT    *The area in front of a building enclosed by flanking buildings or walls.*

FRIEZE    *The middle of the three members of an entablature.*

   CUSHION FRIEZE *is a convex band in place of a regular frieze.*

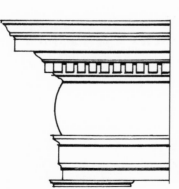

*entablature with cushion frieze*

HEADER    *The end of a brick, or that part of the brick seen when the brick is laid across the wall to bond it.*

   *A* GLAZED HEADER *is a header that is glazed to a dark green or black, so that several glazed headers form a pattern with the stretcher bricks.*

KEYSTONE    *A wedge-shaped stone in the crown of an arch or the center of a lintel to bind the*
*structure.*

*keystones*

LINTEL    *The horizontal top piece of a window or door opening.*

MODILLION    *An ornamental block, larger than a dentil, that is applied to the underside of projecting members of a cornice.*

NEWEL    *The principle post in a banister at the foot of a staircase and at the corners of landings.*

ORDER    *A type of column and entablature. There are five main orders:* TUSCAN, DORIC, IONIC, CORINTHIAN, *and* COMPOSITE.

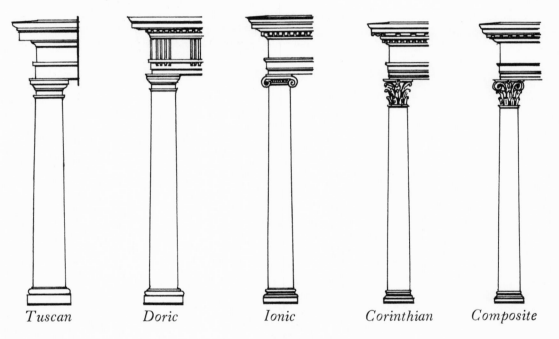

*Tuscan*          *Doric*          *Ionic*          *Corinthian*          *Composite*

PALLADIAN WINDOW, *also called* VENETIAN WINDOW    *A round-headed window or door flanked by lower rectangular windows, and separated from them by columns or piers.*

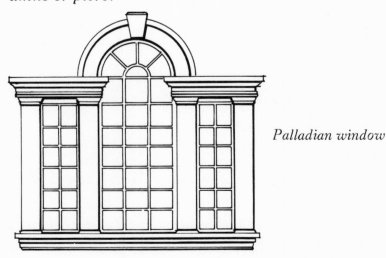

*Palladian window*

PARAPET   *A low wall around the edge of a roof.*

PAVILION   *A projecting part of a façade to give architectural emphasis.*

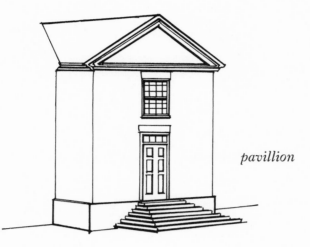

*pavillion*

PEDIMENT   *The crowning motive of porticoes, pavilions, doorways or other architectural features, and usually triangular in form. The most common forms are* TRIANGULAR, OGEE *and* SEGMENTAL; *these are sometimes split to receive some ornament in the center.*

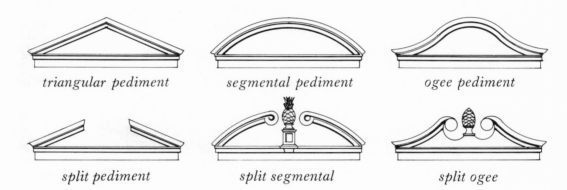

*triangular pediment*       *segmental pediment*       *ogee pediment*

*split pediment*       *split segmental*       *split ogee*

PIER   *A square supporting member, as a square-shaped column or group of columns or pilasters.*

PILASTER   *A flat form of a column applied to a wall.*

PLINTH   *Part of the base of a column; also, the stand for a finial or statue.*

PORTICO   *A covered, usually projecting, colonnade at the entrance of a building, often crowned by a pediment.*

QUOIN   *A squared stone, or similar arrangement of wood or brick, at the corner of a building or of architectural features.*

*quoins*

ROOFS   *The most commonly found roofs are* GABLE, GAMBREL, HIP, GABLE-ON-HIP, HIP-ON-HIP, *or* MANSARD, DECK-ON-HIP *and* JERKIN-HEAD.

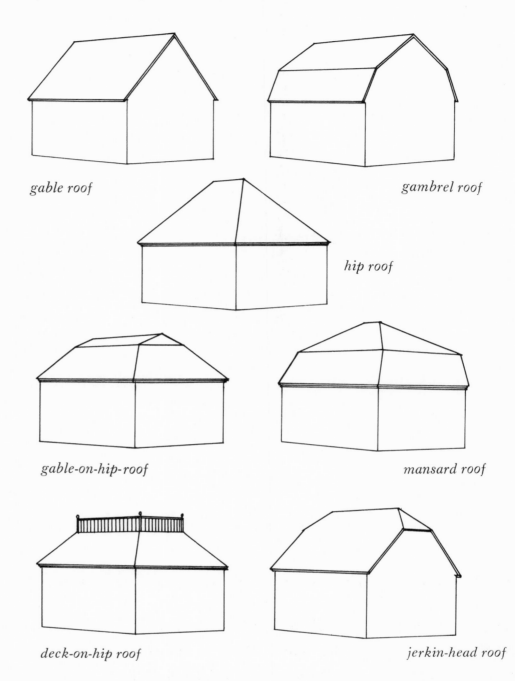

*gable roof*                                                            *gambrel roof*

*hip roof*

*gable-on-hip-roof*                                                *mansard roof*

*deck-on-hip roof*                                                *jerkin-head roof*

RUSTICATION   *Horizontal and vertical channels cut into the joints of stonework to emphasize the joints.*

STRETCHER   *The long face of a brick when laid horizontally.*

VENETIAN WINDOW   *see* PALLADIAN WINDOW.

VOLUTE   *A scroll-like ornament, as on the capital of an Ionic column, sometimes also curled in both directions.*

*volute*

# BIBLIOGRAPHY

*For an over-all view of architecture in the Colonies:*

Fiske Kimbal:   *Domestic Architecture of the American Colonies and of the Early Republic.* Scribners, 1922. This is a rare book, but it has recently been republished by Dover.

Hugh Morrison:   *Early American Architecture.* Oxford, 1952.

Alan Gowans:   *Images of American Living.* Lippincott, 1964.

John Mead Howells:   *Lost Examples of Colonial Architecture.* Helburn, 1931, and Dover, 1963.

Thomas T. Waterman:   *Dwellings of Colonial America.* Chapel Hill, 1950.
Many other titles were of some help, but the above were the best.

*For John Prince:*

Thomas T. Waterman:   *The Mansions of Virginia.* University of North Carolina, 1945, and Bonanza, c. 1960.

Thomas T. Waterman:   *Domestic Colonial Architecture of Tidewater Virginia.* Scribners, 1932.
A trip to Shrewsbury in England is the best way to encounter Prince's work in England.

*For Henry Cary & Son:*

Thomas T. Waterman:   *The Mansions of Virginia,* op. cit.

Marcus Whiffen:   *The Public Buildings of Williamsburg.* Colonial Williamsburg, 1958.

*For Richard Taliaferro:*

Thomas T. Waterman:   *The Mansions of Virginia,* op. cit.

*For John Ariss:*

Thomas T. Waterman:   *The Mansions of Virginia,* op. cit.

*For James Wren:*

Thomas T. Waterman:   *The Mansions of Virginia,* op. cit.

*For William Buckland:*

Rosamond R. Beirne & John H. Scarff:   *William Buckland.* Maryland Historical Society, 1958.

Deering Davis:   *Annapolis Houses.* Architectural Book Publishing Co., 1947, and Bonanza, c. 1960.

*For other Maryland architects:*

Henry C. Forman:   *Early Manor and Plantation Houses of Maryland.* 1934.

Lewis Coffin & A. C. Holden: *Brick Architecture of the Colonial Period in Maryland and Virginia.* Architectural Book Publishing Co., 1919.

*For Architecture of North Carolina:*

Thomas T. Waterman & Frances Benjamin Johnston: *The Early Architecture of North Carolina.* Chapel Hill, 1941.

*For South Carolina Architecture:*

Samuel G. Stoney: *Plantations of the Carolina Low Country.* Carolina Art Association, 1938.

Beatrice St. Julien Ravenel: *Architects of Charleston.* Carolina Art Association, 1945.

*For Sir Christopher Wren:*

Marcus Whiffen: *The Public Buildings of Williamsburg*, op. cit.

Norman Isham: *Trinity Church in Newport, R. I.*
   There are any number of books about Wren's work in England, but none mentions his work in the Colonies.

*For James Porteus and the other Philadelphia architects:*

George B. Tatum: *Penn's Great Town.* University of Pennsylvania, 1961.

Philip B. Wallace: *Colonial Houses.* Architectural Book Publishing Co., 1931, and Bonanza, c. 1960.

Thompson Westcott: *The Historic Mansions and Buildings of Philadelphia.* Porter & Coates, 1877.
   There are many other books on this subject, but the above are the best.
   There are no books dealing satisfactorily with the architects of New York.

*For the Rhode Island architects:*

Antoinette Downing: *Early Homes of Rhode Island.* Garrett & Massie, 1937.

Antoinette Downing & Vincent Scully, Jr.: *The Architectural Heritage of Newport, Rhode Island.* Harvard, 1952. Reprinted 1967.

Carl Bridenbaugh: *Peter Harrison, First American Architect.* Chapel Hill, 1949.

Norman Isham: *Trinity Church in Newport, R. I.*, op. cit.

*For the New Hampshire builder:*

John Mead Howells: *The Architectural Heritage of the Piscataqua.*

*For churches in the Colonies:*

Stephen P. Dorsey: *Early English Churches in America.* Oxford, 1952.

Harold W. Rose: *The Colonial Houses of Worship in America.* Hasting House, 1963.
   There are again many books on this subject, but the above two are the best.

# INDEX

CONTAINING Draughts of Elevations o

above 200 Buildings erected in thefe Colonies

& defigned by the most fkilful Architects be

fore Mr. *Thos. Jefferfon*, including 43 Churche

& other Houfe...                    Schools, Co

leges & Hofpit...                    ate-houfes &

Courthoufes, 8 M...                  blic Buildings

and countlefs                        & Manfions

THE Defigns                          gs were pre

pared by: S...                       ociates; *Joh*

*Prince; J...                        ...ferro; Henr*

*Cary* II; *Edmun...                 ...unday; Joh*

*Smibert; Sam.* C...                 *Ezra Waite*

*John Arifs; Jas. Wren; John Hawks; Wm. Buck*

*land; Horatio Anderfon; Rob.t Twelves; Sam*

*Rhoads; Rob.t ...                   ...cBean; Godfre*

*Malbone; Ric...                     ...v: Bernard; Pete*

*Harrifon; Ch...                     ...imon Duff; Pa...*

*Creagh; Rob.t ...                   ...ay; Jos. Brown*

and divers others who are yet Anonymous